THE COMPLETE BOOK OF
Low-Carbohydrate
COOKING

Lose weight the smart way with a high-protein,
low-carb diet – including more than 150 delicious
recipes designed for fitness and health

Contributing editor:
ELAINE GARDNER

HERMES
HOUSE

This edition is published by Hermes House

Hermes House is an imprint of Anness Publishing Ltd
Hermes House, 88–89 Blackfriars Road, London SE1 8HA
tel. 020 7401 2077; fax 020 7633 9499
www.lorenzbooks.com; info@anness.com

A CIP catalogue record for this book is available from the British Library.

Publisher: Joanna Lorenz
Editorial Director: Judith Simons
Editor: Clare Gooden
Production Controller: Steve Lang
Designer: Nigel Partridge
Recipes: Alex Barker, Joanna Farrow, Yasuko Fukuoka, Brian Glover, Nicola Graimes, Becky Johnson,
Lucy Knox, Jane Milton, Marlena Spieler
Photography: Nicki Dowey, Amanda Heywood, William Lingwood, Thomas Odulate,
Craig Robertson, Simon Smith

10 9 8 7 6 5 4 3 2 1

NOTES
Bracketed terms are intended for American readers.
For all recipes, quantities are given in both metric and imperial measures and, where appropriate, measures
are also given in standard cups and spoons. Follow one set, but not a mixture, because they are not
interchangeable.
Standard spoon and cup measures are level.
1 tsp = 5ml, 1 tbsp = 15ml, 1 cup = 250ml/8fl oz
Australian standard tablespoons are 20ml. Australian readers should use 3 tsp in place of 1 tbsp for
measuring small quantities of gelatine, flour, salt, etc.
Medium (US large) eggs are used unless otherwise stated.

The diets and information in this book are not intended to replace advice from a qualified practitioner,
doctor or dietician. Always consult your health practitioner before adopting any of the suggestions in this
book. Neither the author nor the publishers can accept any liability for failure to follow this advice.
A low-carbohydrate diet is not recommended for children, the elderly or pregnant women.

contents

introduction

A LOW-CARBOHYDRATE DIET is a healthy way of eating, and a good option for achieving rapid, effective weight loss. By making a few simple changes to your lifestyle, incorporating exercise into your routine, and adjusting your eating habits, it can become a successful long-term weight maintenance programme.

Millions of people around the world are adopting a low-carbohydrate diet as a way of losing weight, lowering cholesterol and improving overall health. It is an effective and satisfying diet, on which you can eat a wide variety of delicious foods. A low-carbohydrate diet can be used to tackle weight gain or simply incorporated into your lifestyle as a healthy way of maintaining your ideal weight.

Social, economic and cultural changes, which affect us all, mean that the rate of obesity is increasing, and there is an obsession with weight loss in the Western world. However, improving a person's overall health profile is equally important. A lower carbohydrate, high-protein diet with a healthy proportion of the right types of fat provides a healthier way of eating long-term, combined with weight loss.

It is important to contact your doctor before changing eating patterns or starting any weight loss regime, especially if you suffer from diabetes, high blood pressure or a kidney disorder. A low-carbohydrate diet is not recommended for children, the elderly or pregnant women.

SCIENCE MADE SIMPLE

To lose weight, a very simple formula applies: energy intake must be controlled and output increased in the form of activity. The part of weight management that is often open to debate concerns the amount and ideal proportions of macronutrients (such as carbohydrates, protein and fats) that should be consumed in the diet.

Traditionally, increasing carbohydrate foods was encouraged to add bulk and satisfy hunger; however, the effect of carbohydrates on blood fat levels and insulin response is now better understood, and a lower carbohydrate intake is recommended by many nutritionists. A lower carbohydrate, high protein, healthy fat diet is just as good as other energy controlling diets in reducing weight. The difference is that this diet is more effective in improving body composition: in other words, it enhances the loss of fat while retaining the muscle that is often reduced when losing weight.

Left: For successful weight loss and long-term weight maintenance, a healthy diet is essential. This may involve changing your lifestyle and adopting new eating habits.

Above: *A healthy low-carb diet includes plenty of fresh fish, meat and vegetables, along with essential dairy products.*

A PRACTICAL APPROACH

Too often, diet advice encourages diving into a new way of eating without serious thought or sufficient preparation. It is no wonder that it is difficult to continue with some diets when essential ingredients are missing from regular shopping lists or cupboards are full of foods that should be avoided. This book provides all of the information you need to start and maintain a new eating pattern. As well as explaining in clear and simple terms how the diet actually works, it provides details on getting started, with practical suggestions for implementing the diet, selecting low-carbohydrate snacks, and coping with everyday events, such as eating out at restaurants. These sit alongside great ideas for menu planning and delicious recipes to help make this eating plan really special.

Additionally, the book tackles modern issues in a down-to-earth manner, including vegetarianism and health tips, with an update on newer food items, such as probiotic drinks and yogurt bio-cultures. An extensive guide to ingredients provides background information on the foods you can enjoy and those you should avoid. Step-by-step pictures demonstrate easy and healthy ways of preparing different ingredients to encourage confident cooking. Essential kitchen utensils are examined alongside the top ten healthy cooking methods and quick, simple ideas for using the microwave.

Anyone who has been on a diet before will agree that the most difficult part of weight management is keeping the weight off. Long-term weight maintenance is discussed with suggestions on modifying daily eating patterns, taking account of the need to fit holidays and special occasions into your new lifestyle.

Below: *Leading an active life will enable you to maintain your ideal weight.*

the low-carb approach

ON A LOW-CARBOHYDRATE diet, body composition is improved as the body loses more fat and preserves lean muscle tissue, which would otherwise be lost. Whenever you do any exercise – something that is always recommended on a diet – you will add lean muscle while still losing fat.

By following a diet regime based on lower levels of carbohydrate with a higher protein content, a higher proportion of body fat is lost. This means that more muscle, or lean body mass, is preserved. In turn, this gives the body improved definition and shape, especially if it is toned up through regular exercise. Performing exercise will also help to maintain strength in the muscles.

COMPARATIVE SATIETY OF FOOD

Hunger pangs are often a problem when dieting. High-protein foods make you feel full so they suppress appetite and subsequent energy intake. Even when different types of foods that contain the same number of calories are eaten, those higher in protein are more filling than those containing either carbohydrate or fat, so you should feel less hungry on a high-protein diet.

THE EFFECT ON BONES

There are several ways of maintaining strong bones, and adopting a good diet and taking regular exercise helps to keep bone strength as high as possible. A healthy diet, including plenty of calcium-rich foods, such as milk, yogurt and nuts, and adequate amounts of vitamin D (found in oily fish), is extremely important. After the age of 35, calcium is gradually lost from bones as part of the natural ageing process, so the intake of calcium-rich foods should increase. In women, the loss occurs at a much faster rate after the menopause because of the loss of the protective effects of the female hormone oestrogen.

Below: *High-protein foods make you feel full, meaning there is less chance of giving in to temptation and ruining the diet.*

THE EFFECT ON THE KIDNEYS

For many years now there has been some controversy surrounding whether high protein intake causes damage to the kidneys. Intakes of up to 2.2g protein per kg body weight per day do not appear to have any adverse effect on kidney function. For someone weighing 100kg/220lb, this is the equivalent of eating seven 200g/7oz (130g/4½oz drained weight) cans of tuna a day.

BLOOD FATS

Blood cholesterol

An excess of cholesterol in the blood increases the risk of heart disease. Foods high in saturated fats increase blood cholesterol levels. Foods that contain cholesterol have little effect on blood cholesterol levels. This is because there are two types of cholesterol.

- LDL (low-density lipoprotein) cholesterol can slowly build up in the arteries and cause a heart attack.
- HDL (high-density lipoprotein) cholesterol, sometimes known as "good" cholesterol, carries cholesterol back to the liver, thus lowering the risk of a heart attack.

Blood triglycerides

These are fats that can be made in the body or absorbed from food. Diets that are high in carbohydrates, especially refined carbohydrates such as white rice, bread and pasta, and alcohol, can increase blood triglycerides. People with high levels of blood triglycerides have an increased risk of heart disease, and are more likely to be overweight or have diabetes.

Above: *On a diet that is relatively high in protein, it is important to drink plenty of water – at least eight glasses per day.*

Not cutting down on the amount of protein eaten and choosing food sources wisely provides the benefits that aid weight loss with good health and no risk of kidney damage. However, it is important to remember that the body needs more fluid to break down protein than fat or carbohydrate, so drink at least eight glasses of water per day.

THE EFFECT ON BLOOD SUGAR

When carbohydrate foods are eaten a hormone called insulin is secreted into the bloodstream. This signals the body to remove excess sugar from the bloodstream and store it for future use. When excess insulin is produced this results in a low level of blood sugar, with unpleasant symptoms such as dizziness, tiredness, low energy levels and food cravings. Research has shown that a diet higher in protein produces a lower insulin response. This reduces swings in blood sugar levels and stabilizes them between meals.

Foods such as peas, beans, lentils, fruits and vegetables contain carbohydrate alongside protein, vitamins and minerals. These often contain slowly absorbed carbohydrates, which do not cause large swings in blood sugar, together with essential fibre and valuable antioxidants.

Above: *To ensure your bones stay strong, incorporate regular exercise, such as cycling, into your new healthy lifestyle.*

THE EFFECT ON BLOOD FATS

Eating a diet that is low in carbohydrates, especially avoiding those from simple, refined sources, means that blood triglyceride concentrations can be significantly reduced. For protein sources, eat lean meat, lower fat dairy products,

HOMOCYSTEINE

Homocysteine is a compound made in the body and normally found in low levels in the blood. A higher level of homocysteine is one of several factors that may play a role in damaging the lining of blood vessels, linking it to heart disease. The three vitamins folate, B_6 (found in fruit and vegetables) and B_{12} (the main source in the diet is meat) act to lower homocysteine levels. Eating a diet rich in fruit, vegetables and meat may be a way of minimizing the homocysteine levels in the blood.

white and oily fish, along with nuts, peas, beans, lentils and soya products. Eating these foods can help to lower blood cholesterol levels. A diet that is low in carbohydrate, high in protein, and contains healthy fats, can be extremely beneficial to health and can help achieve weight loss.

Below: *Complex carbohydrates, such as wholemeal (whole-wheat) grains, pasta and beans, provide slow-release energy.*

different types of carbohydrate

THE KEY TO success on a low-carbohydrate diet is not simply cutting out all forms of carbohydrate. Instead, recognize the different types of carbohydrate available and understand which must be avoided completely, which are fine to eat occasionally and which are good, healthy sources of carbohydrate.

Carbohydrates are found in a variety of foods, and they provide energy. Some foods supply additional nutrients, such as valuable vitamins or minerals, or they may provide carbohydrate in a slow-release form that sustains energy levels over a period of time and avoids large swings in blood sugar levels. To promote weight loss, energy intake needs to be kept in check and only the best types of carbohydrates eaten.

FRUITS AND VEGETABLES

Natural sugars can be found in fruits, and these are balanced with healthy amounts of fibre and valuable supplies of vitamins, minerals and antioxidants. Non-starchy vegetables, such as broccoli, cauliflower,

Below: Peas, beans and lentils should be a major part of your low-carbohydrate diet. Try adding them to salads or casseroles.

mushrooms, spinach and cabbage, contain slowly absorbed complex carbohydrates alongside other beneficial nutrients. These can be eaten freely.

Pure fruit and vegetable juices concentrate the complex carbohydrates and natural sugars, so their intake should be limited to one serving per day.

Starchy fruit and vegetables, such as potatoes, bananas and yams, contain large amounts of quickly absorbed carbohydrates and should be avoided.

PEAS, BEANS AND LENTILS

The slow-release carbohydrates found in peas and beans, such as chickpeas or red kidney beans, provide sustained energy. They are also good sources of low-fat proteins, fibre and the essential B vitamins, folic acid and iron. These should be eaten regularly.

Above: A valuable source of fibre and vitamins and minerals, a portion of fruit makes an ideal mid-morning snack.

GRAINS AND CEREALS

All types of grain and cereal contain a considerable amount of carbohydrate. If necessary, small amounts of these wholegrain products can be eaten. Foods such as barley, millet and oats (which are proportionately higher in protein) are recommended.

REFINED CARBOHYDRATES

These are foods that contain refined sugars and flours, such as cakes, biscuits (cookies), sugars, fruit squashes, white bread, white rice or pasta. These foods should all be eliminated from the diet as they contain large amounts of quickly absorbed carbohydrate.

Carbohydrates are also hidden in many processed foods, such as ketchup, sauces, pickles, canned and packet soups, and desserts, and these should be avoided.

GLYCAEMIC INDEX

The glycaemic index (GI) is a measure of how quickly a food raises blood sugar levels in the body. It ranks foods from 0 to 100.

Foods with a high glycaemic index are digested quickly and so cause a rapid flow of blood sugar into the bloodstream. This in turn stimulates the body to produce a large rush of insulin to control the blood sugar.

Foods with a low glycaemic index release glucose more gradually and to a lesser degree, thereby avoiding the large swings in blood sugar levels due to high levels of insulin production. These are the foods to select. Low GI foods also help to satisfy appetite, which is a bonus when trying to lose weight.

FIVE A DAY

Evidence shows that people who eat more fruit and vegetables reduce their risk of coronary heart disease, some cancers and gut problems. As a group of foods, fruit and vegetables are low in fat and energy, and a good source of fibre.

Below: *Refined carbohydrates with few nutrients, such as white bread, pasta and sugar, should be avoided.*

GLYCAEMIC INDEX MEASURE OF SOME COMMON FOODS

Food	Glycaemic Index (GI)
White rice, cooked	87
Baked potato	85
Wholemeal (whole-wheat) bread	71
White bread	70
Baked beans	48
Apple	38
Cooked lentils	30
Peanuts	14

They are also rich in potassium, low in salt, and provide a range of vitamins and antioxidants, which are important for health.

Fruit and vegetables also contain anti-carcinogens called phytochemicals. These neutralize the effects of substances that may promote cancer. Brassicas (such as cabbage and broccoli) are thought to be rich in one such compound called glucosinolates. Other important phytochemicals include lycopene, found in tomatoes, and allium, found in garlic, onions and leeks.

Five portions or 400g/14oz of fruit and vegetables per day is the minimum required to promote health. These five portions will provide minimal energy, and the carbohydrates they contain are balanced by extra nutrients. Only one portion per day should be fruit or vegetable juice. Each of the following counts as one portion:

- 1 piece of fruit (apple, orange or peach)
- 2 small fruits (plums, kiwis, satsumas)
- 1 large slice of melon or pineapple
- 1 cupful of berries
- 2–3 tablespoons stewed or canned fruit
- 1 glass (150ml/¼ pint/⅔ cup) fruit or vegetable juice
- 2 tablespoons raw, cooked, frozen or canned vegetables
- 1 dessert bowl full of salad

Fruit and vegetables should be eaten as fresh as possible. Vegetables should be lightly boiled, steamed or cooked in the microwave to retain their goodness.

Above: *Some fruits and vegetables are very high in carbohydrate so they should be avoided on a low-carb diet plan – these include potatoes, yams and plantains.*

FOODS TO AVOID

Foods that contain high amounts of carbohydrate:
- Bread, cakes and biscuits (cookies)
- Pasta and noodles
- Rice, maize, buckwheat, bulgur wheat and rye
- Starchy fruits and vegetables (banana, yam, potato, sweet potato)
- Cereals, including most refined breakfast cereals

Foods that contain refined sugars:
- Brown and white sugar and honey
- Sweets (candies)
- Fruit squashes and carbonated, sweetened drinks
- Jam (jelly), marmalade, syrup and treacle (molasses)
- Ketchups, pickles and chutneys
- Ice cream

Foods that contain refined starches:
- Canned and packet soups
- Bought custards and desserts
- Ready-made sauces
- Stock (bouillon) granules and cubes

good fats and bad fats

MOST TRADITIONAL diet programmes advise avoiding all fats. However, there are many healthy fats that the body needs to function properly. A low-carbohydrate diet recommends eating these "good" fats to help stabilize cholesterol levels, protect your heart and boost general health.

The fats in food are concentrated sources of energy. On a weight management programme it is essential to limit the amount of fat consumed to keep calorie intake down. However, some fats are essential for health, and including the right type of fat is just as important as reducing the amount of fat.

Omega-3s are the healthy fats to look for. These fats reduce the stickiness of the blood so blood clots are less likely to block arteries. They also reduce the level of triglycerides in the blood, which are a major risk factor for heart disease. Finally, omega-3 fats help the heart to beat regularly so it becomes less prone to the irregular rhythms that doctors consider to be one of the more lethal parts of a heart attack. In summary, omega-3s are the fats to choose for a healthy heart.

Recent evidence has shown that omega-3 fats may also lower the risk of developing some forms of cancer.

Above: *Choose fresh tuna instead of canned, wherever possible, as the canned variety has lost its good omega-3 fats.*

Above: *Tofu is available in many forms, including soft, firm, silken and marinated, and these all contain healthy fats.*

HEART DISEASE – REDUCE THE RISK

Both diet and lifestyle can influence the likelihood of developing heart disease. Some other contributing factors include:

- Smoking
- High blood pressure
- Lack of exercise
- High blood levels of cholesterol and triglycerides
- Obesity

All of the above should be tackled with a combination of regular exercise, a healthy, balanced diet (which should include weight loss if necessary) and help to stop smoking.

SOURCES OF OMEGA-3 FATS

The main source of omega-3 fats is oily fish, such as kippers, herring, mackerel, pilchards, salmon and sardines. Fresh tuna is also an excellent source of healthy fats, but when tuna is canned it loses its good omega-3's. (This does not happen with other canned fish so they remain a great choice.) Try to eat fish at least twice a week as part of your low-carbohydrate diet.

Other foods that contain these beneficial fats are: rapeseed (canola) oil, which can be used in cooking or as a light salad dressing; nuts, such as walnuts, almonds and peanuts; and soya products, such as all types of tofu. Eggs that have been enriched with omega-3 from chickens fed fish meal, flax and algae are also available, and can easily be substituted into your diet.

HOW MUCH FAT TO EAT

One key factor to weight reduction is limiting the amount of fat eaten to under a third of energy intake. On a diet that consists of a 3.5 megajoule/1500 calorie a day total intake, daily fat consumption of around 50g/2oz is recommended.

This fat intake should come predominantly from the healthy heart types of food with small additional amounts from olive oil, seeds (such as sesame, pumpkin and sunflower) and avocados. Those who do not like oily fish or are vegetarian can take omega-3 fats in the form of a supplement. Pure varieties are available containing 0.5–1g omega-3 fats in the form of EPA (eicosapentaenoic acid) and DHA (docosahexaenoic acid) in a daily capsule or liquid form. These are available from pharmacists and health food stores.

DANGER:
AVOID THESE FATS

Foods that contain saturated fat and trans fats raise blood cholesterol levels, which are a major risk factor in the development of heart disease. These foods must be avoided.

Saturated fats are found in:
- Fatty meats
- High-fat sausages
- Crisps (US potato chips)
- Pies and pastries
- Lard (white cooking fat) and butter
- Double (heavy) cream
- Chocolate

Trans fats are found in:
- Hard margarines
- Fatty fast foods
- Pre-prepared meals
- Biscuits (cookies)
- Cakes

Below: *Although fairly high in calories, avocados contain a beneficial oil so should be eaten occasionally.*

FAT AND WEIGHT LOSS

All of the healthy heart fats that you should be eating can easily slot into a diet that provides the dual benefits of working towards weight loss and good heart health.

Oily fish, nuts, enriched eggs and soya, all of which contain these healthy fats, are also good sources of protein and an excellent base for a low-carbohydrate diet. Regularly including these foods rather than building your menu around meat helps to keep your intake of saturated fat down. It is recommended that you eat one or two portions of oily fish per week in addition to other white fish and seafood.

Rapeseed (canola) oil is good for cooking, but when more flavour is required, for example in salad dressings, use a little olive oil. Although the quantity should be limited, it can certainly be used in moderation.

Above: *Try to avoid prepared salad dressings as these are often high in fat. Instead, use a drizzle of olive oil and fresh lemon juice to add flavour.*

LOW-FAT CHEESE

Cheese is slightly too energy rich to be used indiscriminately in a weight-loss programme. Choosing lower-fat cheeses, such as Quark, ricotta and cottage cheese, which contain the majority of the same nutrients, can help lower the amount of fat and energy consumed. Limit the quantity of higher-fat cheeses, such as Parmesan, Cheddar and Stilton, to small amounts. As a guide, hard cheeses are generally higher in fat than soft cheeses.

sources of protein

A HEALTHY DIET must include protein, and when you are cutting back on carbohydrate foods, protein becomes even more important. However, if you increase your intake of protein, be sure to drink plenty of water, as the body needs more fluid to break down protein than carbohydrate or fat.

Protein is an essential part of the diet. The cells of the body must be replaced constantly, and protein is the only nutrient that can build, maintain and repair our cells. It is also needed for the structure of bones, muscle and skin, and for chemicals such as hormones and enzymes in the body. The antibodies that fight illness and infection, and haemoglobin, which transports oxygen around the body, are also proteins.

There are two main sources of protein. Animal sources are meat, poultry, fish and shellfish, eggs, milk, cheese and yogurt. Vegetable sources are peas, beans and lentils, nuts, seeds and meat substitutes, such as mycoproteins (Quorn), soya and textured vegetable protein.

The quality of a protein depends upon its composition and whether it is able to supply the building blocks that the body needs. As a general rule, proteins from animal or fish sources supply all of these building blocks in one food. Vegetable sources have to be combined or eaten together on the same day to provide them all. This is not usually a problem as foods are commonly eaten in combinations. The exception is soya and its products, such as tofu, as it has similar protein quality to animal protein; this is an excellent choice of food.

Below: *Animal and fish sources of protein provide our bodies with the building blocks we need to maintain healthy cells.*

VEGETARIAN OPTIONS

This programme is suitable for vegetarians as well as those who eat meat. The recommendations of what to eat and what to exclude differ slightly, but it is simply a matter of selecting wisely from the choices available (listed below). The energy requirements for vegetarians are exactly the same as for meat-eaters.

Protein:
- Semi-skimmed (low-fat) milk
- Yogurt
- Eggs
- Cheeses made without rennet
- Nuts, seeds and pulses
- Soya and its products (milk, tofu, miso, tahini, tempeh, textured vegetable protein)
- Mycoproteins (Quorn)

Fats:
- Olive oil,
- Rapeseed (canola) oil and spread
- Nuts and seeds

Carbohydrates:
- Fruit
- Vegetables
- Pure fruit and vegetable juices
- Peas, beans and lentils

PROCESSED FOODS

Many processed foods, such as meat or fish pies, burgers, pastries, grill steaks and sausages, contain a large amount of carbohydrate in addition to protein. Bread, rusk and other carbohydrates are often added to these products to bulk them out.

Below: *Natural sources of protein such as nuts and seeds, make a healthy, nutritious and protein-packed snack.*

PROTEIN FOODS TO AVOID

The following processed foods will all contain added sugars, fats or carbohydrates and should be avoided:
- Fish fingers
- Sausage rolls
- Chicken nuggets
- Burgers (unless home-made)
- Breaded products, such as chicken Kiev or goujons
- Grill steaks
- Pies
- Samosas
- Sausages (unless they contain a high proportion of meat)
- Meatloaf

Protein foods that are high in unhealthy fats and should be avoided include:
- Fatty meats
- Crispy chicken or duck skin
- Full-fat (whole) milk

Above: *Eggs, milk, yogurt and cottage cheese are valuable sources of animal protein, especially for vegetarians.*

Additionally, many of these products are high in saturated fat and do not contribute to a diet for a healthy heart.

It is important to avoid foods that are coated with crumbs or batter, including chicken or fish products, as these are loaded with quickly absorbed carbohydrate. Sauces in ready-made dishes, for example casseroles or curries, can also be a problem as many are thickened with sugars, for example sweet and sour sauce, or pure starch. Overall, it is important to avoid processed sources of protein.

QUANTITY OF PROTEIN TO EAT

Protein is not stored in the body, so any extra protein is broken down and used as a source of energy. Protein foods can help reduce the feeling of hunger more than other energy-providing foods, so they are vital for a successful low-carbohydrate diet.

As well as encouraging weight loss, eating lower fat protein foods or those containing healthy fats, can improve your blood fats profile. Aim to include two large helpings of protein foods, plus milk and yogurt, per day.

Below: *Try to avoid processed sources of protein as these often contain added sugars, fats or carbohydrates.*

vitamins, minerals and fluids

ENSURING THAT your diet contains the recommended daily amounts of key vitamins, minerals and fluids is very important. Sip water throughout the day to help keep hunger at bay, while maximizing concentration and well-being, and eat a healthy and varied diet to avoid the need for supplements.

Stores are full of vitamin and mineral supplements, but most people do not need to take these if they eat a varied diet. However, there are times when supplements are useful. For example, vegetarians and vegans who do not eat fortified foods should take a vitamin B_{12} supplement. Those with heart disease or a history of the illness in the family may decide to take an omega-3 supplement daily if they do not eat oily fish.

When trying to lose weight, it is important to vary the diet and not limit foods that provide essential vitamins and minerals. A multivitamin and mineral tablet is the best choice for topping up if you are concerned about nutrient intake, but this is not a substitute for foods and all the extras that they bring, such as antioxidants. Also, some substances work better when they are eaten alongside others. For example, vitamin C functions better when eaten with flavenoids found in fresh fruit and vegetables.

Below: *The easiest way to reduce your salt intake is to avoid processed foods.*

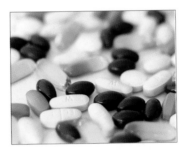

Above: *If you eat a healthy and varied diet, supplements should not be necessary.*

There are many supplements in the form of herbal preparations or tablets that promise weight loss without dieting – do not be fooled by these as there is no quick and easy answer.

FLUID

It is important to drink at least eight glasses or cups of fluid each day to keep properly hydrated. Water should be the first choice, but fresh fruit juice, herbal teas or hot water with lemon are also good options. Diet drinks are fine, but ordinary fizzy drinks and squashes are very high in refined carbohydrates and must be avoided.

Limit coffee and tea to 2–3 cups per day. These should not be drunk last thing at night as they both contain large amounts of caffeine, a stimulant and diuretic.

There is a real danger of dehydration if insufficient liquid is consumed, especially in hot weather. This can be a health risk, with common side-effects such as constipation and headaches, but it can also result in a general feeling of tiredness and lack of concentration. Dehydration also increases the risk of kidney stones and contracting urinary tract infections.

The need for fluid is controlled by the sensation of thirst, and sometimes this can be confused with hunger, leading to consuming more food and energy. Instead of snacking to stave off hunger pangs it can be useful to fill up with fluids.

ALCOHOL

There is no reason why alcohol cannot be included in this new lifestyle, but it does contain a reasonable amount of energy, so it should be limited in quantity. Drinking large quantities of alcohol on a regular basis has other health effects, such as promoting high blood pressure, some cancers, liver disease and depression. The healthy limits for alcohol are 2–3 units per day for women and 3–4 units per day for men. A unit of alcohol is equivalent to 300ml/½ pint/1¼ cups beer, lager or cider, 1 small glass of wine (about 125ml/4fl oz/½ cup), or 1 measure of spirits (25ml/1½ tbsp). As a rule of thumb, sweeter drinks contain more carbohydrate and more calories.

SALT

Although it is calorie-free, salt should not be used excessively as high intakes have been linked to high blood pressure, kidney problems and heart disease.

The main source of salt or sodium in the diet is processed foods, as it is used to improve their flavour, texture and for preservation. By reducing the intake of manufactured foods and eating a diet that is based on fresh fruit and vegetables, pulses, nuts, fresh dairy produce and meat and fish as recommended by this weight-loss plan, salt intake can be kept below the recommended level of 6g per day.

VITAMINS	FUNCTIONS	FOOD SOURCES
Vitamin A	Helps maintain healthy vision and immunity	Liver, dairy products, orange and yellow fruit and vegetables, spinach, oily fish
Vitamin B_1 (thiamin)	Needed for the release of energy from food	Meat
Vitamin B_2 (riboflavin)		Milk, cheese, meat, fish, offal, eggs, yeast extract
Vitamin B_3 (niacin)		Meat, poultry, fish, peanuts, milk, eggs
Vitamin B_6 (pyridoxine)	Maintains healthy skin, blood cells and nervous system	Fish, poultry, meat, vegetables, yeast extract
Vitamin B_{12}	Needed for healthy blood cells and nervous system	Meat, liver, seafood, eggs, milk (including B_{12} fortified soya milk)
Folic acid	Important in pregnancy; helps maintain a healthy heart	Green leafy vegetables, avocado, orange juice, peas, beans and lentils, nuts, liver, offal
Vitamin C	Antioxidant that helps resistance to infection, and promotes healthy gums, teeth, bones, skin and blood cells	Citrus fruit, fresh and lightly cooked vegetables, salad vegetables, fruit juices, berries, kiwi fruit
Vitamin D	Needed for the absorption of calcium and for healthy teeth and bones	Oily fish, eggs, dairy products. Also obtained by the action of sunlight on skin
Vitamin E	Antioxidant that helps prevent damage by free radicals	Nuts, seeds, avocados, vegetable oils, eggs, leafy green vegetables
Vitamin K	Essential for blood clotting	Green leafy vegetables, fruit, dairy foods

MINERALS	FUNCTIONS	FOOD SOURCES
Calcium	Important for strong bones and teeth	Milk (including calcium-enriched soya milk), cheese, yogurt, cream cheese, fish bones (from canned fish), seeds, peas, beans and lentils, green leafy vegetables
Iron	Healthy functioning of red blood cells	Red meat, offal, oily fish, green vegetables, peas, beans and lentils, nuts, seeds
Zinc	Helps in the metabolism of the macronutrients; promotes healthy skin and immune system	Seafood, meat, eggs, dairy products, green vegetables, peas, beans and lentils, nuts
Iodine	Needed for the thyroid hormone, which regulates metabolism	Cow's milk, iodized salt, fish, seafood

assessing your weight

BEING OVERWEIGHT is not only psychologically demoralizing, it is also unhealthy and can lead to serious medical problems. There is no quick solution – losing weight takes time and commitment. Closely monitor how your diet progresses, but do not let yourself become obsessed with the figures.

Being overweight impinges on many aspects of daily life and makes them less enjoyable. Excess weight can also lead to a poorer quality of life with a shorter life span. Obese people are two to three times more likely to die prematurely than those who are leaner and, on average, being obese reduces life span by nine years. There are several simple ways of measuring your weight and checking that you are a healthy weight for your size.

BODY MASS INDEX

A common way of measuring whether an individual is overweight is to record the body mass index (BMI). This is based on your height and weight and can easily be worked out using the simple chart below. Measure height and weight without wearing shoes, draw a line across from the height and up from the weight – the point at which the lines meet shows the BMI category that you fall into.

Another way of working out BMI is by dividing your weight in kilograms by your height in metres squared:

$$\frac{\text{Weight (kg)}}{\text{Height (m)}^2}$$

Body mass index (BMI) is a useful guide for assessing health risk.

- BMI of less than 19 indicates that the person is underweight and may need to put on weight.
- BMI between 19 and 25 indicates a healthy weight, and this is the range in which to stay.
- A BMI of 26 to 30 indicates that the person is overweight. Weight should not rise any further; the person should try and reduce their weight.
- A BMI of over 30 means that health is at risk and the person is classified as obese. It indicates that it is time to lose weight and become more active.

PERCENTAGE BODY FAT

This is often calculated in health clubs or gyms by bio-electrical impedance analysis (BIA). A small current of electricity is passed between electrodes placed on the hands and feet. The amount of lean body tissue is worked out from the drop in voltage caused by the resistance of the body. The amount of fat can then be calculated.

In a normal-weight, healthy adult the amount of body fat varies from 10–25 per cent in males and from 15–35 per cent in females. In cases of obesity, fat can be as high as 60–70 per cent of body weight.

Left: Use this chart to calculate your body mass index (BMI) and decide whether you are a healthy weight.

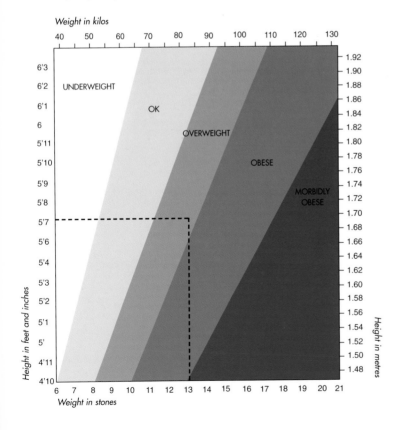

CLOTHES

Often, it is not complicated measurements but clothes that tell the true story. Realizing that tight clothes are becoming more comfortable is a marvellous indicator to boost enthusiasm for maintaining weight loss. The pleasure of being able to go down a size in clothes can be one of the greatest incentives to continue with a healthy weight-loss programme.

WEIGHT-LOSS AIMS

An ideal weight loss is between 0.5–1kg/ 1–2lb per week. This may not seem very much, but the loss needs to be consistent. Over six months this level of weekly weight loss will result in a reduction of over 22kg/ 49lb, or 3½ stone. Even with a weight loss of just 5–10kg/11–22lb or 1½ stone there can be a noticeable improvement in back and joint pain, and a reduction in breathlessness. A loss of just 5–10 per cent of body weight can reduce blood pressure, lower the risk of angina and improve your blood cholesterol levels.

Left: *On a low-carb programme, avoid toast at breakfast and try low-fat natural yogurt with added fresh fruit instead.*

Below: *Weigh youself once a week and record your weight on a chart – you will soon see a downward trend emerging.*

ARE YOU AN APPLE OR A PEAR?

People who carry too much weight around their waist have an increased risk of developing heart disease or diabetes. This body shape is commonly known as an "apple shape". Those who carry excess weight around their hips are "pear shaped", which is less harmful to health.

WAIST MEASUREMENT		
	At risk	High risk
MEN	94cm/37in	102cm/40in
WOMEN	80cm/32in	88cm/35in

SCALES

This is probably the easiest and most common way of measuring weight. Weight should be checked under the same conditions each time – ideally, without wearing shoes, in minimal clothing, at the same time of day and using the same set of scales. Weight fluctuates on a daily basis, so it is important not to get obsessed with the exact readings. Instead, use them as a longer-term indication of progress when losing weight. It may be useful to draw a simple chart on which you can note your weight once per week. Over a period of time the downward trend will gradually begin to show and you will feel proud of your achievement.

problems associated with excess weight

MANY PEOPLE suffer from excess weight at some point in their lives, and it can cause many associated problems, including heart disease, diabetes and joint pain. Losing this excess weight, through a combination of diet and exercise, will reduce the risk of suffering from these medical conditions.

Carrying too much weight is unhealthy. Not only does obesity increase the risk of developing many illnesses and medical problems, it can also increase the severity of some of these conditions.

The risk of heart disease and stroke is doubled in anyone with a body mass index of over 25 and nearly quadrupled if the index reaches over 29; those with a body mass index over 35 have a forty times greater risk of developing type 2 diabetes than non-obese people.

Certain types of cancer, especially those in the bowel and breast (and particularly for women after the menopause), are more likely to occur in the obese. Other problems often linked with being overweight are gall bladder disease, infertility, back and joint pain, arthritis, asthma, incontinence, excess sweating, reduced resistance to infection and greater risk of complications during surgery or other medical intervention.

SYNDROME X

Also known as insulin resistance syndrome, syndrome X has been linked to the current rising levels of obesity and decline in physical activity, which are worldwide problems. It is usually diagnosed when a person suffers from three or more of the following conditions:

- Abdominal obesity (a waist circumference that is greater than 102cm/40in for men, 88cm/35in for women)
- High triglyceride levels
- Low HDL cholesterol levels
- High blood pressure
- High blood glucose levels

People with syndrome X are at greater risk of developing type 2 diabetes and heart disease, and are more likely to die prematurely.

Normally the hormone insulin regulates blood sugar levels; however, in those suffering from syndrome X, cells resist the action of insulin and the body produces more to try to control blood sugar levels.

Obesity, and particularly abdominal fat producing the "apple" shape body, increases the likelihood of insulin resistance. The symptoms can be improved by reducing body weight even by as little as 10 per cent and increasing physical activity.

Above: *Maintaining a normal weight can help to avoid sleep apnoea, a condition where breathing is disrupted.*

Many people who are obese also suffer from sleep apnoea, a dangerous condition in which they stop breathing temporarily while sleeping. This is often associated with loud snoring and occurs when there is a fall in the amount of oxygen in the blood, which can lead to heart failure.

LIFESTYLE PROBLEMS

Normal movement and activity can be a problem due to the burden of excess weight. This can limit work options and cause concerns over safety. Millions of work days every year are lost through sickness as a result of obesity-related problems,

POLYCYSTIC OVARIAN SYNDROME (PCOS)

Many women with PCOS are overweight and at greater risk of developing heart disease and diabetes. This is because they have a tendency to carry excess fat around their middles. PCOS is a hormonal problem in which cysts develop in the ovaries. It can cause the following symptoms.

- Excessive hair growth
- Acne
- Fertility problems
- Thinning of the scalp hair
- High blood pressure

A doctor can prescribe medication, but losing weight will help with the treatment of the symptoms.

therefore employers can be reluctant to recruit obese people. Obesity is also associated with decreased psychological well-being as the social stigma attached to being overweight can lead to depression, isolation and low self-esteem.

Many women and, increasingly, more men are concerned with body image. The media and the fashion industry have been blamed for portraying body images that are too skinny. However, those who are overweight may not be able to wear the clothes they want to, or they may feel so self-conscious that they live in baggy t-shirts.

People simply want to be themselves and enjoy a normal life – this includes running around with the children or wearing a swimming costume without embarrassment. However, being overweight can severely limit these activities.

RELATIONSHIPS

Weight can also affect relationships. Experiencing low confidence due to being overweight increases nervousness and can lead to a reluctance to go out or socialize. Making excuses for staying at home can turn into a downward spiral of receiving fewer invitations from friends or work colleagues. This, in turn, will result in less opportunities to go out and a further deterioration in confidence.

Partners or friends may be concerned about the effect of excess weight on health and personality – someone who suffers all the consequences of gaining weight may not be the person they originally met.

CONTROL

Many problems related to being overweight are associated with lack of control and negative thinking. It is just as important to tackle this psychological aspect of being overweight as it is to tackle diet, and this must be recognized early on in the process of changing your eating habits. Thinking and feeling positive helps develop self-confidence, which is a great starting point for controlling weight.

When changing eating habits it is important to also learn self-control. The first stage of this is planning, deciding what to buy when out shopping or what to eat on any particular day. These plans need to be realistic and achievable.

Above: *Always consult your doctor before making any drastic changes to your lifestyle or eating habits.*

The second stage is sticking to the plan. Think honestly about the influences on your eating habits, such as family and friends, and consider the situations that are associated with less-sensible eating. For example, impulse eating and shopping or special occasions are likely problem areas that often spiral out of control.

Below: *Try to get the support of friends and family when changing eating habits – this will make it easier to maintain control.*

how to start a diet

THE HARDEST PART of adopting a new healthy eating lifestyle or embarking on a weight-loss programme is finding the motivation to get started. There is a lot more involved than many people realize, including clearing out cupboards, buying in the basic ingredients and equipment, and drawing up firm eating plans.

Starting a weight-loss programme or diet may sound easy, but if you rush into it without proper consideration and preparation, there is a real danger that you may not achieve your goals. Preparation, both mental and practical, gives a greater chance of succeeding.

THE STAGES OF CHANGE
The first step in getting started is to decide on your readiness for change. This can be represented by "The Stages of Change".

There are five recognized stages in this model, which everybody needs to progress through: pre-contemplation, contemplation, preparation, action and maintenance. Pre-contemplation is when someone is not actively thinking about weight loss but is aware of the need to do so. Contemplation is when there is active thought about the

Below: Prepare vegetables and keep them in the refrigerator or take them to work so you always have a supply of healthy snacks.

need to lose weight. Preparation refers to getting ready for weight loss, which includes researching the programme. Action is making the decision to lose weight and beginning to implement the starting regime. Maintenance is having the motivation to keep the weight-loss programme going and deciding to continue positively until all of the goals are achieved. Track your progress through these stages.

MOTIVATION
A person's expressed degree of readiness to change is described as their motivation. When starting a diet, it is important to focus on the positive and think about how much slimmer you want to be rather than how fat you are. As a positive incentive, list the reasons for losing weight and all of those things that will be possible when the excess weight has gone.

A useful way to check your readiness for change is to draw a straight line. Label one end "not ready" and the other "ready". In the middle put "unsure". Honestly mark on this line the point you are at. If you are not ready, then it is important to explore why there is this feeling of reluctance. Address any problems before starting the weight-loss programme as it is imperative to remove any barriers or obstacles in your way.

BARRIERS TO CHANGE
Everybody will face barriers to changing their eating habits, and addressing these barriers makes it easier to achieve goals. It is not possible to control and change all barriers and this should be acknowledged.

A common barrier to change is the amount of money available for food. The cost of the diet needs to be compared to the money spent on poorer quality foods, including sweets (candies), chocolates,

GETTING READY: THE CHECKLIST

Deal with the following before starting:
- Assess your readiness for change by listing reasons for losing weight and the things you cannot do due to your excess weight.
- Set realistic targets to help achieve your goals.
- Consider any barriers to change and remove as many as possible.
- Keep a food and feelings chart.
- Clear your kitchen cupboards of unwanted items.
- Check for any useful equipment, such as a blender and steamer, to ensure they are readily accessible.
- Draw up eating plans and shopping lists.
- Ensure basic food items, such as fresh herbs and rapeseed (canola) oil, are purchased.
- Prepare food in advance and freeze it if this helps.
- Practise saying "no" aloud to reject some foods.
- Identify someone to whom you can talk if necessary.
- Set a date to start.

cookies and processed foods. The price of food in local shops and access to cheaper out-of-town supermarkets should also be considered. The ability to prepare suitable foods, facilities and time available are important factors. Many foods, such as salad leaves, cold meats, canned fish and nuts require little time to prepare or cook; they simply have to be added to the shopping list to replace prepared foods.

Lifestyle barriers and situations that tempt a break in diet need to be acknowledged and avoided. If eating out plays a significant role in your life, choosing appropriately from a menu is important. Keeping alcohol consumption under control is also integral to long-term success. Although there will be times when you slip up, special occasions should not be seen as an excuse for breaking the diet. Instead, they should be incorporated into the regime.

Unhappiness, loneliness, boredom or jealousy are all feelings that can propel people into eating more. Emotions should be recognized for what they are to avoid seeking comfort in food. Charting feelings and food can help identify comfort eating. For example, writing down on a daily basis the time, place, company and activity alongside the food eaten can help. Note how you felt before eating – if you were hungry – and how you felt after eating. This can provide clues to genuine hunger and times when eating is a response to other influences. By seeking support from family and friends, and thinking about coping strategies, more control can be gained.

Above: *One of the biggest challenges to your will-power will occur at parties and when eating out with friends or family – try to plan ahead for these situations.*

Below: *Snacks like unsalted nuts need absolutely no preparation, so they are ideal to keep on stand-by, whether at work or at home, in case of hunger pangs.*

SETTING GOALS

There are three main areas to think about when deciding to change – importance, confidence and readiness. Importance is to do with "why?", "is it worthwhile?", "what will change?", and "do I really want to?". Confidence deals with areas such as "how will I do it?" and "will I succeed ?". Low levels of confidence can also affect a person's feelings and thoughts about the importance of change. Both of these affect the readiness to change – the "when" question, with thoughts such as "should I do it now?".

Goal setting is an excellent way to approach the challenge of weight loss. It is similar to planning a long journey in small stages to reduce the overall task into more manageable chunks. The ultimate goal of losing weight can be divided into strategies on how to succeed. For this regime the strategies include eating only healthy fats in the right quantities, taking more exercise,

limiting the consumption of unhealthy, refined carbohydrates and eating large portions of lower-fat protein foods.

These strategies can then be divided into specific targets. Taking a target of eating only healthy fats in the right quantities as an example, ways to achieve this can include eating oily fish twice per week, using rapeseed (canola) oil in cooking, and eating nuts as the basis for a main meal once per week.

Drawing up a list of clearly achievable targets is one way of remaining positive and confident throughout the programme. This makes the ultimate goal easier to grasp. Learn to be in charge of eating by saying "no" with conviction and being assertive about what you do eat.

shopping

ONE OF the biggest factors in your new healthy-eating lifestyle is the weekly shopping trip. Shopping must be a structured event so that the temptations of processed foods and unhealthy snacks are avoided. Read labels carefully and only buy things if you need them as part of your weekly eating plan.

Diet-wise, shopping can be a dangerous time and it should be well planned. Always try to go shopping after a meal, rather than before it when you are still hungry, and always plan ahead with a shopping list.

Portion sizes of ordinary foods are becoming bigger. Products promote big better-value portions and, quite naturally,

Below: Before shopping, work out a menu for each day of the week and buy only those ingredients you need.

these large portions are all eaten. People are encouraged to buy bigger portions by offers on items such as deep-filled sandwiches or double-decker burgers. Sometimes there may be simply no alternative available, or standard-size portions may be more expensive. Multi-packs and two-for-one offers can represent a great cost saving when they are needed, but too often these are simply marketing ploys to make us buy and eat more. Shoppers beware.

Food labels are the source of information to examine. This can take some time so try not to rush food shopping. Labels provide information concerning the main ingredients in the food and the amount of protein, carbohydrate, fat and energy contributed by the food. The information can be very detailed and fairly confusing, so ensure you read it carefully before choosing and buying food. The ingredients are listed in order of weight, so the main ingredient is always at the top of the list.

Many "health" logos and nutrition claims appear on foods. Be sure to understand the meaning of these and do not assume that all products are suitable. For example, a food may claim to be low in saturated fat on the label, but it may still contain high levels of refined carbohydrate.

NUTRITIONAL INFORMATION

It is important to remember the portion size and quantity of the food eaten. Some foods may look extremely high in energy, but if they are eaten in small amounts they can still be suitable for this type of diet. Foods that are eaten more regularly or in larger amounts have a greater effect on the balance of the diet.

A TYPICAL LABEL

Energy content describes the number of calories or joules that the food provides, while the amount of protein is measured in grams. Carbohydrate includes both sugars and starches, but a typical label often does not differentiate between those containing natural sugars or added sugar. Most labels neither indicate whether a food contains a slow-release type of carbohydrate, nor what other nutrients (in the form of vitamins or minerals, for example) it may contain.

When shopping for food, examine labels carefully. The information is incredibly useful in determining whether a food is right for your diet or whether you should avoid it. A typical label will look something like this:

TACO SHELLS (reduced salt)

NUTRITIONAL INFORMATION

Typical values per 100g

Energy	1958kJ/468kcal
Protein	7.2g
Carbohydrate	62.4g
Fat	22.6g
(of which saturates)	3.2g
(monounsaturates)	8.9g
(polyunsaturates)	8.5g
Sodium	15mg

Typical values per shell

Energy	259kJ/62kcal
Protein	1.0g
Carbohydrate	8.3g
Fat	3.0g
(of which saturates)	0.4g
(monounsaturates)	1.1g
(polyunsaturates)	1.1g
Sodium	2mg

Fat describes the total amount of fat found in the food and this is usually broken down into saturates, monounsaturates and polyunsaturates. A good guide is to aim for foods that contain less than 1g saturated fat per 100g portion. Alternatively, choose foods that contain a higher proportion of fat, but from monounsaturated sources.

Sodium indicates the amount of salt a product contains, and this is measured in milligrams. Try to stick to foods that contain less than 100mg sodium per 100g as a high salt intake is bad for your health.

ALTERNATIVES TO PRE-PREPARED PRODUCTS

Today's lifestyles have resulted in the market share of pre-prepared and processed foods rising dramatically. Everyone works to very busy and hectic schedules but being on a diet does not mean missing out on quick and easy foods. Preparing food in advance is the alternative to buying ready-made items. Many of the recommended foods in this programme require little or no cooking;

Above: If you prepare food in advance of meal times, you are less likely to be tempted by quick and easy processed foods.

others can easily be made in advance then stored in the refrigerator or freezer.

Salad dressings are an excellent example. Oil and vinegar-based dressings can be shaken together in a screw-topped jar and stored in the refrigerator for up to one month. Similarly, fresh pesto can be made from basil, pine nuts, garlic, olive oil and Parmesan cheese and stored for up to two weeks in the fridge.

The freezer can be stocked with lean meat and fish that can easily be defrosted overnight and quickly chargrilled to provide a simple and healthy main meal when served with steamed vegetables or salad.

Home-made marinades, stocks and tomato sauces can also be cooked in bulk and frozen in smaller quantities. These can form the basis for soups and provide the finishing touches to many dishes by enhancing plain ingredients.

Below: Make fresh pesto and store it in the refrigerator – it makes a delicious and quick accompaniment to many meals.

the importance of exercise

WHEN TRYING to lose weight, it is important that you exercise as well as controlling your diet. Any exercise is better than none, so do whatever you can, whenever you can. The best way of sticking to a new exercise programme, however, is to make the exercise part of your daily routine.

Exercise is good for you, and it is more important than usual when trying to lose weight. Weight is based on energy balance. If more calories (or energy) are consumed than burned up, there is weight gain; if more energy is used up than is actually eaten, this will help weight loss. Exercise also helps to strengthen muscles while encouraging the body to burn fat, creating a more toned and sleek look.

HEALTH BENEFITS FOR ALL
Regular exercise has been shown to reduce depression and stress, regulate appetite, boost self-confidence, and improve sleep quality. Other conditions that can be improved by regular exercise include heart disease, diabetes and osteoporosis.

Below: *Even pleasurable activities like gardening use up more energy than remaining sedentary, so count as exercise.*

Exercise helps in the prevention and treatment of heart disease and strokes by controlling important risk factors such as high blood pressure and high blood cholesterol. In diabetes, regular activity improves the body's sensitivity to insulin and reduces the risk of developing type 2 (late onset) diabetes. Regular exercise also strengthens bones and prevents osteoporosis. Weight-bearing exercise such as running, jogging, climbing stairs, skipping or aerobics is especially beneficial.

THE BEST EXERCISE
To the question of which exercise is best, the answer is "any exercise that you like". Anything that gets you moving and the heart pumping is good. One of the main problems people face is that they start exercise regimes with good intentions, but over a period of time they lose enthusiasm and stop. This can be due to choosing inappropriate exercise routines.

Walking is the most important weight-loss activity. The pace should be faster than normal but without over-exertion. Walking aids weight loss because it is weight bearing, uses the large muscle groups, makes the body breathe more frequently and deeply, and increases heart rate. Walking can be maintained for a considerable length of time, and it is even better when hills or stairs are involved.

Regular aerobic activity, such as swimming, cycling, dancing, skipping, running, rowing or aerobics, either in a gym using machines or outside, can result in a big energy deficit in the body. The optimum fat-burning exercise is one that uses up the most energy in the limited time available. Those who exercise at lighter levels often do not exercise for long enough to reach the same use of fat.

Above: *Swimming is a very good form of exercise. The body is fully supported by the water, which prevents joint or muscle strain.*

Choosing an enjoyable activity also helps to maintain exercise routines, while exercising with other people can provide the motivation to continue. Find out what is on offer in your local area and commit to something fun. Any exercise that changes a sedentary lifestyle into one that involves getting up and moving will help.

THE AMOUNT OF EXERCISE
It is recommended that everyone takes at least 30 minutes daily exercise on an average of five days per week. For those trying to lose weight this should be increased to 60 minutes per day, five days per week. However, it is important to

remember that any exercise is better than none. It may take a few weeks to build up to 60 minutes per day so do not lose heart.

To help include all these different types of activity, it is a good idea to have different slots (in its broadest sense) for exercise throughout the day rather than limiting it to once a day at a particular time. It is also a good idea to aim for regular aerobic activity and at least one walk of over 30 minutes per day. Learn to look upon weekends and free evenings as an opportunity to do more exercise than usual, rather than a chance to lounge around and watch TV.

LOSING FAT NOT MUSCLE

Wanting to lose weight means wanting to lose fat from your body, not muscle. Recent studies have shown that weight loss diets containing moderate amounts of carbohydrate and higher proportions of protein improve the use of body fat as an energy source while maintaining more muscle. The result is that your body shape will change over time. It is not yet fully understood how this works, but it is thought to be due to an effect on hormone levels.

Exercise is known to increase the metabolic rate and encourage the body to burn fat. Also, more energy is required to maintain body muscle than fat, so people with more body muscle burn up more energy on a weight for weight basis.

BODY IMAGE

Health is often not the main reason that people want to lose weight. The majority want to shed pounds to improve their overall body image. Many are unhappy with their shape and the way they are sometimes treated because of their appearance. Weight loss certainly helps to improve self-esteem and confidence for many people, and it can make people look at someone in a new light. This is in addition to the health benefits. Using exercise as part of a plan to improve body image is excellent as it helps to tone up muscles and improve appearance.

EXERCISE IDEAS

Household chores and normal routines make a valuable contribution to the exercise quota. The following activities can be incorporated into daily life:
- Using the stairs instead of the lift
- Walking rather than taking the bus or car
- Walking one bus stop further away than usual
- Dancing
- Gardening
- Housework, such as window cleaning or shopping
- Playing with the children
- Walking the dog
- Do-it-yourself (DIY)
- Hiding the TV remote control

Below: *Take the dog for a long and energetic walk in the country – a great way to burn off calories after a meal.*

getting support while losing weight

ACHIEVING SUCCESS on your new weight-loss programme is only possible if all barriers to change are overcome. Gaining the support of family and friends is crucial, and by allowing time for preparing food and enjoying breakfast, for example, eating habits will be vastly improved.

Keeping the key points in focus is important in order to lose weight. The mental and physical preparation has been explained, along with the need for a firm commitment, but the area that is too often forgotten is the need to acknowledge and remove all obstacles that may hamper progress.

Losing weight is about energy balance – the amount of energy consumed needs to be lower than the amount of energy burnt up by living plus exercise. For example, 450g/1lb fat contains 3,500 calories, so to lose 450g/1lb per week, there needs to be a calorie deficit between intake and expenditure of 500 calories per day. To increase energy output, at least 60 minutes of activity is required five days a week.

It is important to remember the health messages when losing weight to reduce the risk of illnesses such as heart disease,

Above: *Quick and nutritious fruit smoothies or freshly squeezed fruit juices make a filling and nutritious treat at any time of day.*

type 2 diabetes, cancer and osteoporosis. The choice of food must be taken into consideration. Carbohydrate intake should be reduced to cut back on energy intake and food groups selected wisely to keep blood sugar levels in check. The diet should include five portions of fruit and vegetables per day (from non-starchy sources), a regular intake of peas, beans and lentils, and small amounts of wholegrain cereals or those grains that contain a higher proportion of fats and protein to carbohydrate. Refined carbohydrates, including those hidden in processed foods, should be avoided.

Fats should be limited as they are concentrated sources of energy. Using lean meat, nuts, seeds, soya and skimmed-milk products reduces fat intake considerably.

Including two portions of oily fish per week alongside white fish and shellfish also keeps the fat intake under control and ensures the diet includes a healthier type of fat. Small amounts of rapeseed (canola) oil and olive oil can be used for cooking. Oily salad dressings should be measured to keep a check on the quantity used.

Protein choices should exclude processed foods that contain large amounts of carbohydrates and saturated fats. Two large helpings of lean meat, poultry, fish, eggs, nuts, peas, beans and lentils, soya or mycoprotein (such as Quorn) daily are ideal along with regular consumption of skimmed milk and low-fat yogurt.

Eating a wide variety of good-quality, unprocessed foods ensures that the required intake of vitamins and minerals can be achieved and salt intake will be reduced.

Below: *Studies have proved that people who eat a filling breakfast every morning are less likely to be overweight.*

Below: *Use plenty of herbs and spices when cooking to ensure that food doesn't taste bland and unappetising.*

KEEPING IT TASTY

Try experimenting with new foods and recipes to avoid blandness and boredom as they are the worst aspects of any diet. Aim to try one completely new recipe every week. Shop at different supermarkets or shops to come across new and interesting items.

Use different cooking methods. For example, light the barbecue to grill chicken, or treat yourself to a new kitchen appliance, such as a steamer, and experiment with it.

Enliven food by trying different herbs and spices – as well as standard seasonings, try the herb and spice mixes from different cuisines. Spices are not all hot – the majority are aromatic and warm in flavour.

Change or vary the meal. For example, instead of always having the same packed lunch, try salads, soups, wraps or cheese and fruit. Ask for suggestions from family and friends. Everyone has a favourite and foolproof recipe they will be willing to share.

A FOOD DIARY

Writing a food diary is an excellent way of keeping track of the food you have consumed. Ensuring that everything that passes your lips is written down in a special book is a good way of checking on how well plans have been kept and identifying ways in which you can improve.

Slip-ups are inevitable and should be dealt with in a positive way as they are not the end of the world. Instead of feeling guilty, acknowledge a lapse and start afresh immediately. This is important otherwise a phase of uncontrolled eating could be allowed to develop. Praise and reward success, however small, with non-food indulgences, such as time or money spent on a glossy magazine, a new book or having a long soak in a hot bath. This is much more encouraging than self-criticism for indiscretion.

EATING PATTERNS

People who eat regular meals find it easier to control their weight. This enables the body to keep blood sugar levels more stable, and there is comfort in knowing when the next meal will happen. This way true feelings of hunger and fullness are more easily recognized by the body, which helps to keep binge eating under control.

Breakfast is a must in a regular pattern, and recent studies have shown that those who skip breakfast are 450 per cent more likely to be obese. If time is short in the morning, fruit can be prepared the night before and placed in the refrigerator. Alternatively, a low-fat milkshake or fruit smoothie is ideal first thing in the morning.

Snacking between meals does not in itself encourage weight gain – in fact, those who enjoy at least one snack per day alongside regular meals are less likely to become obese. It is the additional energy that is consumed through poor snack choices and bigger portions that is often to blame. Low-energy, high-nutrient foods, such as fruit, nuts or seeds, are ideal for snacks.

There is no indication that eating late at night contributes to weight gain when the total calorie intake is taken into account. However, eating meals away from home is associated with greater weight, probably because of the larger portions served.

INCLUDE THE FAMILY

Everyone needs support and this may come from family, friends and even work colleagues. It is especially important to involve those in your household as any change in eating habits may affect them. Communication is vital for success, and you have to voice the negative feelings about being overweight, making it clear to everyone why weight loss is so important.

Children must not be put on any weight-reducing regime unless they are under the direct supervision of a doctor or dietician. However, they can be involved with planning suitable meals, preparing shopping lists, cooking and coming up with new ideas to vary the healthy diet. Encourage structured meal times and make eating an occasion for talking and relaxing, rather than grabbing food on the move.

Include the family in an exercise regime. Cycling, swimming or taking a long walk with a picnic can be great fun. Finally, remember to include others in your success. Share your rewards by taking the family out to the cinema, for example, to show them how much you appreciate their support.

Below: Encourage more structured meal times for the whole family. This will help to get their full support and drive you on to achieve your realistic weight-loss goals.

maintaining a diet plan

IT IS EASY to start a diet with good intentions, but difficult in practice to maintain it. Eating out and grabbing snacks on the run are real problems for many dieters, so it is important to understand exactly what you can eat. Keeping a diet interesting can also be difficult, so always look out for new suggestions.

It is not just the reasoning and theory behind a diet that is important but the practical issues that make it work. Planning meals in advance gives a diet structure and definitely promotes sensible choices, but this may not always be possible. Keeping carbohydrate intake under control may be a new and different way of eating, but it is not unusual and should not be too difficult. Starchy sources of carbohydrate, such as rice, potatoes, pasta and bread, should be avoided completely, and there are lots of alternatives for a filling and healthy diet. A meal consisting of protein, such as lean meat, poultry or fish, with two or three different vegetables or salad, is always an excellent and nutritious choice.

Below: *Large flat mushrooms baked with crushed garlic and olive oil are a simple yet delicious vegetable accompaniment.*

IDEAS FOR VEGETABLES

Vegetables can be shredded and stir-fried or cooked by many other methods instead of being boiled. Steaming vegetables or lightly stir-frying vegetable strips retains the goodness and fresh flavour. For a different texture, try coarsely grating vegetables such as carrots and cucumber.

- Large mushrooms can be baked with a spot of olive oil or pesto and used as a base for serving grilled meats, or served as an accompaniment.
- Courgettes (zucchini), (bell) peppers, aubergines (eggplant), carrots and tomatoes are delicious roasted – cooking this way intensifies their flavours.
- Beetroot (beet) and tomatoes can be dressed in balsamic vinegar.
- Bake courgettes, onions and aubergines in a rich garlic and tomato sauce.

Above: *Add interest to a simple bowl of mixed salad with extras such as chopped fruit, cold meat, grated cheese or nuts.*

- Bake leeks in a low-fat cheese sauce seasoned with mustard.
- Beans and lentils make a delicious base for meat or fish, or they can be cooked with spices and served as the main dish with vegetables or salad.
- Different types of salad leaves can be mixed to vary flavours and colours. For interest, introduce stronger flavours with watercress or rocket (arugula).
- A large bowl of mixed salad is an ideal dish. Nuts, peas, beans and lentils, such as chickpeas or kidney beans, grated or chopped vegetables, chopped apples, grated cheese, lean meat or fish can be added in whatever combinations you like. Toss with a small amount of dressing based on olive oil or low-fat yogurt to keep the calories down but avoid overwhelming the fresh ingredients by drenching them with dressing.

ALTERNATIVES TO SANDWICHES

Hot or cold soups can be carried in a flask to make a filling and nutritious meal. A large mixed salad can be carried to work in a sealed container, especially if there is a refrigerator to store food.

Instead of using bread, wrap low-fat cheeses or pates in cold ham or smoked salmon and cut into bitesize pieces. These are excellent with salad.

If there is no alternative, open sandwiches can be prepared on wholemeal bread sliced very thinly – try lean meat, fish or vegetables as a topping. Wraps using soft tortillas can hold lots of filling, while a taco shell is useful for scooping up dips, such as hummus or tzatsiki. Taco shells can be filled with salad for a crunchy snack, and sticks of carrot, cucumber and other vegetables are also good with dips.

SNACK IDEAS

If you need a snack between meals, this is not a bad thing, but remember to differentiate between boredom and hunger. Traditional snacks can be high in energy and low in nutrients so choose from these alternatives:

- Fresh fruit, such as melon wedges or chopped pineapple.
- Unsalted nuts in small amounts.
- Seeds, such as sunflower or pumpkin.
- Vegetable sticks on their own or to use with dips.

- Olives with cucumber sticks.
- Cheese fingers in small quantities.
- Yogurt – use natural as a base for mixing in prepared fruit to avoid the refined carbohydrates in flavoured yogurts.
- Fruit smoothies – whizz them up in a blender in seconds.

EATING OUT

From breakfast on the way to work, a snack at lunchtime or a main meal in the evening, eating out is no longer reserved for special occasions and treats.

American studies have shown that portion sizes have grown, with a cheeseburger increasing in weight from 162g in 1977 to 198g in 1996. The body quickly adjusts to these larger portion sizes, so the danger is that bigger meals may then be served at home.

Drinks are also getting larger. Red wine glasses are now usually 175ml rather than the traditional 125ml, and a shot of spirits has increased from 25ml to 35ml. Not only does this mean more calories but also more alcohol, which makes calculations of units consumed very confusing.

Sensible selections and an awareness of portions and quantities are important when eating out. Sharing dishes is a good way of distributing larger portions, and this is quite acceptable in most restaurants. In Chinese and Japanese restaurants, eating with chopsticks slows down eating and tends to limit the quantity consumed.

Indian food This can be very oily and high in energy. Choose tikka or tandoori meats or fish baked with spices and served with salad. Raita, a yogurt and cucumber dish, or a spicy dish of chopped onions with chilli are good accompaniments. Lassi, a flavoured buttermilk drink, is suitable but choose those flavoured with herbs or spices. Pulses can be a good choice and are delicious served with onions, tomato and yogurt. Indian sweets are high in refined sugars so avoid them.

Left: Serve vegetable sticks with fresh dips based on cottage cheese or yogurt, for example with garlic and herbs.

Above: *The average glass of wine served in restaurants today is larger than in the past, which means more calories.*

Italian food For an appetizer, choose Parma ham with melon, tricolore salad, stuffed mushrooms, tuna with beans, hearty bean and vegetable soups or traditional antipasto misto. Grilled meat or fish and salad or vegetables are good choices for the main course. Avoid pasta, risotto or pizza.
Chinese and East-Asian food Traditional soups with shredded meats, seafood and vegetables are a meal in one bowl, but soups thickened with starch or containing noodles should be avoided. Lettuce leaves are used as wraps for shredded meats and vegetables. Crispy Beijing duck is suitable as the pancakes contain as little as 4.5g carbohydrate each. Spare ribs or satay prawns, beef or chicken are good choices. Stir-fried vegetables are used as a base for many dishes, but some come in thickened sauces. Steamed fish is popular and tofu is an excellent alternative to meat or fish.
Turkish and Greek food This is mainly based on grilled meat or fish, served with salad, which is ideal. Be careful with dips, such as hummus, as these may be generously dressed with oil.
Mexican food Guacamole with grilled meat or fish is suitable. Choose salads and salsas, and mild jalapeno chillies or (bell) peppers. Fajitas and refried beans are fine but limit the number of taco shells or tortilla wraps. Avoid tortilla chips with sour cream and deep-fried tortillas.

keeping the weight off

TO MAINTAIN weight loss, significant lifestyle changes must take place. Once the weight has dropped off, it is possible to slowly reintroduce small amounts of carbohydrate, but it is important not to slip back into old eating habits and routines. Regular exercise also remains a huge factor for success.

Much has been written about how to lose weight initially but not as much on maintaining the loss. There is no one ideal solution to healthy weight maintenance, but studies have shown that there are common factors among those people who are successful in keeping the weight off.

One of the most important factors is increasing levels of physical activity. Those who habitually participate in high levels of exercise as part of their lifestyle maintained more of the weight loss than those whose exercise levels were lower. Once the weight has been lost, the amount of exercise can be reduced gradually from 60 minutes to 30 minutes for 5 days per week. It is still important to continue with aerobic activity, however, such as cycling, running, dancing and walking whenever possible.

Below: *When considering reintroducing carbohydrates, try a light couscous salad with fresh vegetables and herbs.*

Individuals who were successful in losing considerable amounts of weight (greater than 20kg/44lb or greater than 5 per cent of their initial body weight) during a weight-loss programme were more likely to sustain long-term loss. These were people who had lost the weight gradually and consistently at the recommended rate 0.5–1kg/1–2lb per week. The longer the weight remained off, the less likely it was to be regained again, suggesting that skills and behaviour patterns acquired in achieving weight loss had become part of a successful and permanent lifestyle change.

BEING IN CONTROL

Taking control of eating habits and not feeling guilty about eating certain foods has a positive effect on keeping weight off.

Above: *Serve oatcakes instead of bread to enjoy with cheese, patés and cold meats – ideal for buffet-style meals.*

Weight control is about long-term change. The idea of being "on a diet" is not the ideal way of thinking because as soon as you come "off the diet", the weight is regained. The long-term goal is to change old habits, attitudes and behaviour by maintaining the short-term goals that have been achieved. Continuing to monitor weight weekly but not obsessively, using scales or clothes as a guide, is a useful way of checking weight maintenance.

The key is to realize that it is not possible to return to old eating habits, and it may take time to feel confident about controlling weight at the new level.

EATING PATTERNS: LONG-TERM CHANGES

Continuing to eat regular meals, including a substantial breakfast, light lunch and healthy dinner, and paying attention to portion sizes is important. Eating out is acceptable within reason, and is often unavoidable, but you must select food carefully, and fast food should still be avoided. The quality of the food intake should remain good, with fruit and vegetables retaining the primary place in your diet, alongside lean meat, fish, dairy products, nuts, peas, beans and lentils, and seeds. This maintains the healthy profile.

After the initial weight-loss period, the quantity of carbohydrate you consume can be increased gradually until your weight stabilises at a healthy level. When reintroducing carbohydrates to your diet, start with small helpings of wholegrain cereals, such as wholemeal (whole-wheat) bread, brown rice or pasta, starchy fruit and vegetables, and foods with a low glycaemic index. Initially, these should be introduced once per day. Refined carbohydrates that have few nutritional benefits, such as confectionery, carbonated drinks, squashes and sugars, should still be limited and avoided wherever possible.

SPECIAL OCCASIONS AND HOLIDAYS

Lifestyle changes should be permanent rather than temporary. This means that it is essential to maintain the new positive and healthy lifestyle on special occasions as well as during holidays. If weight does begin to creep back on, acknowledge it and don't just try to ignore the problem. Examine why you have regained some weight and take control of the situation without feeling guilty. Getting back on track again is extremely important. You will then be able to manage stress and confront problems head on, rather than eating uncontrollably to try and make a problem disappear.

Life is not just about eating and drinking, and it is now important to find some new point of focus. This may be a new exercise regime or hobby that was impossible when overweight, a new interest, such as studying or taking evening classes, a new job or travelling abroad. Whatever this new focus is, you will be physically confident and able to take control.

Below: *Continue enjoying a high level of exercise to maintain weight loss, and involve family and friends to provide motivation.*

REINTRODUCING GOOD CARBOHYDRATES

When weight loss has been achieved, wholegrain sources of good-quality carbohydrates can be reintroduced. These should be included once per day and the quantities increased gradually until weight stabilises. As a guide, they should be kept to under 20 per cent of intake, so that less than one fifth of the food on your plate is starchy. The following are ideal foods to introduce:

- Wholemeal (whole-wheat) pasta in a salad or served with tomato sauce, lean minced meat or vegetables.
- Aubergines (eggplant), (bell) peppers or marrow (large zucchini) stuffed with brown rice and vegetables.
- Wholegrain cereals, such as muesli (granola), with added fruit and possibly some wheatgerm.
- Couscous with lots of fresh herbs and salad vegetables, for example it could be used to make a tabbouleh-type salad.
- Thinly sliced wholegrain bread toasted into croutons to serve with soup or salad.
- Crunchy oatcakes to eat instead of bread with patés, cold meats or cheeses.
- Sweet potato baked and served with home-made crunchy coleslaw.
- Wholegrain noodles stir-fried with vegetables and tofu or fresh seafood, such as prawns.
- Barley or quinoa cooked with stock and vegetables, and served with lean grilled meat or fish.
- Banana or grapes with other fruits, such as apple, mandarin, kiwi and pineapple, in a fruit salad.

Refined sources of carbohydrates, such as cakes, biscuits (cookies) and sweets (candies) should still be limited as far as possible.

meal planners

Meal planner 1	Monday	Tuesday	Wednesday
Breakfast	Apricot and Ginger Compote served with Natural Yogurt	Freshly squeezed orange juice Griddled Tomatoes on Toast	Tomato juice Hot oat porridge
Lunch	Chicken and Avocado Soup Sunflower and pumpkin seed mix Fresh pineapple chunks	Soufflé Omelette with Mushrooms Mixed Green Leaf and Herb Salad Strawberries	Hummus dip with a selection of raw vegetables Handful of unsalted mixed nuts Fresh Fruit Salad
Dinner	Paper-wrapped and Steamed Red Snapper Spinach and Roast Garlic Salad Steamed baby sweetcorn	Barbecue-cooked Lamb Steaks with Red Pepper Salsa Radicchio and Chicory Gratin Fresh melon wedge	Roasted Vegetable Soup Steamed Mussels with Thai Herbs Pistachio Kulfi Ice Cream

Thursday	Friday	Saturday	Sunday
Strawberry and Honey Smoothie	Natural yogurt with stewed apple slices	Fresh pineapple juice	Poached rhubarb pieces
	Frittata with Sun-dried Tomatoes	Warm Salad with Poached Egg	Savoury Scrambled Eggs

Seafood Salad	Carpaccio with Rocket	Roasted Garlic and Butternut Squash Soup with Tomato Salsa	Figs with Prosciutto and Roquefort
Kiwi fruit	Orange and chickpea salad		Lamb Pot Roast with Tomatoes, Green Beans and Onions
	Fresh cherries	Mackerel and ricotta paté with taco shells and vegetable sticks	Braised fennel and leeks

Italian Sausages with Pancetta and Beans	Devilled Chicken	Duck and Sesame Stir-Fry	Pink Grapefruit and Avocado Salad
Steamed broccoli and cauliflower	Grilled mushrooms with pesto	Steamed oriental vegetables	Fresh passion fruit
	Anchovy and Roasted Pepper Salad	Satsumas	

Meal planner 2	Monday	Tuesday	Wednesday
Breakfast	Porridge with Dates and Pistachios	Frozen Melon Reduced-fat Edam cheese and apple	Orange juice Egg-stuffed Tomatoes
Lunch	Cold chicken topped with guacamole and salad Red cabbage coleslaw Figs and Pears in Honey	Lentil and Nut Loaf Okra with Coriander and Tomatoes Fresh peach	Chicken Satay with Peanut Sauce Pak Choi and Lime Dressing Shredded carrot
Dinner	Tomato and Fresh Basil Soup Pan-fried Tofu with Caramelized Sauce Beansprout salad	Skewered Lamb with Coriander Yogurt Broccoli with Garlic Roasted aubergines	Salmon with Leeks and Peppers Asparagus and Bacon Salad Poached pear

Thursday	Friday	Saturday	Sunday
Raspberry and oatmeal blend	Grapefruit with cinnamon	Cranberry juice	Apple juice
	Omelette Arnold Bennett	Herrings in Oatmeal with Bacon	Poached Eggs Florentine

Bean Salad with Tuna and Red Onion	Pork on Lemon Grass Sticks	Devilled Kidneys	Steak with Warm Tomato Salsa
Fresh lychees	Fried Spring Greens	Bed of lentils	Mushrooms with Chipotle Chillies
	Fruit Platter with Spices	Watercress salad	Steamed French beans

Red Chicken Curry with Bamboo Shoots	Mushrooms with Garlic and Chilli Sauce	Steamed Lettuce-wrapped Sole	Cheese-topped Roast Baby Vegetables
Courgette ribbons with mint raita	Pear, chickpea and walnut salad with yogurt dressing	Mexican-style Green Peas	Green salad
Mango and Lime Fool		Raspberries	

the low-carb
kitchen

MANY PEOPLE ARE WARY of a low-carbohydrate diet, seeing it as a restrictive way of living. This section takes a close look at the essentials of a successful low-carb diet, from the equipment you'll need to get started, to the ideal cooking methods and the ingredients that should form the bulk of your diet, and proves that it is anything but restrictive. From fresh fruit and vegetables to meat, fish, dairy foods and nutritious vegetable proteins such as nuts and tofu, there is a wide range of suitable foods that should be combined for a healthy, balanced diet.

kitchen basics

PREPARE YOUR kitchen by investing in a few basic pieces of equipment, and you'll find sticking to your new diet much simpler. Items like a blender are indispensable for creating fresh soups, sauces and smoothies, and a griddle pan will be used over and over again for cooking meat, fish and vegetables.

The correct equipment for preparing food, although not essential, does make cooking easier and in many cases more enjoyable. Even though the following equipment is recommended, it is probably wise to purchase items gradually, having considered how often they will be used, rather than rushing out and buying them all at once.

MEASURING EQUIPMENT

Kitchen scales Not all recipes require weighing, but accurate quantities are essential for some dishes. When trying to lose weight, it may be helpful to know exactly how much of a certain food has been eaten. Scales should be simple – digital or with weights as preferred, and adjustable for use with or without a bowl. They must also be handy, easy to clean and, most importantly, easy to use. Consider the accuracy and precision required – for example, some digital scales weigh to the nearest gram while others are accurate to 5 or 10 grams.

Below: *Getting your portion sizes correct is crucial when dieting, so invest in a measuring jug and a set of measuring spoons.*

Above: *Create fresh low-carb dressings with a useful salad-dressing bottle – any leftovers can simply be refrigerated.*

Cup measures American cup measures are used for dry ingredients and liquids. They can be used instead of scales for many foods or instead of a measuring jug (pitcher) for liquids.

Measuring jug (pitcher) or cone These measure fluids accurately, which can be important, especially when working with small amounts of concentrated ingredients. Choose a measure with clear increments that are easy to read. Many show measurements in millilitres, pints and cups.

Spoon measures Table cutlery is not suitable for measuring as the spoons vary in size. A set of measuring spoons may be in either metric or imperial, or some have metric scoops on one end of the handle and imperial at the other.

Salad-dressing bottle This is a large, bottle with a stopper and dressing recipes

marked on the side. The idea is to pour in the suggested quantities of each ingredient, cover and shake thoroughly to make a delicious dressing. Any excess can then be refrigerated in the covered bottle for up to 2 weeks, ready for quickly finishing a salad.

PREPARATION EQUIPMENT

Knives Sharp knives are an essential tool in the kitchen. The most practical choice is a serrated vegetable knife for chopping and a larger, heavier cook's knife for cutting. Check that the handles are comfortable to hold and that the blades are stainless steel.

Kitchen scissors These are useful for trimming and cutting bacon and herbs, as well as opening stubborn packets.

Chopping boards These are necessary to prevent damage to knives and worktops, and for hygienic food preparation. They should be colour-coded for preparing different types of foods, such as raw poultry or meat, salads or cooked foods. This is to prevent cross contamination of bacteria from raw to cooked food and flavour transfer, reducing the potential for food poisoning and improving hygiene in the kitchen for overall safety and protection.

Blender This is the one essential electric gadget. It saves time when making soups by blending them to smooth, consistent purées; it produces a better texture than pushing mixtures through a sieve (strainer); fruit can be puréed to make a coulis-style sauce; and smoothies or shakes can be whizzed up easily for a quick breakfast or snack. Blenders are particularly good for whizzing tender fruit, such as berries or pears, with milk, yogurt or even a probiotic drink, which contains good bacteria. Using a blender to make a smoothie retains the fibre component of the fruit, which is important for healthy digestion as well as cardiovascular health.

Above:
*Delicious
sauces or fruit
smoothies are quick and easy to
make with a blender.*

COOKING UTENSILS

Wok A large Chinese frying pan, this is ideal for stir-frying vegetables, strips of lean meat or poultry. A large, deep-sided non-stick pan with two handles is the best choice. These are available for use on both gas and electric stoves and many have a flat base for stability, although a round-bottomed wok is more authentic.

Right: *Cooking with a
griddle pan ensures
you use only
minimal fat.*

Above: *Steam fresh vegetables by slotting this stainless-steel basket inside a pan.*

Heavy griddle pan Essential for cooking vegetables, meat and fish, this gives food an attractive chargrilled look. A griddle pan needs only small amounts of fat, and the ridges allow any surplus fat to drain away. This makes it an extremely healthy way of cooking.

Ovenproof roasting dishes These are a good investment for roasting lots of vegetables or portions of fish as well as meat. They should be fairly heavy with a non-stick coating and a non-scratch surface.

Electric steamer This is a luxury item that will certainly be appreciated by anybody on a low-carbohydrate diet. Steaming ensures that no vital nutrients are lost in cooking so this method is perfect for tasty, vitamin-packed vegetables or fish. A stainless-steel steaming basket that opens and closes like a water lily and fits neatly inside pans is an economical alternative.

MAKING A SMOOTHIE

1 Prepare the fruit as necessary by washing it, peeling it if the skin is inedible, and carefully removing any stones, cores and large pips.

2 Place the fruit and chosen liquid, whether milk, fruit juice or water, in the blender and whizz together thoroughly. Add the fruit and liquid at the same time to ensure even blending.

3 Taste the smoothie and add any flavourings, such as herbs or spices, before blending again briefly.

cooking methods

SOME COOKING methods are healthier than others. These are the ones that tend to use a minimum amount of healthy oil, retain vitamins and minerals and result in great flavour, appearance and texture. Try to vary the cooking methods you use, rather than sticking to one, as this will add interest to your diet.

Marinating A marinade is a liquid flavoured with herbs, spices or aromatics in which ingredients are left to marinate before cooking. This adds flavour, tenderizes foods and keeps them moist so that additional fat is not needed. Lemon juice and herbs are often used for fish, orange juice and thyme for pork, pineapple for gammon (smoked or cured ham), yogurt and spices for meats cooked Middle-Eastern style, and soy sauce with ginger for Asian flavours.

Poaching This is a method of cooking food gently in hot liquid, such as water, stock or skimmed milk, without additional fat. It is commonly used for eggs and fish, and for East-Asian soups. Some fresh fruits can also be poached in wine. Any nutrients, such as vitamins and minerals, that have leached out from the food are consumed when the cooking liquor is served as part of the dish.

Steaming Vegetables and fish are often cooked in this way. Ingredients are not in direct contact with the water, and so they retain their flavours, juices and nutrients. Oil and fat are not needed. Time steaming carefully to avoid overcooking the food.

Griddling The griddle pan should be extremely hot. This ensures that the surface of the food is immediately sealed, which helps to retain juices and flavour, and also gives an attractive striped appearance. The griddle needs to be brushed with a small amount of rapeseed (canola) oil before cooking, so a few extra calories are added.

Grilling (broiling) Food is browned quickly and the juices are sealed in. Fat naturally present in food melts and drips out when ingredients are cooked slowly, so this is an ideal method of reducing the energy content of food. Foods containing very little fat, such as tofu or vegetables, should be brushed with a little oil or marinated before cooking to prevent them from drying out.

Stir-frying This is a fast method of cooking that retains vitamins. Ingredients should be cut into pieces approximately the same size, then added to a small amount of hot, flavoured oil, such as sesame oil. Meat and fish should be fully cooked; vegetables should retain their crunch.

Roasting Vegetables, such as aubergines (eggplant), tomatoes, miniature corn, (bell) peppers and courgettes (zucchini) are ideal for roasting with a teaspoon of olive oil. When roasting meat and poultry, discard any fat.

Casseroling One-pot meals cooked in a casserole are extremely practical. Casseroles can be left to cook for long periods or prepared ahead of time. They retain the natural goodness of the food and any excess fat can be skimmed off the surface before serving. Long, slow simmering tenderizes meat, while rich sauces transform simple ingredients into delicious dishes.

Casseroles vary from rich, winter stews flavoured with herbs and wine, to light vegetable, bean and lentil mixtures laced with garlic, tomatoes and yogurt, or seafood casseroles with saffron.

Microwaving Food is cooked by electromagnetic waves that cause any liquid molecules in the food to vibrate and create heat. Microwave ovens are ideal for heating pre-cooked food or defrosting frozen food; some microwaves also use conventional heat sources to brown food. The best role of the microwave is to cook vegetables quickly, so that they retain their vitamins, nutrients and texture.

Cooking "en papillotte" This involves wrapping food in paper before cooking. Fish, meat, poultry or vegetables retain their moisture, flavour and nutrients as they steam in their own juices. Non-stick baking parchment is perfect for foods to be steamed or baked; foil should be used on a barbecue.

Below: *When food is griddled, the surface is sealed, retaining juices and flavour*

Below: *Be adventurous with casseroles; experiment with different herbs and spices.*

the store cupboard

THERE ARE some basic ingredients that every cook should have in the kitchen cupboard, especially one who is on a low-carbohydrate eating programme. Once you've stocked up on these, experiment with different cooking methods such as roasting, griddling and preparing casseroles.

There are a few essential ingredients that keep for long periods of time, which you should always have ready in the store cupboard. The majority are seasonings and flavourings to transform ordinary recipes into great ones. This is not a comprehensive list, merely some suggestions to get started.

Anchovies These are great when making a tomato-based sauce as they melt into the sauce giving a delicious rich flavour with not a hint of fishiness.

Balsamic vinegar This rich vinegar can be used on its own to dress salads without any oil. Adding a teaspoon to roasted vegetables enhances their flavour.

Capers Useful in sauces, salads or snacks.

Lemon juice Bottled lemon juice is useful for times when fresh is not available.

Mustard Essential for salad dressings.

Olive oil This is essential for cooking or making salad dressings. Although it is a healthy oil, it is still very high in calories so should be limited in use and measured to keep the quantities under control.

Olives Whether green or black, stuffed or unstuffed, these are good in salads and for snacking in between meals.

Above: *Use olive oil sparingly as it is high in calories, despite being a healthy oil.*

Above: *Freshly ground black pepper adds flavour and kick to finished dishes.*

Pepper If there is only one item in your store cupboard, it should be a pepper mill filled with fresh black peppercorns. Pepper enhances flavours without the negative health impact of salt.

Spices Gradually build up your selection of spices according to taste, rather than buying them all. Nutmeg and cinnamon are useful ingredients in savoury dishes as well as sweet.

Thai fish sauce This is useful for bringing an Eastern flavour to some dishes.

Tomato purée (paste) This enriches and thickens sauces, and boosts their flavour.

White wine vinegar This is an essential ingredient for vinaigrette salad dressings.

Worcestershire sauce A dash of this flavourful sauce can be used to add a piquant, slightly sharp edge to many dishes.

WINDOW BOX HERBS

Herbs are an essential flavouring and garnish for most recipes. Fresh herbs are better than dried, and a window ledge is an ideal place to grow a selection. Try the following:

- Parsley, preferably flat leaf.
- Coriander (cilantro) works especially well in chicken or fish dishes.
- Basil is essential for tomatoes and to give an Italian flavour.
- Sage is great with liver or turkey.
- Mint is refreshing with fruit.

SHOPPING LIST ESSENTIALS

The following is a list of essential items that every chef should have on their shopping list, irrespective of what is being cooked. They are all fresh, perishable ingredients so must be replaced regularly.

- Garlic
- Chilli peppers
- Fresh root ginger
- Lemons
- Onions
- Pesto
- Plain low-fat yogurt
- Half-fat crème fraîche
- Parmesan cheese

fruit

AN ESSENTIAL part of any diet is fresh fruit, packed full of vitamins and minerals. To make sure you eat enough fruit, experiment by adding it to savoury salads and main courses, rather than just grabbing it as a snack or dessert. Remember that some fruits contain more natural sugars than others.

Apples Cultivated for more than 3,000 years, apples are a popular and versatile fruit. They can be enjoyed raw as a snack, eaten with cheese, grated into salad with nuts or added to a fruit salad. They can also be stewed and served as a sauce with pork, or baked and served as a classic dessert. Although fairly low in vitamin C, apples are rich in soluble fibre and pectin, both of which may help to lower cholesterol levels in the blood.

Berries Strawberries, raspberries, blackberries, blueberries and other berries are luscious, delicate fruits that need gentle handling. Look for bright and firm berries that show no signs of bruising, wetness or mildew. Fat, juicy berries are all wonderful served with thick, low-fat yogurt or crème fraîche. They can also be pushed through a sieve (strainer) or whizzed in a blender to

make a delicious coulis or sauce. Strawberries make an attractive base for a summer fruit salad, salsa or a salad with mint and cucumber. All berries can be made into mousses, fools or smoothies, or used to decorate fruit cocktails or puddings. Cranberries are hard, bright shiny berries with an acidic, slightly spicy flavour. They are most commonly used for making cranberry sauce, often served with turkey, or bought as juice in a refreshing, nutritious drink that is rich in vitamin C. All berries are abundant in nutrients. For example, blueberries contain valuable amounts of fibre, vitamin C and B vitamins along with flavenoids that can aid the body's defences against infection. Raspberries also contain high levels of folate, potassium and zinc, making them a healthy choice.

Blackcurrants and redcurrants These contain a useful amount of calcium and are one of the best possible sources of vitamin C. The stems and flower ends should be removed during preparation, unless the berries are going to be sieved (strained). Generally, currants are best used cooked otherwise they are extremely tart.

Cherries These make a simple, tasty and refreshing dessert. They also provide a delicious and unusual start to a meal in the form of a chilled soup, which is light and easy to digest. Pitted cherries can be used in salads and are delicious with almonds in a yogurt dressing to accompany rich game meats. They provide valuable amounts of the antioxidant vitamin C, which helps resistance to infection.

Above: *Try making either a delicious chilled plum soup or a rich sauce with juicy Victoria plums.*

Below: *Apples are extremely filling and make a healthy, convenient snack.*

POACHING FRUIT

1 Prepare the poaching liquid – red wine, grape juice or canned fruit juice are ideal. Add any flavourings, such as cinnamon, cloves or a vanilla pod.

2 Boil the liquid for 2 minutes. Reduce the heat, add the prepared fruit and simmer gently until tender. The time will depend on the type and size of fruit.

3 Allow the poached fruit to cool before serving with low-fat crème fraîche or yogurt.

Peaches These may be white or yellow fleshed. Make sure you select unblemished fruit as peaches bruise easily. They can be skinned in the same way as tomatoes, and at their peak they are best served plain as a tasty dessert or snack. They are also delicious with fresh raspberry purée, in a sundae with nuts and crème fraîche, as peach brûlée or poached in brandy. They are a traditional accompaniment for gammon (smoked or cured ham), or they can be blended with tomato juice and tarragon to make a light, refreshing soup. Peaches are a valuable source of vitamin A in the form of carotene, and they contain useful amounts of a whole range of vitamins and minerals.

Pears These do not keep very well, so buy them slightly underripe and store at room temperature for a day or two. When they are ready for eating they will give slightly to pressure at the stalk end and have a delicate flavour with natural sweetness and melting flesh. Pears complement ripe cheese, such as brie, or they can be used in a salad with a yogurt and herb dressing. They are also excellent poached as a dessert. Pears contain soluble fibre, vitamin C and potassium.

Below: *Add flavour to casseroles or fish dishes with a squeeze of lemon or lime juice.*

Plums These are classed as either cooking or dessert varieties. Some cooking varieties have extremely dry flesh with little flavour and are best stewed with cinnamon. Dessert plums, such as greengages or Victoria, are sweet and juicy, and they can also be used for cooking. Plums make excellent chilled soups and are also the main ingredient of plum sauce – a thick, dark sauce that is often used in Chinese cooking and goes well with any roasted meats, but particularly duck or lamb. Plums are relatively low in calories and rich in vitamins and minerals, and so are ideal for anybody trying to lose weight.

Lemons These are indispensable for their juice and rind, which accentuates the flavour of other foods and gives a subtle tang. Lemon juice is often used instead of vinegar in salad dressings. It helps to preserve the colour of other fruits or vegetables that discolour easily when exposed to air. They make an attractive garnish, and lemon wedges are an essential accompaniment for many foods, such as fish. Preserved lemons are often used to add tartness to stews and casseroles.

Oranges These are valued for their high vitamin C content and also for the oils that they contain. The rind is used for its flavour and the flesh may be added to salads or used with meat and poultry. Orange juice is used as an ingredient in both sweet and savoury recipes, as a marinade or braising agent, or served as a refreshing drink. Oranges go particularly well with almonds or cashew nuts. When orange segments are added to a fruit salad, the acidity of their juice helps to prevent certain other fruits, such as apples or pears, from oxidizing and discolouring.

Grapefruit These sharp and refreshing citrus fruits are often served as an appetizer or as a light, healthy breakfast. Grapefruit can also be used in salads with ingredients such as avocado and watercress, or served hot, sprinkled with ground cinnamon and browned under a grill (broiler). Pink grapefruit are sweeter and juicier than white ones. Like other citrus fruits, grapefruit is high in vitamin C and low in calories.

SEGMENTING AN ORANGE

1 Using a sharp knife, cut a thin slice of peel off each end of the orange.

2 Working your way around the whole orange, carefully remove all the peel and white pith.

3 Cut between the membrane casings around the segments and the orange flesh to loosen each segment and remove it in one piece.

4 Repeat this until only the casings and core of the orange remain.

Limes These sour green citrus fruits have a distinctive flavour and can be used instead of lemon in many dishes. Lime juice is essential in some recipes, such as guacamole, where it also prevents the avocado from turning brown. A squeeze of lime juice in sparkling water on ice makes a refreshing summer drink.

Pineapple Widely available fresh, canned or as juice, pineapple is refreshing in either sweet or savoury salads. It goes well with strong cheeses and can be used extensively in meat dishes. It contains a natural enzyme called bromelin, which softens meat fibres, so the fresh fruit is ideal to use in a sauce or marinade for tough meat (the enzyme is destroyed by heating, so canned fruit does not have the same effect). Tender ingredients, such as chicken, should not be allowed to marinate for too long as its texture can become soft, grainy and unpleasant. Some types of fish, such as snapper, also go well with fresh pineapple. Pineapple contains useful amounts of magnesium, zinc and fibre as well as valuable antioxidants, which may neutralize cell damage by free radicals.

Below: *Watermelon is very low in calories. A refreshing fruit, it is perfect cut into wedges and served at hot summer parties.*

Mangoes Named the "king" of tropical fruits, mango has smooth, aromatic flesh that is delicious eaten on its own as a snack. It has a large flat stone (pit) in the middle, which must be removed before eating. When buying a mango, choose one that is tender all over and yields slightly in the palm of your hand. An extremely versatile fruit, mango goes well with savoury ingredients, such as cold meats, and can also be used in salsas, pickles or chutneys. It is especially good cooked with chicken curry and served with courgette (zucchini) ribbons and lemon slices. They are also a tasty addition to many desserts, especially tropical fruit salads. Mangoes are very high in vitamin A.

Passion fruit These are small and oval in shape with a dark purple, leathery skin. Try to buy them when the skin is wrinkled as this denotes ripeness. To eat, simply cut the passion fruit in half and scoop out the fragrant, full-flavoured green pulp with a teaspoon. The black crunchy seeds should be eaten along with the pulp. Sweet, aromatic passion fruit is delectable in fruit salad or any other dessert, and it is a good source of carotene and iron.

Below: *When buying passion fruit, look out for extremely dark wrinkly skin as this indicates the freshest, ripest fruit.*

PREPARING A MANGO

1 Carefully slice off the mango flesh down each side of the stone.

2 Make criss-cross cuts into the flesh on the flat cut side of each fruit half.

3 Push out the flesh from the middle. This turns the mango inside out and makes the flesh stand proud. Slice the chunks off the skin.

4 To remove any fruit left on the stone, peel away the skin around the edge and scrape off the flesh.

Lychees These small exotic fruits are about the size of a plum with a hard, red, knobbly skin. The skin can be cracked and pulled away easily to reveal a ball of flesh that is translucent white and juicy with a pleasant, aromatic scent. There is a large stone (pit) in the middle of the fruit, which must be removed. Lychees make a wonderful addition to exotic fruit salads, or they can be blended with other fruits, such as melon or apple, for a tasty fruit smoothie. They are high in vitamin C.

Melon This has a high water content and is one of the most refreshing fruits. There are many different varieties, including honeydew, cantaloupe, watermelon and Galia, and all should be eaten when ripe. To determine whether a melon is ripe, smell it and press the end of the fruit. It should have a strong fragrance and yield a little. Melons are commonly eaten as a light appetizer, often flavoured with ginger or green peppercorns. They are also often served with thin slices of air-dried ham, such as prosciutto. Melon makes a tasty addition to a savoury salad with crab meat or prawns (shrimp), or it can be eaten as a dessert piled with summer fruits, such as redcurrants, strawberries or raspberries. All melons are low in calories.

Above: *Fresh pineapple juice can help to tenderize tough cuts of meats and is often used as a marinade.*

Pomegranates These are large, thick-skinned berries full of jewel-like seeds surrounded by a shiny pink pulp. The seeds are arranged in irregular compartments divided by tough skin. Cut the pomegranate in half and scrape the seeds out using a teaspoon or sharp knife. The seeds make an attractive topping for desserts or salads and are used extensively in meat dishes in the Middle East. Pomegranates can also be crushed to make a refreshing juice.

Rhubarb This trimmed stem of the rhubarb plant should be cooked before eating, and the leaves must not be eaten, whether raw or cooked, as they are poisonous. Any tough outer skin should be peeled off if the stems are large and coarse. Rhubarb can be gently stewed with a little sugar until soft and tender and is

Above: *Shiny pomegranate seeds can be scraped out with a sharp knife or scooped out with a teaspoon and eaten immediately.*

best flavoured with ginger, orange or cashew nuts. Rhubarb contains valuable calcium but also has large amounts of oxalic acid, which prevents the body from absorbing minerals, such as calcium and iron. It is therefore inadvisable to eat rhubarb more than twice a week.

Below: *Melons with bright golden flesh, such as the cantaloupe, contain large amounts of carotene.*

vegetables

IT IS IMPORTANT that we all eat enough vegetables, and there are so many types available that they need never get boring. Try to experiment regularly with new recipes that feature more unusual varieties, or discover different ways of serving old favourites like cauliflower and cabbage.

Salad leaves There are many varieties of salad leaves available, including frisée lettuce, firm red radicchio, which has crisp leaves and a bitter flavour, crisp romaine lettuce, or peppery rocket (arugula). Buy leaves as fresh as possible and tear them by hand. Lettuce contains 95 per cent water and is very low in calories.

Watercress This strong-tasting, tangy leaf is good in mixed salads. It can be blended to create delicate soups and sauces and can also be used in stir-fries. It is a valuable source of iron and carotene.

Spinach This is a delicious dark green leafy plant that can be eaten raw when young but is better cooked when older and slightly tougher. Cooked spinach is a good base for baked eggs, grilled meat or poached fish. Spinach is often added to curries with lamb or paneer, Indian cheese. It is rich in vitamin A, iron and calcium but it also contains oxalic acid, which stops the body absorbing some of these minerals.

Cabbage This everyday vegetable comes in a variety of forms, all extremely versatile either as side dishes or salads. Coleslaw, the traditional white cabbage salad made with grated carrot, onion and occasionally fennel, is delicious made with red cabbage as well. Red or white cabbage is extremely good cooked with pineapple, (bell) peppers and onion, or it can be pickled and served as a condiment. Crisp varieties such as Chinese leaves (Chinese cabbage) and pak choi (bok choy) are popular choices for stir-frying. Savoy cabbage can be wrapped around savoury fillings, such as minced (ground) meat, and then baked in a rich tomato sauce. Cabbage contains carotene, iron, calcium and varying amounts of vitamin C but little energy, so it makes a nutritious addition to the diet menu.

Below: A good low-carb dish is traditional French ratatouille, made with roughly chopped aubergine, courgettes and peppers.

Broccoli Another versatile and nutritious vegetable that should be eaten regularly, broccoli is good stir-fried, roasted or simply steamed. It can be used as a base for baked dishes, such as chicken in a mushroom sauce, or served cold with chopped, roasted almonds. It contains large amounts of vitamin A, folic acid and iron.

Cauliflower This popular vegetable has a delicious flavour and crunchy texture, but be careful not to overcook it as it may turn mushy. It is best to cut cauliflower into fairly small, even-sized florets so that they each take the same time to cook. Indian spices complement cauliflower extremely well, as do cheese, nutmeg or tomato. Raw cauliflower florets are great as crudités for scooping up dips or snacking. Full of valuable nutrients, including potassium, fibre, vitamins C and E, folate and carotene, cauliflower is a healthy choice.

Aubergine (eggplant) Often overlooked, this vegetable readily absorbs robust flavours and has a firm, velvety texture. Aubergines complement vegetarian or meat dishes well, especially lamb, and they are often served stuffed with minced lamb or layered in a bake with meat sauce as in the Greek dish moussaka. Chickpeas, tomatoes and mushrooms also go well with aubergines to make interesting bakes and salads. Baby aubergines are tasty when roasted in the oven with a teaspoon of olive oil and cumin seeds. Roasted aubergine flesh can be made into a vegetable dip seasoned with lemon juice and parsley. Traditional varieties contained bitter juices that had to be removed by standing in salt (degorging), but this is not necessary with modern varieties. However, degorging does prevent aubergines from absorbing too much oil during cooking, so it can be useful for reducing the calories.

Above: *Peppers roasted with a little olive oil and garlic make a delicious light lunch.*

Peppers (sweet bell peppers) Brightly coloured and fresh in flavour, these are useful raw in salads, with other vegetables as crudités, or as a garnish. They can be cooked in casseroles, stir-fried or threaded on to kebabs. They can also be stuffed or roasted with a little olive oil. Raw peppers are high in vitamin C and carotene.

Chilli peppers These range in hotness from mild to very fiery, but they all need careful handling. Cut the chillies and remove the seeds under running water using the point of a sharp knife. Do not touch your face afterwards (especially your eyes) as the juices are a severe irritant. Remember to wash your hands thoroughly afterwards.

Below: *Tomatoes are a versatile ingredient, used in soups, sauces and salads.*

Above: *Fresh chilli peppers, raw or cooked, add delicious fire and spice to many dishes.*

Tomatoes An indispensable flavouring and salad ingredient, tomatoes can be used in a variety of ways. Cherry tomatoes are perfect in salads, roasted with balsamic vinegar, hollowed out and stuffed with ricotta cheese, or dunked into dips. Large beefsteak tomatoes are ideal for stuffing or slicing into salads. Plum tomatoes have an intense, sweet flavour that makes excellent soups and sauces. Passata, or sieved (strained) tomatoes, is readily available bottled, sometimes with herbs or spices added, and is a useful store-cupboard item for making a quick sauce for fish, meat or pasta. Dried tomatoes, particularly the sun-blushed variety, combine well with garlic and fresh herbs for an unusual salad. Tomato purée (paste) is useful for enriching and thickening sauces. A valuable source of vitamins E, C and carotene, tomatoes also contain the antioxidant lycopene, which may help protect against some types of cancer.

Avocado This delicately flavoured fruit-vegetable is best eaten when the flesh has ripened to the consistency of soft butter and is light yellow-green in colour. Avocado is delicious halved and served with a teaspoon of vinaigrette or stuffed with fresh prawns (shrimp) or crab meat. Avocados can also be used to make a delicately flavoured soup, added to a leafy green salad, or served with cooked cold meat in a light yogurt dressing. Traditional Italian "tricolore" salad combines avocado with plump mozzarella cheese and juicy ripe tomatoes. Avocado is the main ingredient in the traditional Mexican dip, guacamole. It can also be served hot, either lightly baked or grilled (broiled). Avocados are rich in protein, vitamin A and vitamin B, with virtually no carbohydrate content at all. They also contain a beneficial type of oil that cannot be found in other fruits. Although fairly high in calories, avocados are an extremely healthy ingredient and should be eaten regularly.

HALVING AND STONING AN AVOCADO

1 Cut the avocado in half lengthways around the stone (pit).

2 Holding one side in each hand, twist the halves in opposite directions to separate them.

3 Carefully remove the stone with the point of a sharp knife. Unless serving immediately, add fresh lemon juice to the cut surface to prevent discoloration.

Right: *Fennel is often served as a popular accompaniment to roast meats.*

Courgettes (zucchini) These are baby marrows and are at their most tender when they are between 10–15cm/ 4–6in long. They can be cooked whole, sliced, cut into matchsticks or ribbons or coarsely grated. Courgettes are good when lightly steamed, seasoned and served with fresh herbs. Combined with aubergines (eggplant), onions and tomatoes they make the classic French dish, ratatouille. More simply, they can be served in a tomato sauce or added to stir-fried dishes. Larger courgettes can be stuffed, for example with minced (ground) meat, and baked or added to casseroles.

Onions These ancient vegetables have numerous culinary uses as a flavouring, raw or cooked. Onions can also be served as a vegetable in their own right, either roasted, baked or boiled. Red onions have a milder flavour and more colourful appearance.

Below: *Spring onions are delicious added to salads or stir-fried with other vegetables.*

Spring onions (scallions) are popular in salads and stir-fries. Although onions contain few nutrients, their main value health-wise lies in the natural antibiotic properties of the compounds they contain, for example allicin. These are reputed to help fight infections, have valuable cleansing and healing properties, may lower blood cholesterol levels and may even help protect against cancer.

Leeks Providing useful amounts of iron as well as the antioxidants carotene and vitamins E and C, leeks are a good choice in casseroles and soups. They can be steamed and served hot or cold, dressed with fresh parsley and a little vinaigrette dressing.

Celery This crunchy vegetable adds a distinctive flavour to soups and casseroles. It can be braised with bacon, carrot and onion in a simple and tasty vegetable dish to serve with roasted meats or alongside cheese. For buffets, raw celery stalks can be filled with low-fat cream cheese, puréed avocado or a seafood mixture. Celery is delicious combined with apple, carrot or pear in a fresh healthy juice. Stalks can also be eaten alone as a low-carb snack. Celery consists of 95 per cent water, so it is extremely low in calories, and it contains a small amount of a range of valuable vitamins and minerals.

Fennel Similar in texture to celery, this has a delicate aniseed-like flavour, and almost all of the plant is edible. Choose firm, pale green fennel for the best flavour. The stalks are used as a vegetable, either raw or cooked, and can replace celery in Waldorf salads and similar dishes. Fennel leaves are sometimes used as a garnish and the seeds are often added to meat products, such as sausages, as a spice.

Asparagus Whether served hot or cold, as a side dish or appetizer, asparagus spears are delicious dressed with a teaspoon of

COOKING ASPARAGUS SPEARS

1 Wash the asparagus spears thoroughly, then cut off any tough and woody stem ends with a sharp knife. Scrape the spears at the base to make them roughly even in thickness

2 Tie the asparagus spears in bundles of up to ten and stand them in a pan containing about 2.5cm/1in of fresh boiling water

3 Arrange a dome of foil over the top of the pan to cover the tips. Fold it down tightly around the rim to keep in the steam. Simmer for about 10–15 minutes, until the asparagus spears are tender but still firm.

tangy vinaigrette. They may be served as an accompaniment to meat, chicken or fish dishes, used in an omelette; or added to a stir-fried dish or salad. They sometimes have an astringent taste. Asparagus is rich in folate, an essential B vitamin.

Above: *Rich in vitamin C, petits pois are often at their best when bought frozen.*

Above: *Large flat mushrooms can be stuffed and grilled for a tasty appetizer.*

Peas Petits pois (baby peas) are the smallest and sweetest of shelled peas and are good frozen. They are cropped in peak condition and frozen within hours of picking, which means they retain more nutrients, especially vitamin C, than shop-bought fresh peas. Peas are a colourful and tasty addition to many dishes. They provide a good source of protein as well as vitamins and minerals.

Mangetout (snow peas) These are a variety of pea with edible pods, eaten before the peas are formed. Ideally, they should be briefly steamed to enhance their sweet flavour and crunchy texture. They are also good in stir-fries or served raw for dipping. Take care not to overcook mangetout.

Green beans Often overlooked, green beans can be used in a variety of ways. They can be steamed, fried in a little rapeseed (canola) oil with chopped onion and flaked almonds, added to stir-fried dishes, served hot as an accompaniment to meat, poultry or fish dishes with a teaspoon of vinaigrette dressing, or served with hard-boiled eggs, fresh tuna and anchovies in a classic Niçoise salad. Green beans provide useful amounts of carotene and B vitamins. Remember to ensure that those with strings along the edge are trimmed before cooking.

Okra This contains a natural, gummy substance that can act as a thickening agent in soups, sauces and stews. Okra may also be eaten uncooked in salads, in curries or stuffed with spices. Okra is especially high in magnesium, which is essential for cell functioning and enzyme reactions within the body.

Corn Baby or miniature corn are a must for stir-fries and Chinese cooking, and go well in salads or grilled on the barbecue. They add colour, texture and fibre to meals as well as providing health-promoting vitamins and minerals.

Mushrooms These are rich in the essential B vitamins niacin, pantothenic acid and biotin. Flat mushrooms are excellent for grilling, stuffing or making into paté. Dried shiitake mushrooms are often used in Chinese cooking but must be soaked before use.

Below: *Add baby corn to stir-fries for colour and flavour.*

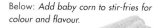

ADDING SPICES TO OKRA

Okra can be stuffed with spices, then simmered in a curry sauce, baked in a tomato sauce, or stir-fried.

1 Choose small, firm pods and cut off their stalk ends.

2 Carefully make a slit along the length of each pod.

3 Mix a variety of ground spices, such as coriander, cumin and a pinch of chilli powder. Use a teaspoon to place a little of this mixture in each pod.

meat, poultry and game

ON A LOW-CARBOHYDRATE programme, when a good protein intake is recommended, meat can be an important part of the diet. Always opt for lean cuts to reduce the amount of fat being consumed and choose healthier ways of cooking, such as grilling, casseroling or stir-frying.

MEAT

Red meat is often perceived to be high in fat with no place in a weight-loss regime. However, the fat content of meat is far lower than it was 25 years ago. Visible fat can easily be trimmed off a piece of meat before cooking, or on the plate, reducing the fat content by as much as 79 per cent. However, this cannot be done with meat products such as bought burgers or sausages, where the high fat content is mixed in the product and cannot be reduced. Red meat also contains a number of important nutrients, including protein, iron, zinc, vitamin D and B vitamins. Always try to select the leanest cuts of meat available, which will reduce the saturated fat content as much as possible, and try to use a low-fat cooking method such as grilling (broiling), stir-frying or casseroling.

White meat is lower in iron than red meat, but it is still a rich source of nutrients, particularly protein and B vitamins. The pork available from supermarkets and butchers' shops today is leaner than ever before. Bacon and gammon are traditionally high in salt from the curing process but low-sodium varieties are now readily available.

A popular way of preparing meat is to make kebabs. Cut ingredients to roughly the same size so that they cook evenly and thread them onto a skewer for grilling. The combinations are limitless and the pieces of meat can be interspersed with vegetables. The ingredients may be marinated or you could use rosemary twigs or lemongrass sticks instead of skewers to add extra flavour.

Beef Generally, meat cut from the back of the carcass, including steak, is the most tender and therefore suited to fast cooking methods, such as grilling, stir-frying and cooking on a barbecue. The areas that work the hardest in the live animal, for example the shoulders and lower legs, provide slightly tougher cuts, such as silverside

Above: *Lamb contains valuable vitamins and minerals, such as iron and zinc.*

(pot roast) and stewing steak. These cuts should ideally be casseroled or braised as the long, slow cooking allows them to tenderize. When buying minced (ground) beef, choose extra lean mince with less than 5 per cent fat. Although it is more expensive than the standard variety, the low fat content means there will be less wastage, so a smaller amount is needed.

Above: *If using minced beef, for example to prepare a meal of spicy low-carb chilli con carne, select the extra lean variety if possible, as it contains minimal amounts of fat.*

Above: *Use thin strips of lean pork, with all fat removed, for healthy stir-fries.*

Lamb Your butcher will need to trim lamb on request as it has a generous covering of fat. Select a lean joint or cut, such as leg steaks, to keep the fat content down and the protein and iron content up. Fat drips off during the cooking process and more can then be trimmed off after cooking if necessary. Lamb works perfectly in casseroles with a mixture of vegetables, beans and lentils. If the meat is being casseroled, any excess fat can simply be skimmed off the top before serving.

Pork The pigs farmed for pork today are much leaner than in the past, so lean pork is a healthy option on any diet. Cuts that cook quickly include leg, loin chops or the fillet, which does not have any covering of visible fat and is popular for cubing, for example for making kebabs, or for stir-frying. Pork marries well with tart fruit, such as apples, apricots, pineapple or cranberries, either made into sauces or served in whole pieces. It also provides many valuable minerals, such as copper, manganese and selenium.

Below: *Cured sausages, such as spicy Spanish chorizo, can be enjoyed on a low-carb diet, but do not over-indulge.*

Above: *Lean rashers of bacon can be grilled until crisp and tasty, then cut into strips and added to salads.*

Bacon This is pork that has been preserved by curing. Salt is combined with flavourings and either rubbed directly on to the meat or injected into it, after which the bacon may be smoked to give it a different flavour. Bacon is very versatile and makes a tasty addition to salads. It can also be wrapped around chicken breast fillets or portions of fish, such as salmon, or even scallops, to keep them juicy and moist while cooking and impart a delicious flavour.

Gammon (smoked or cured ham) This is the name given to the whole cured hind leg of a pig. Gammon can be bought in large pieces or in slices, also known as gammon steaks or rashers.

MEAT PRODUCTS

There are a variety of different meat products available. These tend to be much higher in saturated fat than the meat itself and, as a result, lower in protein, vitamins and minerals. Wherever possible, try to make these products yourself to control the fat content. Commercial products often contain carbohydrate in the form of rusk or filler, used to provide bulk or to bind the meat, so look out for this on the list of ingredients.

Sausages There are two main types of sausage: dry sausages, such as salami, are cured and can be eaten uncooked; wet sausages are fresh products that must be cooked before eating. Most types of sausage are made from a blend of minced pork, with seasonings and preservatives. The fat content of sausages varies greatly, but low-fat varieties are available. The ingredients are controlled by law and must be stated on the packet, so check before buying. It is fine to enjoy sausages occasionally, but limit your intake and buy those with a high meat content wherever possible as these are less likely to contain bulking ingredients.

Burgers The majority of burgers from shops or fast food outlets are high in salt and saturated fat so should be avoided. However, home-made burgers consisting of lean minced (ground) meat with finely chopped onion and herbs are delicious and they provide a good source of iron. Different types of lean meat can be used to make more unusual burgers, such as chicken, turkey or venison.

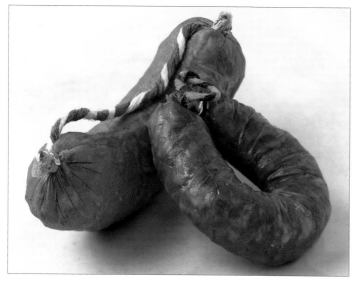

POULTRY

All domestic birds that are reared for the table are described as poultry. They are an excellent source of protein and B vitamins, with the majority of fat being found in the skin. Removing the skin from a chicken breast portion before cooking, for example, can reduce its fat content from 11 per cent to just over 1 per cent. Alternatively, the skin can be removed after cooking to keep calories down. When using frozen poultry it is important to thaw it thoroughly in the refrigerator before cooking.

SKINNING A CHICKEN BREAST

1 Cover your fingers with kitchen paper to prevent the skin from slipping.

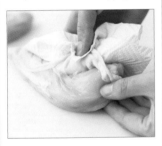

2 Insert one finger under the skin and grip it with the kitchen paper, then pull the skin away from the meat.

3 Use a knife to cut off any small pockets of white fat left on the meat.

Above: *It is worth spending a bit more for a free-range chicken as the flavour is much better.*

Chicken The most common poultry, eaten throughout the world, chicken is inexpensive, plentiful and versatile. Free-range chickens that are grain-fed and reared slowly by traditional methods have the best taste and are worth the extra cost for their firm texture and superior flavour. Corn-fed chickens are easily recognized by their bright yellow skin, which loses its colour during cooking. Chicken can be bought in portions, such as leg, thigh or breast, or a whole bird can be bought for roasting or casseroling. Always cook chicken well, so there is no sign of raw flesh.

Turkey Leaner than chicken, turkey is prone to dryness if not cooked carefully. Breast meat can be flattened and wrapped around a lean ham and cheese stuffing before being grilled slowly. Strips can be marinated and used in stir-fries. The darker thigh meat is more flavoursome and moister. Turkey rashers are a manufactured product that can be grilled, then chopped and sprinkled on salads instead of bacon for a tasty source of protein. When buying a whole turkey, look for a plump, well-rounded breast and legs, and clear, soft and evenly coloured skin.

Duck Modern breeding methods have brought leaner ducks to the supermarket, with a good proportion of breast meat and only a fine layer of fat under the skin, most of which melts during cooking anyway, leaving the meat succulent and well-flavoured. Duck is a rich meat and is traditionally balanced by tart accompaniments, such as orange, plums or cherries. Although it is not recommended to eat duck every day, due to its high fat and energy content, it can be eaten occasionally.

Below: *The fat underneath duck skin melts during cooking, leaving the meat moist and tender.*

GAME

In the kitchen, game means any edible animal not raised on a farm, although nowadays, furred game such as deer and rabbit can be farmed. The health benefits of game are beginning to be recognized and, as it becomes more widely available in supermarkets, it is becoming more popular. With exceptionally nutritious meat that is an excellent source of protein, iron and B vitamins, some varieties of game, such as venison and rabbit, can also be very low in fat and cholesterol, so they are excellent choices for anybody trying to lose weight.

Venison This is a lean, dark and fine-textured meat with a strong flavour and very little fat. Care must be taken to ensure venison stays moist during cooking and some cuts, such as neck, shoulder and shin, benefit from being marinated, particularly in spiced red wine, then cooked very slowly and gently to tenderize the meat and bring out the rich flavour. Prime cuts such as haunch, loin, fillet or best end tend to be more juicy and tender and therefore need less cooking – this meat can even be served rare.

Rabbit The flesh is pale and mild but the flavour of rabbit is slightly stronger than chicken. The meat of the doe (female) rabbit is more tender than that of the buck (male). Rabbit is excellent when casseroled with a mustard-flavoured sauce, cider or sweet dried fruit, such as prunes or apricots.

Below: *Lamb's kidneys (bottom) have a more delicate flavour than pig's kidneys (top) and are tasty when lightly grilled with spices.*

Above: *Fine-textured calf's liver has a more delicate flavour than the more economical lamb's liver.*

OFFAL

Nutrient-dense and a good source of protein, iron and B vitamins, the fat content of offal is minimal, but it does contain some cholesterol. For the majority of people, however, cholesterol eaten in food has little effect on blood cholesterol levels, and it is more important to reduce the quantity of saturated fat eaten in the diet. Most offal is rich and highly flavoured, which is often due to the high blood content of the organs. Always leave sealed pre-packed offal in its container and use it by the date shown on the packet. Offal bought loose should be transferred to a deep dish and covered tightly with clear film (plastic wrap) or a close-fitting lid. Store it in the refrigerator and use within 24 hours of purchase.

Liver Exceptionally high in vitamin A, liver has a very short shelf life and must be eaten very soon after purchase. The strength of flavour will depend on the type, with calf's liver being the most delicate and highly prized, and ox liver being the strongest. To draw out any bitterness in liver and to tone down its flavour if you find it overpowering, try soaking it in milk for a couple of hours before cooking – be sure to dry it out before cooking. Chicken livers freeze well and are excellent for making paté, or they can be lightly sautéed and added to salads for a delicious source of protein.

Kidneys Small, tender and quite delicate in flavour, lamb's kidneys can be wrapped in strips of bacon and cooked on a barbecue. Alternatively, they can be seasoned with mustard or Indian spices and lightly grilled. Kidneys are a traditional ingredient in beef casserole and also mix well with tomatoes and mushrooms. For a tasty variation on the traditional French dish, ratatouille, add pieces of grilled kidney for a quick and nutritious one-pot meal.

PREPARING LIVER

1 Remove the liver from its container as soon as possible, unless it is in a sealed packet, and put it in a shallow dish (deep enough to catch any drips). Cover with clear film (plastic wrap) or foil and place in the refrigerator.

2 If required, add some milk to the dish 1–2 hours before cooking to cover the liver. Leave the liver to soak until you are ready to start cooking – this will remove any bitterness.

3 Pour away the milk, dry the liver gently on kitchen paper and prepare as required for the recipe.

fish and shellfish

AS MORE exotic species find their way into the supermarkets, the choice of fresh fish available today is wonderful. A valuable source of protein, vitamins and minerals, essential oils and healthy fats, fish should be eaten at least three times a week as part of your low-carbohydrate diet.

WHITE FISH

A rich source of protein, vitamins and minerals, white fish contains little fat and is low in calories. The majority of fish is sold prepared ready for cooking, for example with scales and insides removed. Fish is often bought in cuts such as fillets and steaks. Most fishmongers are happy to complete any preparation required on whole fish. In general, fish requires little cooking as its delicate flavour and texture is easily spoilt. The lack of fat in white fish means it is best cooked gently by a moist method, such as poaching or steaming.

Monkfish A firm white fish, monkfish can be marinated to keep it moist during grilling (broiling) or poached in milk or yogurt with herbs. Cubes of monkfish can be wrapped in bacon and skewered as a kebab.

Cod This is a large white fish with a firm texture and delicate flavour. Cod is a versatile fish and most methods of cooking are suitable for it, but it is particularly good stuffed and baked. Cod roe is a delicacy in its own right, whether fresh or smoked.

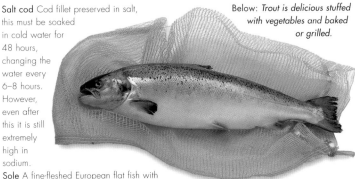

Below: *Trout is delicious stuffed with vegetables and baked or grilled.*

Salt cod Cod fillet preserved in salt, this must be soaked in cold water for 48 hours, changing the water every 6–8 hours. However, even after this it is still extremely high in sodium.

Sole A fine-fleshed European flat fish with a delicate flavour, Dover sole is considered to be the true sole; lemon sole is less expensive but also a good-quality fish. Fillets can be rolled around a herb stuffing and then poached. A sauce made from white wine or tomatoes is perfect for baking sole fillets to ensure they remain moist.

Halibut One of the largest flatfish, this has close-textured, firm white flesh. Sold in fillets, steaks and other small portions, most cooking methods are suitable, but halibut is often baked with onions and tomatoes.

OILY FISH

Fats known as omega-3 fats, which help the heart beat more regularly and prevent heart disease, are present in oily fish. The average person should eat at least one 100g/4oz serving of oily fish per week to help prevent heart disease, while those with existing heart disease should eat two or three servings each week. Oily fish is also a good source of protein and vitamins A and D.

Sardines Young pilchards, these are superb cooked on a barbecue and served with lemon juice or in a salad with lettuce, beetroot (beet) and egg. Sardines are usually canned, and are a useful standby ingredient for dishes such as paté.

Salmon Known as the king of fish, salmon can be prepared in many ways. It can be grilled and served with a citrus sauce, cooked in baking parchment with herbs, skewered with bacon and red onions, stir-fried with mangetout (snow peas) and ginger, or added to a tasty seafood soup.

Trout With attractive pale pink flesh, trout is high in omega-3 fats, naturally low in sodium and calories, and a useful source of vitamins. Whole trout, cooked over a grill (broiler) or barbecue, is easy to eat as the flesh falls away from the bones, but it can also be flaked and added to salads.

Right: *Canned sardines are perfect for quick salads or snacks.*

CHOOSING FRESH FISH

Look for the following signs of freshness when selecting fish:
- Clean shiny scales
- Vivid markings
- Pink or bright red gills
- Bright eyes
- A fresh smell
- Firm flesh that springs back when pressed
- Translucent flesh when buying fillets

Reject fish that looks dry or shrivelled, smells strongly or is displayed in damaged packets that should be sealed.

Tuna Fresh tuna is high in healthy omega-3 fats but when the fish is canned the levels are reduced to those found in white fish. Although canned tuna is still a healthy choice it does not count as an oily fish. Pregnant women should limit the amount of tuna they eat to two fresh tuna steaks per week or four medium-sized cans, because tuna contains mercury and high levels of this can harm an unborn child's developing nervous system.

Herring This small fish is most often pickled in flavoured vinegar or served in one of a variety of tangy sauces as a delicious appetizer or light meal, accompanied by chopped onions and capers. Herrings are a typically Scandinavian dish.

Mackerel An inexpensive and underrated fish, mackerel can be easily incorporated into everyday meals. Smoked mackerel fillets make a delicious salad, especially with apple and beetroot (beet), or a tasty paté with fresh lemon juice and ricotta cheese. Fresh mackerel can either be grilled or baked and served with a sharp gooseberry sauce, or roasted fennel. It is also good Chinese-style, baked with soy sauce and ginger. Canned mackerel can be used in the same way as canned sardines.

CANNED FISH

Many oily fish, such as sardines, mackerel, herrings, pilchards and salmon, are available canned in oil (olive oil is best), spring water, brine, tomato sauce, curry sauce or other flavourings. The fish heads are removed before canning but the bones are still in the fish. After the canning process is complete, the cans are left for up to two years to mature, during which time the bones soften and become edible. As a result, canned oily fish are a good source of calcium. They also provide omega-3 fats (tuna is the exception as it loses its omega-3 fats when canned), vitamins A and D, and protein in a relatively cheap and convenient form.

Above: *Prawns should be lightly cooked, otherwise they can become tough.*

SHELLFISH

An excellent low-fat source of protein, shellfish does contain some cholesterol, but this has little effect on blood cholesterol levels as these are affected more by saturated fat intake.

Prawns (shrimp) These are popular in many sizes, from tiny British prawns to larger tiger prawns and king prawns (jumbo shrimp). Raw prawns are grey or blue in colour and turn pink when cooked gently and briefly – if they are overcooked they tend to become tough. Prawns are ideal for grilling on the barbecue. They are also good with a spicy peanut satay sauce, poached in soup with vegetables or other shellfish, stir-fried with cashew nuts or simply baked with garlic.

Mussels These must be alive when bought in their shells and should be purchased from a reputable source. They are usually steamed in a small amount of liquid – typically white wine – with flavourings such as onion, chilli or garlic; grilled with garlic, parsley and lemon juice; baked with tomatoes and onions; or served in a salad. Mussels become rubbery when overcooked, so add them towards the end of the cooking time when making a casserole-style dish. Mussels are also available ready-cooked and chilled or frozen.

PREPARING AND STEAMING MUSSELS

1 Scrub the mussels under cold running water and pull or scrape off any tufts of hair – known as the beard – that protrude from the shell.

2 Tap any mussels that are slightly open with the back of a knife and discard them if they do not close. Discard any mussels that float in liquid or have broken shells.

3 Pour about 1cm/½in liquid, such as water or white wine, into a large pan and add the required flavourings, such as tomatoes, fresh herbs, garlic, chilli or other spices. Rinse the mussels and add them to the pan.

4 Cover and cook over a high heat for 6–10 minutes, until the mussels are open, shaking the pan frequently.

5 Be sure to discard any shells that have not opened.

Scallops These delicious and delicate shellfish can be poached, stir-fried, skewered and grilled (broiled), or steamed Chinese-style with black beans and spring onions (scallions). Try wrapping scallops in pieces of prosciutto before cooking, to retain the moisture. They can be bought fresh or frozen, usually removed from their shells, with or without the orange coral (roe), and ready for cooking.

vegetable protein

HIGHLY NUTRITIOUS vegetable proteins are important foods for anybody on a low-carbohydrate weight loss diet, but particularly for vegetarians, who miss out on the protein content of meat and fish. Add a bit of variety to your diet and try a few of the more unusual ingredients listed here.

PEAS, BEANS AND LENTILS

Grown all over the world, these are staple and economical foods. They have to be washed and, in some cases, soaked before cooking. Numerous varieties are also available canned, including chickpeas and red kidney beans. They are rich in protein, iron, calcium and B vitamins, with virtually no fat and lots of fibre, so they are a great food to include in the eating plan.

Chickpeas These have a rich, nutty flavour and are the basis for many dishes, such as dips (hummus) and felafel, spicy deep-fried balls. They are often used in salads and stews. Chickpea flour is known as gram flour in Indian cooking and used to make bhajis. They are a rich source of phytoestogens.

Above: *Use red kidney beans to make a traditional Mexican chilli con carne.*

Above: *Try adding chickpeas to a fresh green salad to add protein and flavour.*

SOAKING AND COOKING TIMES FOR PEAS, BEANS AND LENTILS

When soaking, cover the beans in plenty of cold water and leave for 6–8 hours or overnight. Drain and rinse again. To cook, place the beans in a large pan with plenty of water. Boil hard for 10 minutes to destroy any natural toxins that can cause stomach upsets (particularly found in red kidney beans) then simmer without a lid for the recommended time or until tender.

- All types of lentils, mung beans and split peas cook without soaking for 25–30 minutes.
- Flageolet and cannellini beans soak and cook for 30–60 minutes.
- Soya beans soak and cook for 1½–3 hours.
- Red kidney beans, chick peas and other beans soak and cook for 1–1½ hours.

Red kidney beans These are readily associated with Mexican cooking, in which they are used to make traditional dishes such as refried beans and chilli con carne. Red kidney beans are also excellent when served cold in a mixed salad or added to stews.

Mung beans Small, round and green, these are the beans that are sprouted to create Chinese beansprouts. They are excellent in crisp salads, and when sprouted are also a delicious addition to stir-fries.

Lentils The most common type of lentils are red lentils, but many other varieties are also available, including green and brown and Puy lentils, which are very dark, almost black, and are generally considered to have the best flavour. Lentils do not require soaking before use. They are often used as a main ingredient or thickening agent in soups,

casseroles and stews, spicy Indian-style dhal or salads. Lentils can also be used to replace meat in some traditional recipes, or they are served as a simple, nutritious accompaniment to grilled meats or fish. Lentils can be flavoured liberally with fresh or dried herbs and spices.

Below: *There are many varieties of lentils, but Puy lentils are considered to have the best flavour, and they retain their shape well when cooked.*

SOYA

Soya beans are a versatile food source with the highest nutritional value of all beans. They supply protein, B vitamins and unsaturated fats, and, as part of a diet low in saturated fat, 25g/1oz soya protein per day can help reduce blood cholesterol. It also provides phytoestrogens, which have health-promoting properties and may help prevent some cancers and improve osteoporosis.

Tofu This is made from soaked, mashed and strained soya beans. It is white, milky and set in custard-like squares. Its texture can be soft (silken tofu) or firm. Fresh tofu should be kept covered with water in the refrigerator. Vacuum-packed, long-life tofu can be stored unopened at room temperature. Firm tofu can be stir-fried, used in stews and soups, crumbled into salads or cooked on a barbecue. Soft tofu can be beaten for use in dips, dressings or sweet dishes, such as fruit fools. Plain tofu absorbs the flavours of other ingredients well during cooking. Smoked and marinated tofu are also available.

PHYTOESTROGENS

Phytoestrogens, such as isoflavones, are naturally occurring plant derivatives that are found in soya beans, chickpeas and some other legumes. They mimic oestrogen in the human body and are particularly useful for menopausal women. A lot of research is taking place into their effect on health, and they have been associated with some of the following benefits:

- Improved symptoms of osteoporosis, possibly due to the slowing of bone demineralization.
- A reduction in the risk of cardio-vascular disease due to a blood cholesterol lowering effect.
- A lower risk of some cancers, such as breast and prostate cancer.
- The improvement of menstrual symptoms.
- The reduction of hot flushes in menopausal women.

Miso This Japanese paste is made from fermented soya beans. It is very salty and should be used sparingly, for example in stews or spread on vegetables before grilling. It can also be dissolved in water and used as a base for soup.

Tempeh This is made by fermenting cooked soya beans in banana leaves. It has a strong flavour and needs to be soaked or marinated with ingredients that have equally strong flavours before grilling or stir-frying.

Textured vegetable protein (TVP) This is manufactured from soya beans into different shapes and forms. It has a firm, sponge-like texture and can be flavoured to resemble meat or left as a natural soya product. TVP needs to be rehydrated with water or stock for a few minutes before being incorporated into recipes. It is available as chunks or resembling minced (ground) meat. It is fortified with vitamin B_{12} and is therefore a nutritious alternative to meat, or it can be combined with meat to extend a modest quantity and so reduce the overall saturated fat content. TVP can be treated in the same way as the cuts of meat it resembles, but it does not take up flavours as readily as other soya products.

Soya flour High in protein and low in carbohydrate, this can be stirred into sauces, soups and gravies to add bulk and nutrients. It is not suitable as a thickening agent and has a distinct flavour so should be combined with strong-flavoured ingredients, otherwise it can overwhelm a dish.

MYCOPROTEIN (QUORN)

This is related to fungi and is a good source of protein that is low in fat and energy and contains fibre. Mycoprotein is often found in ready-made vegetarian meals. Prepared cuts and shapes of mycoprotein are extremely useful for cooking. It readily absorbs and retains the flavours of aromatics and sauces so is ideal for casseroles, curries or stir-fries.

IDEAS FOR USING TOFU

- Mash the tofu and make it into burgers with onion, herbs, spices and garlic.
- Use as a salad dressing: blend with chopped fresh coriander (cilantro) leaves and lemon juice.
- Thread cubes on to skewers with mushrooms, tomatoes and (bell) peppers; marinate in soy sauce and mustard before grilling.
- Whip with fresh herbs and Tabasco sauce as a dip for carrot sticks and other crudités.

- Blend with fresh fruit, such as strawberries or raspberries, to make a fruit fool.
- Stir-fry with Chinese mushrooms, bamboo shoots, pak choi (bok choy) and cashew nuts.
- Poach in a clear broth with seafood and vegetable strips for a simple, light meal.

Left: *Textured vegetable protein (TVP) is available either cubed or minced.*

NUTS

All nuts are a good source of fibre, iron, calcium and B vitamins. Their flavours and textures vary according to type, as does their use. They are also an excellent source of protein and make a good alternative to animal protein foods, such as meat. However, they should not be eaten more than once a day as a snack when trying to lose weight as they can contain a concentrated source of calories.

Almonds Best known for their use in sweet dishes, these are also excellent served as a topping for baked or grilled trout, sprinkled into a salad or over vegetables, such as French beans or broccoli. They are the best wholefood source of vitamin E and contain unsaturated fats.

Peanuts Probably the most popular of all nuts, peanuts supply minerals, such as selenium and zinc, as well as the phytochemical resveratrol which may help protect against cancer and heart disease. The fat content is mainly unsaturated, and unsalted peanuts are a valuable and healthy choice in the diet. The nuts can be added to salads and stir-fries, while peanut butter can be used as a base for delicious sauces for chicken, seafood and beef. Look for fresh peanut butter without additives or additional fat in the form of palm oil.

Below: Coconut contains saturated fat so should only be eaten occasionally.

Walnuts A traditional ingredient in Waldorf salad (with apple and celery), walnuts can be used extensively in cooking, in both savoury and sweet dishes. They are a valuable source of omega-3 fats.

Pine nuts Small and creamy in colour, these can be used plain or lightly roasted. They are one of the ingredients in traditional pesto and can be toasted and added to many dishes, such as omelettes or sprinkled over salads or vegetables.

Coconut The fruit of the coconut palm, this can be used to flavour curries, soups and stir-fries or in a savoury sauce for vegetables. The fat content of coconut is saturated, and it is high in calories, so it should be used sparingly.

SEEDS

These add variety to a dish in terms of both taste and texture, but try to avoid the salted variety. Add flavour to seeds by browning them in a dry frying pan, in the oven or under a grill (broiler).

Sesame seeds These are rich in protein, iron and zinc, and can be generously sprinkled over salads and cooked vegetables as a crunchy topping. Sesame seed paste (tahini) is used to make hummus, the popular chickpea dip, and is also useful for flavouring soups and casseroles.

Below: Packed with minerals, unsalted peanuts make an ideal snack or ingredient.

CHOPPING NUTS

1 Place the nuts on a sturdy board and use a sharp knife. Hold the point down and keep it in one place, then pivot the knife around in a semi-circle from the point as you chop.

2 To save time, a food processor, blender or electric coffee grinder can also be used to reduce nuts to the required texture.

Pumpkin seeds Used in salads or stir-fries, pumpkin seeds are also good as a snack, or they can be sprouted. They are a good source of omega-3 fats.

Sunflower seeds These are best lightly roasted and used in savoury baked goods or salads. They are a particularly good source of vitamin E and thiamin (vitamin B_1). Also try lightly toasting pumpkin and sunflower seeds together for a delicious snack.

Alfalfa seeds These are tiny legumes which, when sprouted, are rich in protein, vitamin C and valuable B vitamins. They have a low energy content.

grains and cereals

ALL GRAINS AND CEREALS contain large amounts of carbohydrate. Unrefined or wholegrain versions of these products are a better choice as they release energy into the bloodstream slowly. However, some grains have a higher protein to carbohydrate ratio, and these are a good choice.

Cereal grains have been cultivated throughout the world for centuries. They are inexpensive and readily available, and certain types of grain are an important part of a low-carb diet.

Oats Available rolled, flaked, as oatmeal or oatbran, oats are one of the best sources of soluble fibre in the diet. They are also linked with beneficial reductions in blood pressure and blood cholesterol. They have a low glycaemic index and satisfy hunger pangs for longer, so they can reduce energy intake throughout the day. Eat oats as porridge made with water or skimmed milk. This is lower in calories than commercial breakfast cereals and is easy to make. Oats can also be sprinkled into yogurt for extra fibre.

Wheatgerm This tiny wheat seed is extremely rich in B vitamins, vitamin E, proteins and fatty acids. It is available

Above: *Wheatgerm, rich in vitamin E, is a perfect addition to nutritious fruit smoothies.*

ready-toasted for adding to porridge and yogurt. It will only keep for a short time and should be stored in the refrigerator.

Barley This small round grain is high in fibre and makes a useful addition to soups, stews or salads instead of rice. It can be simmered with onions, garlic, tomatoes and other vegetables or flavourings to make pilaff.

CEREAL PRODUCTS

The following are a selection of products that contain lower levels of carbohydrate than traditional staples. They bring variety to a low-carb diet plan.

Taco shells Made from corn, these are good as a scoop for dips, for making a crispy sandwich or filled with grilled meat and salsa. On average each shell contains 60 calories and 8g carbohydrate.

Wraps (tortillas) These thin rounds of unleavened bread are made from wheat flour. They can be wrapped around sweet or savoury fillings to make light meals. A wrap with a diameter of around 20cm/5in contains 130–160 calories and 27–30g/1–¼oz carbohydrate.

Asian rice wrappers These can be used to wrap any filling. Their carbohydrate content is approximately 4.5g per pancake.

Below: *Try low-carbohydrate Asian rice wraps instead of traditional flour tortillas.*

USING WRAPS

For a quick snack or a light lunch on the move, create a low-carb "sandwich". Instead of using bread, place strips of meat, pieces of fish, grated cheese, egg or chopped vegetables inside a flour tortilla wrap or an Asian rice wrapper.

1 Lay the wrap flat on a surface and place the filling down the middle.

2 Fold in the sides and ends towards the ingredients and roll up tightly from the longer side to make a large cigar shape.

3 Cut in half at an angle and eat immediately with your fingers.

dairy foods and eggs

MILK, EGGS, and ingredients derived from these foods, can be high in saturated fats, but they contain valuable nutrients such as protein, calcium, vitamins and minerals, so they are very important for health. Choose low-fat versions wherever possible and do not over-indulge.

MILK

Containing almost every nutrient the body needs for good health, milk is the most complete form of food. In particular, it is a prime source of calcium, high-quality protein and B vitamins. The amount of fat in milk varies and is carefully controlled by legislation. Lower-fat varieties contain just as much calcium and protein, and also most of the vitamins of full-fat (whole) milk, so they are an excellent choice for losing weight. Full-fat milk contains 4 per cent fat, semi-skimmed (low-fat) 1.7 per cent fat and skimmed milk between 0.1 and 0.3 per cent fat. Buttermilk is low in fat, containing just 0.5 per cent, and it can be used in cooking or for making refreshing drinks. The majority of milk consumed is heat treated to destroy disease-carrying bacteria.

Below: *On a weight-loss programme, always opt for low-fat varieties of milk.*

Most milk comes from cows, but goat's milk is becoming more popular. Goat's and sheep's milk have similar compositions to cow's milk, with the milk from sheep being slightly more energy dense. Goat's and sheep's milk are often suggested as alternatives to cow's milk, however the proteins in them are potential allergens, and they are not generally recommended for individuals who are allergic to cow's milk.

Milk is an extremely versatile ingredient. It can be used for milkshakes and smoothies, in sauces, as a poaching liquid for fish, in soups, or for making yogurt.

Soya milk is made from soya beans, and both sweetened and unsweetened varieties are available. Its energy and fat content are similar to semi-skimmed milk, but the micronutrient content varies. Soya milk is not naturally rich in calcium and, while some products are fortified, on average 23 per cent less calcium is absorbed into the body from soya milk than from cow's milk due to the presence of phytates. It is also lower in phosphorus, zinc and vitamins A, B$_{12}$ and D. Oat, rice and nut milks are also available. These are lower in protein and have a variable fat content.

CREAM

This is the part of the milk that contains all the fat. If fresh milk that has not been homogenized is left undisturbed, the cream rises to the surface. Cream is classified according to its thickness and the proportion of butter-fat it contains. Single (light) cream contains no less than 18 per cent fat; whipping cream contains a minimum of 35 per cent fat; and double (heavy) cream contains a minimum of 48 per cent fat. The choice of cream is usually dictated by its use, for example, single cream cannot be whipped.

Above: *It is better to eat small amounts of real cream than synthetic cream substitutes.*

Cream is composed of saturated fat with traces of vitamins and minerals. The energy value depends on the fat content. Synthetic cream substitutes are available, but these are still high in saturated fat, so it is better to eat small quantities of the real thing.

ALTERNATIVES TO CREAM

- Sour cream has a similar fat content to single cream, with a thick texture (although it cannot be whipped) and a sour flavour.
- Smetena is a mixture of single cream and skimmed milk.
- Crème fraîche is a sharp-tasting cream that is higher in calories than sour cream. It is useful for cooking as it does not separate. Low-fat crème fraîche is a good compromise when looking for a rich flavour with a lower energy content.
- Soya cream has the consistency of single cream.
- Parev is a blend of water and vegetable oils. It is a kosher cream replacement.

PROBIOTICS

Yogurts and drinks containing specific strains of beneficial bacteria (often called bio-cultures) have become increasingly available in the shops. These are known as probiotics and there is evidence that they can help with the following:

- Irritable bowel syndrome
- Excessive bloating
- Infectious diarrhoea
- An improved immune system
- Respiratory infections and colds
- Recurrent thrush
- Constipation
- Lowering cholesterol levels

YOGURT

This is made by fermenting milk with bacteria, which causes it to clot and set. Natural yogurt has the same food value as the milk from which it is made, so it is a good source of protein, calcium and many vitamins and minerals. Types of yogurt vary from full-fat Greek (US strained plain) yogurt to low-fat yogurt made from skimmed milk.

Commercial fruit yogurts vary widely in fat content and can contain sweeteners. It is much healthier to use low-fat natural yogurt and add your own chopped fresh fruit, berries or fruit purées. Yogurt can also be made from soya milk.

Below: *Yogurt contains the same protein, calcium and vitamin and mineral content as milk, making it a valuable food.*

CHEESE

Amazingly versatile either as an ingredient or as a main food, there are hundreds of different cheeses. They are all made from milk and supply protein, calcium, vitamins A, B, D and E as well as zinc. The fat in cheese is saturated, and the content can vary from low to high. For a weight-loss regime use low-fat varieties or small quantities of a strongly flavoured cheese, such as Parmesan or extra-mature (sharp) Cheddar.

Parmesan This cheese has a strong, sharp flavour, and only small amounts are needed. For the best flavour, buy a piece and grate or shave it as required. Parmesan is delicious flaked over salad or vegetable bakes.

Gruyère This has a nutty flavour with a smooth texture. Used in fondue for its fine flavour and good melting qualities, it is high in fat, so limit the amount you eat.

Cheddar Traditionally a strong cheese, mild varieties are available. Its high energy content means intake should be limited. Low-fat varieties contain about 15 per cent fat.

Ricotta This bland, unsalted Italian soft cheese has a relatively low fat content. Layer it in a vegetable bake or use instead of cream cheese.

Cottage cheese Made from skimmed milk, this is low in fat but with a creamy flavour and lumpy texture. It is ideal in salads or stuffed in vegetables.

Goat's cheese With a distinct flavour and not too high in fat, goat's cheese makes a tasty appetizer grilled (broiled) on mushrooms.

Below: *With high-fat cheeses like Cheddar, make sure you eat no more than a small matchbox-sized portion a day.*

Above: *Crumbly feta is a traditional Greek ingredient with a fairly sharp flavour.*

Quark This is a low-fat cheese that can be used instead of cream.

Feta Originally from Greece, feta has a crumbly texture with a sharp, tangy flavour, and is fairly high in fat. Skewer small cubes of feta with diced pork and grill.

Mozzarella This fairly bland, fresh cheese is good in salads and not too high in fat. Buffalo's milk mozzarella is the best variety. Always tear this cheese rather than cutting it.

Brie A soft cheese that is fairly high in fat, brie is made in a large flat round. Wrap it in foil and bake on the barbecue or mash with walnuts to make a dip.

Stilton Ripened by the growth of green moulds, this high-fat, strong-tasting cheese is a useful ingredient in dips, dressings and soups. It is also delicious crumbled on salads.

EGGS

These are an important source of protein, vitamins and minerals, and they make a valuable contribution to a healthy diet. The energy content of eggs is relatively low, and it is adding fat during frying or baking that increases this. Whereas a boiled or poached egg provides just 90 calories, a fried egg contributes about 110 calories, so it is important to choose lower-fat methods of preparation.

fats and oils

WHILE IT is important to cut back on the amount of fat we consume, to avoid it completely would be almost impossible. Instead, focus on restricting your intake, whether cooking, drizzling or spreading, and choose healthier fats and oils wherever possible to reduce the negative effects.

All types of fat, by definition, are "fattening" as they are a concentrated source of energy. Weight for weight they contain twice as many calories as proteins and carbohydrates, so whatever oil or spread is used, whether it be margarine, butter, olive oil or nut oils, it is wise to limit the quantity consumed.

The main difference between types of fat is the proportion of saturated and unsaturated fats. Scientific evidence shows that diets that are high in saturated fat can raise total and low-density lipoprotein (LDL) cholesterol, which is directly associated with coronary heart disease. The cardio-protective effect of the Mediterranean way of eating has been demonstrated, and this diet recommends unsaturated sources of fat, such as olive or rapeseed (canola) oil, in preference to saturated fat.

Below: Butter is high in saturated fat and should only be eaten rarely. Opt for low-fat spreads or margarine wherever possible.

BUTTER

Made from cream, butter contains 82 per cent fat, which is mainly saturated, and calcium, with good quantities of vitamins A and D. As an indication of how much fat butter contains, it is worth noting that the cream from over 10 litres/18 pints of milk is required to make less than 450g/1lb butter. Butter can be flavoured with savoury ingredients, such as garlic, herbs, lemon or lime juice, mustard, chilli or even coconut, and served over lean grilled meat, vegetables or fish. It can also be flavoured with other ingredients, such as brandy, almonds or chocolate, and served as an accompaniment to desserts. Butter is bought either salted or unsalted (sweet). Salted butter keeps for longer as the salt has a preserving effect. Unsalted butter has a sweet flavour, but it is slightly more bland than salted butter. Due to its high fat content, however, the quantity and frequency with which butter is eaten should be strictly limited.

CHOLESTEROL-LOWERING SPREADS

There are a number of margarines and low-fat spreads available that have added plant sterols and stanols. These plant extracts are natural components taken from vegetable oils, and when they are eaten regularly they can help reduce the total and low-density lipoprotein (LDL) cholesterol (the bad cholesterol) circulating in the blood. Plant sterols and stanols do not have any effect on the levels of high-density lipoprotein (HDL) cholesterol (the good cholesterol) or triglycerides.

Scientific studies into low-cholesterol spreads have shown that approximately three portions of plant sterols or stanols per day can give up to a 10–15 per cent reduction in LDL cholesterol levels within just three weeks.

Plant sterols and stanols do not contribute to the total energy value of the food – it is only the fat itself that does this. For anybody at risk of developing coronary heart disease or those trying to lose weight and reduce their blood cholesterol levels, these spreads, although slightly more expensive than normal low-fat spreads, can be a very good choice. They can be found in most large supermarkets or health food stores.

Many dairy products have had plant sterols and stanols added to them, especially the following:
• Margarine
• Low-fat spread
• Yogurt
• Cream cheese

Above: *Check the label on low-fat spreads carefully as the fat content varies depending on the oil and fat sources used.*

MARGARINE

Instead of butter, consider using margarine. It is composed of between 80 and 90 per cent oil, with the addition of vitamins A and D. The composition of the margarine depends entirely on the specific blend of oils used to make it, and this can vary tremendously between brands, so it is important to check individual product labels for the composition before buying them.

SPREADS

Lower-fat spreads contain less fat than either margarine or butter, and so they are less energy rich (but some only marginally so). The fat content of spreads varies enormously from between 5 per cent and 70 per cent, but the individual profile of each product depends on the type of oil and fat sources from which it is made. As with margarine, it is important to check labels thoroughly when shopping.

Right: *Select oils for cooking and salad dressings carefully, and use in moderation as they are a concentrated source of energy.*

When low-fat spreads are used for cooking, they may behave differently to full-fat products, such as butter or margarine. Always use a heavy pan over a low heat when heating low-fat spreads, to avoid burning, spitting or spoiling, and stir all the time. Low-fat spreads are not suitable for frying. Remember also that the keeping qualities of recipes made using low-fat spreads may be reduced slightly, because of the lower fat content of those spreads.

Olive oil spreads are made from a percentage of olive oil and therefore contain a greater amount of unsaturated fats. They have a delicious, distinctive flavour. The majority are also extremely low in trans fats so can help reduce the risk of developing coronary heart disease.

OILS

For low-fat or fat-free cooking it is best to avoid roasting and frying as these can increase the fat content of food. Instead poach, grill (broil), bake, steam or microwave food, as none of these cooking methods involves the addition of fat. When oil is needed, however, it is important that you choose the healthiest types.

All pure oils are very high in energy and, while they do have health benefits, they should be used in moderation, especially when trying to lose weight or maintain weight loss. Oils gradually lose their flavour and become rancid over time, so it is important to store them in an airtight bottle or container in a cool dark place, but not in the refrigerator.

Olive oil This is virtually 100 per cent oil with no additions and is used widely in Mediterranean cooking or as a salad dressing. It is made by pressing ripe olives. When a label says "virgin olive oil", the oil has come from the first cold pressing and has not been chemically treated. As well as tasting delicious, olive oil is high in unsaturated fats and low in saturated and trans fats, so it can help reduce the risk of developing coronary heart disease.

Rapeseed (canola) oil This is a bland oil but an extremely healthy choice. It is a good source of omega-3 fats and therefore useful for general cooking, especially if you are not keen on oily fish. Try adding herbs, spices or blanched cloves of garlic to rapeseed oil to give it a bit more flavour.

Nut oils There are many nut oils available, including walnut, hazelnut, groundnut and almond oils. These each have their own distinctive flavour and can be overpowering if used in large quantities. They can be mixed with rapeseed (canola) oil to make a delicious salad dressing.

sauces and dressings

A FRESH SALAD or a simple piece of grilled fish is ideal for a low-carbohydrate diet, but take care not to smother it in a dressing or sauce that is high in sugar, salt or fat. Wherever possible, make sauces or dressings yourself rather than using ready-made, so you can control the ingredients.

SALAD DRESSINGS

A good salad dressing is important to brighten up any salad. Traditional dressings are based on a mixture of delicately flavoured oils and vinegars, with added herbs or seasonings, such as mustard, lemon juice, garlic, chillies or honey.

TO MAKE FRENCH DRESSING

1 Mix 45ml/3 tbsp olive oil and 10ml/ 2 tsp vinegar in a screw-top jar.

2 Screw on the lid, shake vigorously until well blended, then add seasoning or other flavourings to taste.

3 Store in the refrigerator for up to one month.

Due to the large oil content, salad dressings can be high in calories, so do not use too much. A maximum of 25ml/1½ tsp per portion will keep the energy content down, while adding enough flavour. Ready-made, fat-free dressings are also available. For creamier dressings, opt for those based on low-fat natural yogurt, fat-reduced mayonnaise or low-fat crème fraîche flavoured with garlic, herbs or lemon juice.

SAVOURY SAUCES

Sauces add the finishing touch to many dishes, bringing colour, moisture and essential flavour. Sauces may be served alongside the main ingredients, to be added at the table, or ingredients may be cooked directly in the sauce. Home-made sauces are generally tastier and allow you to control the ingredients, but there are a number of good-quality commercial products available, which are worth using.
Fresh tomato sauce Made from tomatoes simmered with onion, this is low in calories and bursting with healthy lycopenes and carotenes. It can be flavoured with fresh basil, parsley, garlic, mushrooms or chilli and made with canned tomatoes or passata (bottled strained tomatoes) for speed.
Red (bell) pepper sauce Red peppers can be cooked in the same way as tomatoes, with garlic and onions, then blended to make a rich red sauce that is great served with grilled meat or fish.
Pesto This uncooked herb, garlic and Parmesan paste can be added to soups, spread on vegetables for grilling, mixed into yogurt to make a tasty dressing or dip, or stuffed inside fish or chicken. It is extremely versatile and flavoursome. The energy content of pesto can be high due to the olive oil and cheese, so limit the portion size to 25ml/1½ tsp per person.

Above: A salad dressing made from fresh lemon juice is a tasty and healthy option.

Below: Choose a low-calorie tomato salsa to spice up simple meat or fish dishes.

QUICK IDEAS FOR SALAD DRESSINGS

- Low-fat yogurt mixed with tahini (sesame seed paste).
- Lime juice whisked with olive oil in the proportions 1:3.
- Balsamic vinegar shaken with olive oil in the proportions 1:3, and flavoured with crushed garlic.
- Chopped watercress in reduced-fat mayonnaise with grated lemon rind.
- Avocado blended with 15ml/1 tbsp lemon juice or white wine vinegar and 5ml/1 tsp Dijon mustard, spiced with hot chilli sauce, if you like.

- Low-fat crème fraîche mixed with mint or ready-made mint sauce.
- Fresh orange juice – this makes a good dressing for grated carrot, apple and celery.
- Lemon juice flavoured with a pinch of hot chilli powder or chopped fresh chilli (good poured over tomatoes).
- White wine simmered with chopped shallots, mustard seeds and 5ml/1 tsp Dijon mustard and served warm.
- Thai fish sauce mixed with fresh garlic, lime juice and herbs.

Raita This is an Indian accompaniment based on yogurt. The most common is cucumber raita, which is usually flavoured with mint. Tomato, onion and other vegetables or fruit, or a mixture, can be added to yogurt to make raita. Simple flavouring, such as curry paste, coriander or mint, can be used to season the yogurt instead of vegetables. These sauces are refreshing and excellent with spicy dishes or salads. The yogurt provides a good source of calcium and protein, and, if low-fat yogurt is used, raita has few calories.

SALSAS

These sauces have become very popular as accompaniments for grilled meat or fish. They are almost mini salads for which the ingredients are chopped together and

dressed with lime or lemon juice, occasionally with a little added olive oil. The ingredients of a salsa are varied to suit the main dish, typically tomatoes (fresh, canned or dried), onion, (bell) peppers, chillies, fruit, vegetables, such as aubergine (eggplant) or courgette (zucchini), peas, beans or lentils, fresh herbs or spices. They are health promoting, usually with few calories, and an excellent choice for a weight-loss menu.

SWEET SAUCES

These can transform simple desserts into elegant final courses. For example, a raspberry purée or coulis goes well over fresh or poached pears, and a blackberry or blackcurrant sauce is delicious on stewed apple. Fresh fruit dipped into melted chocolate is a treat for special occasions.

Below: *Mint or cucumber raita, made with low-fat natural yogurt, is a healthy choice.*

Below: *Try dipping fresh fruit in melted chocolate for a quick, indulgent dessert.*

MAKING FRESH PESTO

This fresh basil paste can be made in advance and stored in the refrigerator. To liven up dishes, add a spoonful to fish or chicken, savoury wraps or cheese. Pesto can also be made with rocket (arugula) or chopped parsley to which 5ml/1 tsp of dried basil can be added for flavour. Use walnuts instead of pine nuts, if you prefer.

1 In a food processor or a blender, or using a traditional mortar and pestle, blend a large handful of fresh basil leaves with 30ml/2 tbsp pine nuts, 2 garlic cloves and some olive oil.

2 Fold in 30ml/2 tbsp freshly grated Parmesan cheese and plenty of ground black pepper.

3 The pesto can be stored in an airtight container in the refrigerator for up to two weeks. If it starts to dry out, drizzle a little extra olive oil on top of the pesto to preserve it.

breakfasts

FOR GOOD HEALTH, A SUSTAINING breakfast is an essential start to the day. Many classic breakfast foods, such as cereal or bagels, which can contain large amounts of carbohydrate, are simply not an option on a low-carbohydrate diet. However, there are lots of other quick, simple and nutritious choices that are just as tasty. Try combining one or two of the breakfast basics, or make the most of weekend mornings by enjoying a leisurely breakfast of poached eggs Florentine or herrings in oatmeal with bacon.

basic breakfast eggs

EGGS ARE HIGH IN PROTEIN and an essential part of many low-carbohydrate breakfasts. Quick and easy to prepare, simply choose your favourite and combine with grilled meat or fish for a healthy, nutritious and filling start to the day.

Boiled eggs

1 When cooking chilled eggs until firm, it is best to put them into cold water to boil. Alternatively, lower the eggs with a spoon into simmering water, taking care not to crack them on the base of the pan.

2 Heat the water until bubbling gently, then allow 4 minutes for soft eggs, 5–6 for semi-firm (yolks still soft) and 8–10 for hard. If the eggs were lowered into simmering water, allow slightly longer.

3 Remove the egg from the pan using a slotted spoon and place in an eggcup. Cut off the top with a small sharp knife. Tap the shell firmly and evenly with the blade to prevent too much shell from crumbling.

Poached eggs

1 Pour about 2.5–4cm/1–1½in water into a frying pan. Add 15ml/1 tbsp vinegar and bring to the boil. Reduce the heat to keep the water bubbling gently.

2 Crack the egg into a cup or small dish, then gently tip it into the bubbling water. Cook the egg for 1 minute undisturbed, then spoon a little water over the centre of the egg to cook the yolk. The egg is cooked when it can be loosened easily from the bottom of the pan.

3 Lift the egg from the water and trim off any rough edges. Allow any water to run off the egg and pat dry with kitchen paper before serving.

Fried eggs

1 Heat 30–45ml/2–3 tbsp oil in a frying pan over a medium heat. There is no need to add oil to a non-stick pan.

2 Crack the egg into the pan and allow it to settle and start bubbling gently around the edges before adding another. Try not to let the eggs touch in the pan.

3 Cook for a further 1 minute, until the white has turned opaque and the edges are just beginning to brown. Carefully lift the cooked egg out of the pan. If you prefer a firmer egg, flip it over using a fish slice, being careful not to split the yolk, and cook for a further minute, until the yolk has hardened.

basic breakfast grills

GRILLING IS THE HEALTHIEST way to cook meat and fish – the fat drips off, leaving the food delicious and crispy. It is important to fill yourself up early in the day, so don't be tempted to skip breakfast, even if you are in a hurry.

Grilled bacon

1 Bacon can be fried, but it is better grilled as it gives a delicious crispy result. Trim any excess fat from the edges of the bacon rashers using kitchen scissors.

2 Preheat the grill (broiler) to a medium heat, then lay the rashers on a rack and grill (broil) for between 4 and 8 minutes, turning occasionally. The fat will drip away from the bacon as it cooks, so this is the best cooking method to use if you are on a healthy, low-fat diet.

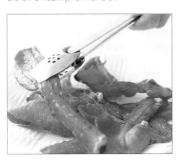

3 When the rashers are cooked and crispy, remove them from the grill and place them on a sheet of kitchen paper to soak up any excess fat.

Grilled sausages

1 Preheat the grill to medium. Using a pair of kitchen scissors, snip the string of sausages apart.

2 Lightly prick each sausage three or four times with the point of a sharp knife. This will prevent them from bursting while cooking, but it is not necessary if you are using sausages that have been made with natural casings.

3 Place the individual sausages on a rack in the grill pan and cook well away from the heat source under the preheated grill. Cook thick sausages for about 10 minutes, turning frequently until evenly browned. Thin sausages will need less time.

Grilled kippers

1 Kippers (smoked herrings), as with all fish, taste better cooked on the bone, but you can buy kipper fillets if you prefer.

2 Preheat the grill, then line the grill pan with foil. Lightly brush the foil with a little sunflower oil.

3 Carefully remove the heads and tails from the kippers with sharp kitchen scissors, then lay the fish on the foil, skin-side up. Grill them for about 1 minute, turn them over, brush the flesh with a little more oil to prevent the kippers from drying out, and grill for a further 4–5 minutes, until cooked through. Serve immediately with lemon juice and cayenne pepper.

raspberry and oatmeal blend

A SPOONFUL of oatmeal gives substance to this tangy, invigorating drink. If you can, prepare it ahead of time because soaking the raw oats helps to break down the starch into natural sugars that are easy to digest.

2 Put the soaked oats in a blender or food processor and add all but two or three of the raspberries, the honey and about 30ml/2 tbsp of the yogurt. Process until smooth, scraping the mixture down from the side of the bowl if necessary.

3 Pour the raspberry and oatmeal smoothie into a large glass, swirl in the remaining yogurt and top with raspberries. Store the smoothie in the refrigerator until you are ready to drink it – it will thicken up so you might need to add a little juice or mineral water before serving.

Makes 1 large glass

25ml/1½ tbsp medium oatmeal
150g/5oz/scant 1 cup raspberries
5–10ml/1–2 tsp clear honey
45ml/3 tbsp natural (plain) yogurt

NUTRITION NOTES

Per portion:

Energy	184kcal/778kJ
Protein	6.7g
Fat	2.6g
saturated fat	0.7g
Carbohydrate	35.5g
Fibre	12.9g
Calcium	157mg

1 Spoon the oatmeal into a large heatproof bowl, then pour in about 120ml/4fl oz/½ cup boiling water and leave to stand for about 10 minutes or until the water has been completely absorbed.

COOK'S TIP

If you don't like raspberry pips (seeds) in your smoothies, simply press the fruit through a sieve with the back of a wooden spoon to make a smooth purée, then process with the oatmeal and yogurt as before. Alternatively, you could try using redcurrants instead of the raspberries.

Although a steaming bowl of porridge cannot be beaten as a warming winter breakfast, this smooth, oaty drink makes a great, light alternative in warmer months. It is a good way to make sure you get your fill of wholesome oats for breakfast.

strawberry and honey smoothie

THIS ENERGIZING BLEND is simply bursting with goodness. Not only is tofu a good source of protein, it is also rich in minerals and contains nutrients that protect against diseases. Store any leftovers in the refrigerator for the following morning.

Makes 2 glasses

250g/9oz firm tofu
200g/7oz/1¾ cups strawberries
45ml/3 tbsp pumpkin or sunflower seeds, plus extra for sprinkling
30–45ml/2–3 tbsp clear honey
juice of 2 large oranges
juice of 1 lemon

NUTRITION NOTES

Per portion:

Energy	325kcal/1368kJ
Protein	15.7g
Fat	13.7g
saturated fat	2.5g
Carbohydrate	38.8g
Fibre	3.2g
Calcium	90mg

1 Roughly chop the tofu, then hull the strawberries and chop them. Reserve a few strawberry chunks for garnish.

2 Put all of the ingredients into a blender or food processor and blend until completely smooth and creamy, scraping the mixture down from the side of the bowl, if necessary.

3 Pour into tumblers and sprinkle with extra seeds and strawberry chunks.

COOK'S TIP

Almost any other fruit can be used instead of the strawberries. Those that blend well, such as mangoes, bananas, peaches, plums and raspberries, are good substitutes.

porridge with dates and pistachios

FULL OF VALUABLE FIBRE and nutrients, dates give a natural
sweet flavour to this warming winter breakfast dish.

Serves 4

250g/9oz/scant 2 cups fresh dates
225g/8oz/2 cups rolled oats
475ml/16fl oz/2 cups semi-skimmed
(low-fat) milk
pinch of salt
50g/2oz/½ cup shelled, unsalted
pistachio nuts, roughly chopped

1 Halve the dates and remove the stones
and stems. Cover with boiling water and
leave to soak for 30 minutes, until soft.
Strain, reserving 90ml/6 tbsp of the water.

2 Remove the skin from the dates
and place them in a food processor
with the reserved soaking water. Process
to a smooth purée.

3 Place the oats in a pan with the milk,
300ml/½ pint/1¼ cups water and
a pinch of salt. Bring to the boil, then
reduce the heat and simmer gently for
4–5 minutes until thick, creamy and
thoroughly cooked, stirring frequently.

4 Ladle the porridge into warm serving
bowls, then top with a spoonful of the
date purée and sprinkle with the roughly
chopped pistachio nuts. Serve immediately,
while still piping hot.

NUTRITION NOTES

Per portion:

Energy	452kcal/1905kJ
Protein	14.2g
Fat	14.2g
saturated fat	2.2g
Carbohydrate	69.7g
Fibre	4.0g
Calcium	197mg

apricot and ginger compote

FRESH GINGER ADDS WARMTH to this stimulating breakfast
dish and complements the flavour of the plump, juicy apricots.

Serves 4

350g/12oz/1½ cups dried
unsulphured apricots
4cm/1½in piece fresh root ginger,
finely chopped
200g/7oz/scant 1 cup natural
live yogurt

NUTRITION NOTES

Per portion:

Energy	186kcal/789kJ
Protein	6.7g
Fat	0.5g
saturated fat	0.3g
Carbohydrate	41.0g
Fibre	21.0g
Calcium	170mg

1 Cover the apricots with boiling water,
then leave to soak overnight.

2 Place the apricots and their soaking
water in a large, heavy pan. Add the
finely chopped root ginger and gently
bring to the boil.

3 Reduce the heat and simmer gently for
10 minutes or until the apricots are soft
and plump and the water becomes syrupy.
Strain the apricots, reserving the syrup, and
discard the chopped ginger.

4 Serve the cooked apricots warm
with the reserved syrup and a spoonful
of natural yogurt.

COOK'S TIP
Fresh ginger freezes well. Peel the
root and store it in a plastic bag in the
freezer. You can grate it from frozen,
then return the root to the freezer until
the next time you need it for a recipe.

egg-stuffed tomatoes

THIS SIMPLE DISH is just the kind of thing you might find in a charcuterie in France. It is easy to prepare at home and makes a light and nutritious breakfast or a simple lunch.

Serves 4
175ml/6fl oz/¾ cup low-fat crème fraiche
30ml/2 tbsp chopped fresh chives
30ml/2 tbsp chopped fresh basil
30ml/2 tbsp chopped fresh parsley
4 hard-boiled eggs
4 ripe tomatoes
salt and ground black pepper
salad leaves, to serve

NUTRITION NOTES

Per portion:	
Energy	99kcal/416kJ
Protein	9.8g
Fat	5.5g
saturated fat	1.8g
Carbohydrate	2.6g
Fibre	0.5g
Calcium	31mg

1 In a small bowl, mix together the crème fraiche and herbs, and then set aside. Using an egg slicer or sharp knife, cut the eggs into thin slices, taking care to keep the slices intact.

2 Make deep cuts to within 1cm/½in of the base of each tomato. (There should be the same number of cuts in each tomato as there are slices of egg.)

3 Fan open the tomatoes and sprinkle with salt, then insert an egg slice into each slit. Place each stuffed tomato on a plate with a few salad leaves, season and serve with the herb crème fraiche mixture.

COOK'S TIP
For the best flavour, use the freshest, ripest tomatoes you can find.

griddled tomatoes on toast

LITTLE COULD BE SIMPLER and tastier than this breakfast dish. Tomatoes are rich in vitamin C and the thinly sliced wholegrain toast provides fibre and slowly-absorbed complex carbohydrate.

1 Brush a ridged griddle pan with a little olive oil and heat. Lay the slices of tomato on the pan and cook for about 4 minutes, turning once.

2 Meanwhile, lightly toast the thin slices of wholegrain bread. Place the tomatoes on top. Drizzle the tomatoes with a little olive oil and balsamic vinegar. Season with salt and pepper and serve with shavings of Parmesan cheese, if you like.

Serves 4

olive oil, for brushing
and drizzling
6 tomatoes, thickly sliced
4 thin slices wholegrain bread
balsamic vinegar, for drizzling
salt and ground black pepper
shavings of Parmesan cheese,
to serve (optional)

COOK'S TIPS

• To reduce the total amount of carbohydrate in this dish, try to cut the bread as thinly as possible.
• Using a ridged griddle pan reduces the amount of oil required for cooking and imparts the smoky flavour of foods that have been cooked on a barbecue.

NUTRITION NOTES

Per portion:	
Energy	105kcal/438kJ
Protein	3.2g
Fat	3.8g
saturated fat	0.7g
Carbohydrate	15.5g
Fibre	2.4g
Calcium	28mg

savoury scrambled eggs

HIGH IN PROTEIN and low in carbohydrate, these tasty scrambled eggs make a nutritious breakfast that will keep you going throughout the morning.

Serves 2

2 slices wholegrain bread
25g/1oz/2 tbsp butter
2 eggs and 2 egg yolks, beaten
60–90ml/4–6 tbsp semi-skimmed
(low-fat) milk
salt and ground black pepper
anchovy fillets, cut into strips, and paprika,
to garnish
anchovy paste or Gentleman's Relish,
for spreading

1 Toast the bread, then remove the crusts and cut the toast into triangles or squares, if you like. Keep warm.

2 Meanwhile, melt the butter in a pan over a very low heat.

3 Pour the eggs and milk into the butter and stir in a little salt and pepper. Heat very gently, stirring constantly, until the mixture begins to thicken. Remove the pan from the heat and continue to stir until the mixture becomes very creamy.

4 Place the toast on two plates and divide the eggs equally among them. Garnish each portion with strips of anchovy fillet and a generous sprinkling of paprika. Serve immediately, with anchovy paste to spread on the toast.

NUTRITION NOTES

Per portion:	
Energy	220kcal/919kJ
Protein	13.7g
Fat	13.3g
saturated fat	3.8g
Carbohydrate	13.0g
Fibre	1.1g
Calcium	112mg

poached eggs florentine

THE CLASSIC COMBINATION of eggs and spinach is high in protein and packed with vitamins and minerals. It is tasty and sustaining and makes an ideal weekend brunch if you have an active day ahead of you.

3 To make the sauce, melt the butter in a small pan, add the flour and cook for 1 minute, stirring constantly. Gradually blend in the hot milk, beating well. Cook for 2 minutes, stirring constantly. Remove from the heat and stir in the mace and 75g/3oz/¾ cup of the Gruyère cheese.

4 Break each egg into a cup and slide into a pan of lightly salted simmering water. Poach for 3–4 minutes. Lift the eggs out using a slotted spoon and drain on kitchen paper.

5 Place a poached egg in the middle of each dish and cover with the sauce. Sprinkle with the remaining cheeses and bake for 10 minutes, or until just golden. Garnish with shavings of Parmesan cheese and serve immediately.

Serves 4

675g/1½lb spinach, washed and drained
pinch of freshly grated nutmeg
4 eggs
15ml/1 tbsp freshly grated Parmesan cheese, plus shavings to garnish
salt and ground black pepper

For the sauce

25g/1oz/2 tbsp butter
25g/1oz/¼ cup plain (all-purpose) flour
300ml/½ pint/1¼ cups hot milk
pinch of ground mace
115g/4oz/1 cup grated Gruyère cheese

VARIATION

To make a low-fat version of this dish, omit the Gruyère cheese from the recipe. It will work just as well.

1 Preheat the oven to 200°C/400°F/ Gas 6. Place the spinach in a large pan with a little water. Cook for 3–4 minutes, then drain well and chop finely.

2 Return the spinach to the pan, add the nutmeg and seasoning and heat through. Spoon into four small gratin dishes, making a well in the middle of each.

NUTRITION NOTES

Per portion:	
Energy	366kcal/1404kJ
Protein	25.9g
Fat	24.8g
saturated fat	12.4g
Carbohydrate	11.3g
Fibre	3.7g
Calcium	747mg

omelette arnold bennett

A CREAMY, SMOKED HADDOCK soufflé omelette is low in carbohydrate and perfect for a leisurely weekend breakfast. Fish is an excellent source of protein; the cream, butter and cheese make this dish high in fat so save it for a special occasion.

3 Mix the egg yolks with 15ml/1 tbsp of the remaining cream. Season, then stir into the fish. In a separate bowl, combine the cheese and remaining cream.

4 Whisk the egg whites until stiff, then fold into the fish mixture. Heat the remaining butter in an omelette pan, add the fish mixture and cook until browned underneath. Pour the cheese mixture over and grill (broil) until bubbling. Garnish with watercress and serve.

COOK'S TIP
Try to buy smoked haddock that does not contain artificial colouring for this recipe. Apart from being better for you, it gives the omelette a lighter, more attractive colour.

Serves 4

175g/6oz smoked haddock fillet, poached and drained
50g/2oz/4 tbsp butter, diced
175ml/6fl oz/¾ cup whipping cream
4 eggs, separated
40g/1½oz/⅓ cup mature (sharp) Cheddar cheese, grated
ground black pepper
watercress, to garnish

1 Remove and discard the skin from the haddock fillet. If there are any small bones remaining, remove them with tweezers and discard, then carefully flake the flesh using a fork.

2 Melt half the butter with 60ml/4 tbsp of the cream in a non-stick pan, then stir in the flaked fish. Cover and set aside to cool. Preheat the grill (broiler).

NUTRITION NOTES

Per portion:	
Energy	429kcal/1795kJ
Protein	15.0g
Fat	40.5g
saturated fat	24.7g
Carbohydrate	1.7g
Fibre	0g
Calcium	126mg

soufflé omelette with mushrooms

A LIGHT, MOUTH-WATERING omelette makes a great morning meal. Mushrooms contain barely any carbohydrate, but are wonderfully satisfying and a source of B vitamins and minerals.

Serves 2

2 eggs, separated
15g/½oz/1 tbsp butter
flat leaf parsley or coriander (cilantro)
   leaves, to garnish

For the mushroom sauce

15g/½oz/1 tbsp butter
75g/3oz/generous 1 cup button (white)
   mushrooms, thinly sliced
15ml/1 tbsp plain (all-purpose) flour
75–120ml/2½–4fl oz/⅓–½ cup milk
5ml/1 tsp chopped fresh
   parsley (optional)
salt and ground black pepper

2 Stir the flour into the mushrooms, then slowly add the milk, stirring constantly. Bring to the boil and cook until thickened. Add the parsley, if using, and season with salt and pepper to taste. Keep warm.

3 Beat the egg yolks with 15ml/1 tbsp water and season with a little salt and pepper. Whisk the egg whites until stiff, then fold into the egg yolks using a metal spoon. Preheat the grill (broiler).

4 Melt the butter in a large frying pan and pour the egg mixture into the pan. Cook over a gentle heat for 2–3 minutes. Place the frying pan under the grill and cook for a further 2–3 minutes, until the top is golden brown.

5 Pour the mushroom sauce over the top of the omelette and fold it in half. Cut the omelette in half, and slide each portion on to a warmed plate. Serve immediately, garnished with parsley or coriander leaves.

1 First, make the mushroom sauce. Melt the butter in a frying pan and add the sliced mushrooms. Cook gently over a low heat, stirring occasionally, for 4–5 minutes, until tender and juicy.

NUTRITION NOTES

Per portion:

Energy	244kcal/1020kJ
Protein	10.6g
Fat	17.5g
saturated fat	10.4g
Carbohydrate	8.5g
Fibre	0.7g
Calcium	106mg

stuffed thai omelettes

LOW IN CARBOHYDRATE and saturated fat, the subtle combination of fragrant coriander and hot chilli in these omelettes will instantly invigorate and kick-start a sluggish system.

Serves 4

30ml/2 tbsp vegetable oil
2 garlic cloves, finely chopped
1 small onion, finely chopped
225g/8oz/2 cups minced (ground) pork
30ml/2 tbsp Thai fish sauce
2 tomatoes, peeled and chopped
15ml/1 tbsp chopped fresh
    coriander (cilantro)
ground black pepper
sprigs of coriander (cilantro) and red
    chillies, thinly sliced, to garnish

For the omelettes
5–6 eggs
15ml/1 tbsp Thai fish sauce
30ml/2 tbsp vegetable oil

1 Heat the oil in a wok, add the garlic and onion, and cook for 3–4 minutes, until soft. Add the pork and cook, stirring, for about 8 minutes until lightly browned.

2 Stir the fish sauce, tomatoes and pepper into the pork; simmer until slightly thickened. Mix in the coriander.

3 To make the omelettes, whisk the eggs and fish sauce together. Heat 15ml/ 1 tbsp of the oil in an omelette pan or wok. Add half the beaten egg mixture and tilt the pan to spread the egg into an even shape.

4 Cook until the omelette is just set, then spoon half the filling into the centre. Fold into a neat square parcel by bringing the opposite sides of the omelette towards each other – first the top and bottom, then the right and left sides.

COOK'S TIP
For a milder flavour, discard the seeds and membrane of the chillies because this is where most of their heat resides.

5 Carefully invert the parcel on to a warmed serving dish folded side down, and keep warm. Make a second omelette parcel with the remaining oil, eggs and filling and invert it on to the serving dish.

6 Cut each omelette parcel in half, and serve immediately, garnished with sprigs of fresh coriander and thinly sliced red chillies.

NUTRITION NOTES

Per portion:	
Energy	309kcal/1291kJ
Protein	23.4g
Fat	22.8g
saturated fat	4.5g
Carbohydrate	4.1g
Fibre	0.9g
Calcium	64mg

frittata with sun-dried tomatoes

THIS ITALIAN OMELETTE, made with tangy Parmesan cheese, can be served warm or cold. It is perfect as a filling breakfast or as a delicious snack at any other time of day.

Serves 4

6 sun-dried tomatoes
60ml/4 tbsp olive oil
1 small onion, finely chopped
pinch of fresh thyme leaves
6 eggs
25g/1oz/⅓ cup freshly grated Parmesan
  cheese, plus shavings to serve
salt and ground black pepper
thyme sprigs, to garnish

1 Place the tomatoes in a bowl and pour over hot water to cover. Leave to soak for 15 minutes. Lift out the tomatoes and pat dry on kitchen paper. Reserve the soaking water. Cut the tomatoes into thin strips.

2 Heat the olive oil in a frying pan. Cook the onion for 5–6 minutes. Add the thyme and tomatoes and cook for a further 2–3 minutes.

3 Break the eggs into a bowl and beat lightly. Stir in 45ml/3 tbsp of the tomato soaking water and the Parmesan and season to taste. Raise the heat under the pan. When the oil is sizzling, add the eggs. Mix quickly into the other ingredients, then stop stirring. Lower the heat to medium and cook for 4–5 minutes, or until the base is golden and the top puffed.

4 Take a large plate, invert it over the pan and, holding it firmly with oven gloves, turn the pan and the frittata over on to it. Slide the frittata back into the pan, and continue cooking for 3–4 minutes until golden brown on the second side. Remove the pan from the heat. Cut the frittata into wedges, garnish with thyme sprigs and parmesan, and serve immediately.

NUTRITION NOTES

Per portion:	
Energy	335kcal/1400kJ
Protein	12.6g
Fat	30.8g
saturated fat	6.4g
Carbohydrate	2.2g
Fibre	0.2g
Calcium	127mg

herrings in oatmeal with bacon

OILY FISH ARE AN EXCELLENT SOURCE of omega-3 fatty acids, which are essential for good health. They make a delicious, sustaining breakfast to take you through the day. For extra colour and flavour, serve with grilled tomatoes.

Serves 4
50g/2oz/½ cup medium oatmeal
10ml/2 tsp mustard powder
4 herrings, about 225g/8oz each,
   cleaned, boned, heads and tails removed
30ml/2 tbsp sunflower oil
8 rindless bacon rashers (strips)
salt and ground black pepper
lemon wedges, to serve

1 In a shallow dish, combine the oatmeal and mustard powder and season. Press the herrings in the mixture to coat.

2 Heat the oil in a large frying pan and fry the bacon until crisp. Drain on kitchen paper and keep hot.

3 Gently lay the herrings in the pan. You may need to cook them in two batches to avoid overcrowding the pan. Cook the fish for about 3–4 minutes on each side, until crisp and golden.

4 Using a fish slice (metal spatula), lift the herrings from the pan and place on warmed serving plates with the bacon rashers. Serve immediately with lemon wedges for squeezing over.

NUTRITION NOTES

Per portion:	
Energy	675kcal/2821kJ
Protein	48.7g
Fat	46.9g
saturated fat	11.4g
Carbohydrate	10.5g
Fibre	1.9g
Calcium	146mg

devilled kidneys

THIS TRADITIONAL ENGLISH breakfast dish is a great way to start the day for anyone on a low-carbohydrate diet. It is packed with protein, low in fat and contains a negligible amount of carbohydrate.

Serves 4

25g/1oz/2 tbsp butter
1 shallot, finely chopped
2 garlic cloves, finely chopped
115g/4oz/1½ cups mushrooms, sliced
1.5ml/¼ tsp cayenne pepper
15ml/1 tbsp Worcestershire sauce
8 lamb's kidneys, halved
   and trimmed
30ml/2 tbsp chopped fresh parsley

COOK'S TIP
If you prefer not to eat spicy food first thing in the morning, omit the cayenne pepper. The dish will be just as tasty but milder on the palate.

1 Melt the butter in a frying pan, then add the shallots, garlic and mushrooms and cook for about 5 minutes. Stir in the cayenne pepper and Worcestershire sauce and cook for 1 minute more.

2 Add the kidneys to the pan and cook for 3–5 minutes on each side. Sprinkle with chopped parsley, divide among warm serving plates and serve immediately.

NUTRITION NOTES

Per portion:

Energy	190kcal/794kJ
Protein	31.2g
Fat	7.3g
saturated fat	3.3g
Carbohydrate	0.2g
Fibre	0.4g
Calcium	18mg

soups

LIGHT AND NUTRITIOUS SOUPS, whether served as a first course or as a simple lunch, can work perfectly as part of a low-carbohydrate diet. They are quick and simple to prepare, making it easy to include them as an essential part of your eating plan. Try making a large batch of your favourite soup and freezing individual portions, which can then be defrosted as you need them. Choose from traditional soups, such as creamy stilton and watercress soup or hearty Italian ribollita, or try something more exotic, such as aromatic hot and sour soup.

lime and avocado soup

THIS DELICIOUS AND VERY PRETTY SOUP is perfect for dinner parties and has a fresh, delicate flavour. You might want to add a dash more lime juice just before serving for added zest.

Serves 4

2 large ripe avocados
300ml/½ pint/1¼ cups crème fraîche
1 litre/1¾ pints/4 cups well-flavoured
  chicken stock
5ml/1 tsp salt
juice of ½ lime
small bunch of coriander (cilantro)
ground black pepper

1 Halve the avocados, remove the stones (pits) and peel. Chop the flesh coarsely and process in a food processor with 3–4 tbsp of the crème fraîche until smooth.

2 Heat the chicken stock in a pan. When it is hot, but below simmering point, add the remaining crème fraîche and the salt.

3 Add the lime juice to the avocado mixture and process briefly to mix, then gradually stir the mixture into the hot chicken stock, ensuring it is thoroughly combined. Heat gently but do not let the mixture approach boiling point.

4 Roughly chop the coriander. Pour the soup into individual heated bowls and sprinkle each portion with chopped coriander and freshly ground black pepper. Serve immediately.

NUTRITION NOTES

Per portion:	
Energy	524kcal/2165kJ
Protein	6.8g
Fat	52.3g
saturated fat	22.3g
Carbohydrate	6.8g
Fibre	2.0g
Calcium	15mg

cream of courgette soup

THE JOYS OF THIS SOUP are its delicate colour, creamy texture and subtle taste. Be careful not to add too much salt when cooking, as the Dolcelatte cheese is already quite salty.

Serves 4

30ml/2 tbsp olive oil
15g/½oz/1 tbsp butter
1 medium onion, roughly chopped
900g/2lb courgettes (zucchini), trimmed
    and sliced
5ml/1 tsp dried oregano
about 600ml/1 pint/2½ cups
    vegetable stock
115g/4oz Dolcelatte cheese, rind
    removed, diced
300ml/½ pint/1¼ cups single
    (light) cream
salt and ground black pepper
fresh oregano and extra Dolcelatte,
    to garnish

1 Heat the oil and butter in a pan until foaming. Add the chopped onion and cook gently, stirring frequently, for about 5 minutes, until softened but not brown.

2 Add the courgettes and oregano and season to taste with salt and black pepper. Cook over a medium heat, stirring frequently, for about 10 minutes.

3 Pour in the stock and bring to the boil, stirring constantly. Lower the heat and partially cover the pan. Simmer gently, stirring occasionally, for about 30 minutes, then stir in the diced dolcelatte until it has completely melted.

4 Pour the mixture into a blender or food processor. Process until smooth, then press through a sieve (strainer).

5 Add two-thirds of the cream. Stir over a low heat until hot, but not boiling. Add more stock if the soup is too thick. Taste for seasoning, then pour into heated bowls. Swirl in the remaining cream. Garnish with fresh oregano and extra cheese and serve immediately.

NUTRITION NOTES

Per portion:

Energy	461kcal/1916Kj
Protein	13.6g
Fat	39.0g
saturated fat	19.0g
Carbohydrate	16.0g
Fibre	0.4g
Calcium	238mg

tomato and fresh basil soup

THE CLASSIC COMBINATION of tomato and basil works particularly well as a soup. Make this in late summer when fresh tomatoes are at their most flavoursome.

Serves 4

15ml/1 tbsp olive oil
25g/1oz/2 tbsp butter
1 medium onion, finely chopped
900g/2lb ripe plum tomatoes, chopped
1 garlic clove, chopped
750ml/1¼ pints/3 cups chicken stock
120ml/4fl oz/½ cup dry white wine
30ml/2 tbsp sun-dried tomato purée (paste)
30ml/2 tbsp shredded fresh basil
150ml/¼ pint/⅔ cup single (light) cream
salt and ground black pepper
fresh basil, to garnish

1 Heat the oil and butter in a large pan until foaming. Add the onion and cook gently for about 5 minutes, stirring frequently with a wooden spoon, until softened but not brown.

VARIATION

This soup can also be served chilled. Pour it into a container after sieving (straining), cool to room temperature, then chill in the refrigerator for at least 4 hours. Serve in chilled bowls.

2 Stir in the chopped tomatoes and garlic, then add the chicken stock, white wine and sun-dried tomato purée, with salt and pepper to taste. Bring to the boil, then lower the heat, half cover the pan and simmer gently for 20 minutes, stirring occasionally to stop the tomatoes from sticking to the base of the pan.

3 Pour the soup into a blender or food processor, add the shredded basil, then process until fairly smooth. Press through a sieve (strainer) into a clean pan.

4 Add the cream and heat through very gently, stirring. Do not allow the soup to overheat. Check the consistency and add a little more stock or water if necessary, then taste for seasoning. Pour into heated bowls and garnish with basil. Serve immediately.

NUTRITION NOTES

Per portion:	
Energy	204kcal/850kJ
Protein	3.8g
Fat	16.8g
saturated fat	8.3g
Carbohydrate	10.0g
Fibre	3.6g
Calcium	72mg

stilton and watercress soup

A GOOD CREAMY STILTON and plenty of fresh peppery watercress bring maximum flavour to this smooth soup. It is very rich so should be served in small portions.

Serves 6
600ml/1 pint/2½ cups vegetable stock
225g/8oz watercress
150g/5oz stilton or other blue cheese
150ml/¼ pint/⅔ cup plain yogurt

NUTRITION NOTES

Per portion:

Energy	212kcal/884kJ
Protein	13.7g
Fat	15.5g
saturated fat	9.2g
Carbohydrate	4.9g
Fibre	1.9g
Calcium	326mg

1 Pour the vegetable stock into a pan and bring almost to the boil. Remove and discard any large stalks from the watercress. Add the watercress to the pan and simmer gently for about 2–3 minutes, until tender, being careful not to let it boil.

2 Crumble the cheese into the pan and simmer for 1 minute more, until the cheese has started to melt. Process the soup in a blender or food processor, in batches if necessary, until very smooth. Return the soup to the pan.

3 Stir in the yogurt and check the seasoning. The soup will probably not need any extra salt as the blue cheese is already quite salty. Heat the soup gently, without boiling, then ladle into warm bowls.

COOK'S TIP
Vegetarian varieties of some cheeses are available in large supermarkets and health food shops.

roasted garlic and butternut squash soup with tomato salsa

THIS IS A WONDERFUL, RICHLY FLAVOURED DISH. A spoonful of the hot and spicy tomato salsa gives extra bite to the sweet-tasting garlic and butternut squash soup.

Serves 4

2 garlic bulbs, outer papery skin removed
75ml/5 tbsp olive oil
a few fresh thyme sprigs
1 large butternut squash, halved and seeded
2 onions, chopped
5ml/1 tsp ground coriander
1.2 litres/2 pints/5 cups vegetable or chicken stock
30–45ml/2–3 tbsp chopped fresh oregano or marjoram
salt and ground black pepper

For the salsa

4 large ripe tomatoes, halved and seeded
1 red (bell) pepper, halved and seeded
1 large fresh red chilli, halved and seeded
30–45ml/2–3 tbsp extra virgin olive oil
15ml/1 tbsp balsamic vinegar
pinch of caster (superfine) sugar (optional)

1 Preheat the oven to 220°C/425°F/ Gas 7. Place the garlic bulbs on a piece of foil and pour over half the olive oil. Add the thyme sprigs, then fold the foil around the garlic bulbs. Place on a baking sheet with the butternut squash and brush the squash with 15ml/1 tbsp oil. Add the tomatoes, pepper and fresh chilli for the salsa.

2 Roast the vegetables for 25 minutes, then remove the tomatoes, pepper and chilli. Reduce the temperature to 190°C/375°F/Gas 5 and cook the squash and garlic for about 20–25 minutes more, or until the squash is tender.

3 Heat the remaining oil in a large, heavy pan and cook the onions and ground coriander gently for about 10 minutes, or until softened.

4 Skin the pepper and chilli and process in a food processor or blender with the tomatoes and 30ml/2 tbsp olive oil. Stir in the vinegar and season to taste, adding the sugar and the remaining oil if necessary.

5 Squeeze the roasted garlic out of its papery skin into the onions and scoop the squash out of its skin, adding it to the pan. Add the stock, 5ml/1 tsp salt and plenty of black pepper. Bring to the boil and simmer for 10 minutes.

6 Stir in half the oregano or marjoram, cool the soup slightly, then process it in a blender or food processor. Alternatively, press the soup through a sieve.

7 Reheat the soup, then season before ladling it into warmed bowls. Top each with a spoonful of salsa and sprinkle over the remaining chopped oregano or marjoram. Serve immediately.

NUTRITION NOTES

Per portion:	
Energy	307kcal/1290kJ
Protein	3.5g
Fat	26.8g
saturated fat	3.7g
Carbohydrate	13.7g
Fibre	1.7g
Calcium	46mg

sherried onion and almond soup

THE SPANISH COMBINATION of onions, sherry and saffron gives this pale yellow soup a beguiling flavour that is perfect as the opening course of a special meal.

Serves 4

40g/1½oz/3 tbsp butter
2 large yellow onions, thinly sliced
1 small garlic clove, finely chopped
pinch of saffron strands (about 12 strands)
50g/2oz blanched almonds, toasted and finely ground
750ml/1¼ pints/3 cups good chicken or vegetable stock
45ml/3 tbsp dry sherry
salt and ground black pepper
30ml/2 tbsp flaked (sliced) almonds, toasted, and chopped fresh parsley to garnish

1 Melt the butter in a pan over a low heat. Add the onions and garlic, then cover the pan and cook gently for 15–20 minutes, until the onions are soft and golden.

2 Add the saffron and cook for 3–4 minutes, then add the almonds and cook for another 2–3 minutes, stirring constantly. Pour in the stock and sherry and season. Bring to the boil, then lower the heat and simmer gently for 10 minutes.

VARIATION

This soup can also be served chilled. Use olive oil rather than butter and add a little more stock to make a thinner soup.

3 Process the soup in a blender or food processor until smooth, then return it to the rinsed pan. Reheat slowly, without allowing the soup to boil, stirring occasionally. Taste for seasoning, adding more salt and pepper if required.

4 Ladle the soup into heated bowls, garnish with the toasted flaked almonds and a little chopped parsley, and serve immediately.

NUTRITION NOTES

Per portion:	
Energy	222kcal/922kJ
Protein	4.6g
Fat	19.0g
saturated fat	5.8g
Carbohydrate	6.5g
Fibre	3.6g
Calcium	68mg

chicken and avocado soup

ORGANIC AVOCADOS RIPEN NATURALLY over a longer period of time than non-organic, producing really rich-flavoured fruit. Combined here with chicken and spring onions they add a creaminess to this delicious soup.

Serves 6

1.5 litres/2½ pints/6¼ cups chicken stock
½ fresh chilli, seeded
2 skinless, boneless chicken breast fillets
1 avocado
4 spring onions (scallions), finely sliced
400g/14oz can chickpeas, drained
sea salt and ground black pepper

1 Pour the chicken stock into a large pan and add the chilli. Bring to the boil, add the whole chicken breast fillets, then lower the heat and simmer for about 10 minutes, or until the chicken is cooked.

2 Remove the pan from the heat and lift out the chicken breasts with a slotted spoon. Leave to cool a little, then, using two forks, shred the chicken into small pieces. Set the shredded chicken aside.

3 Pour the chicken stock into a food processor or blender and add the chilli. Process the mixture until smooth, then return to the pan.

COOK'S TIP
Handle chillies with care as they can irritate the skin and eyes. It is advisable to wear rubber gloves when preparing them and wash your hands afterwards.

4 Cut the avocado in half, remove the skin and stone (pit) with a sharp knife, then slice the flesh into 2cm/¾in pieces. Add it to the stock, with the sliced spring onions and chickpeas.

5 Return the shredded chicken to the pan, add salt and freshly ground black pepper to taste, then heat gently. When the soup is heated through, spoon into warmed bowls and serve immediately.

NUTRITION NOTES

Per portion:	
Energy	146kcal/613kJ
Protein	12.3g
Fat	6.6g
saturated fat	1.1g
Carbohydrate	9.2g
Fibre	2.0g
Calcium	26mg

roasted vegetable soup

ROASTING THE VEGETABLES gives this hearty winter soup a wonderful depth of flavour and a beautiful rich colour. The filling root vegetables make this a satisfying main course dish.

Serves 6

60ml/4 tbsp olive oil
1 small butternut squash, peeled, seeded and cubed
2 carrots, cut into thick rounds
1 large parsnip, cubed
1 small swede, cubed
2 leeks, thickly sliced
1 onion, quartered
3 bay leaves
4 fresh thyme sprigs, plus extra to garnish
3 fresh rosemary sprigs
1.2 litres/2 pints/5 cups vegetable stock
salt and ground black pepper
sour cream, to serve

1 Preheat the oven to 200°C/400°F/ Gas 6. Pour the oil into a large bowl, add the vegetables and toss until well coated.

NUTRITION NOTES

Per portion:	
Energy	132kcal/557kJ
Protein	2.1g
Fat	10.2g
saturated fat	1.4g
Carbohydrate	8.5g
Fibre	2.4g
Calcium	49mg

2 Spread out the vegetables in a single layer on one large or two small baking sheets. Tuck the bay leaves, thyme and rosemary sprigs among the vegetables.

3 Roast the vegetables for about 50 minutes, turning them occasionally to make sure that they brown evenly. Remove from the oven, discard the herbs and transfer the vegetables to a large saucepan.

4 Pour the stock into the pan and bring to the boil. Lower the heat, season to taste, then simmer for 10 minutes. Transfer the soup to a food processor or blender and process until thick and smooth.

5 Return the soup to the pan and heat through. Serve in heated bowls, adding a swirl of sour cream to each portion. Garnish with the extra thyme sprigs.

ribollita

RIBOLLITA IS AN ITALIAN SOUP, rather like minestrone, but made with beans instead of pasta. It is traditionally served ladled over a rich green vegetable, such as spinach.

Serves 6

45ml/3 tbsp olive oil
2 onions, chopped
2 carrots, sliced
4 garlic cloves, crushed
2 celery sticks, thinly sliced
1 fennel bulb, trimmed and chopped
2 large courgettes (zucchini), thinly sliced
400g/14oz can chopped tomatoes
30ml/2 tbsp home-made or bought pesto
900ml/1½ pints/3¾ cups vegetable stock
400g/14oz can haricot (navy) or borlotti
   beans, drained
salt and ground black pepper

For the base

15ml/1 tbsp extra virgin olive oil, plus
   extra for drizzling
450g/1lb fresh young spinach
ground black pepper

1 Heat the oil in a large pan. Add the chopped onions, carrots, crushed garlic, celery and fennel and fry gently for about 10 minutes. Add the courgettes and fry for a further 2 minutes.

NUTRITION NOTES

Per portion:	
Energy	168kcal/707kJ
Protein	5.2g
Fat	10.2g
saturated fat	1.1g
Carbohydrate	14.7g
Fibre	4.8g
Calcium	70mg

VARIATION

Use other dark greens, such as chard or cabbage, instead of the spinach; simply shred and cook until tender, then ladle the soup over the top.

2 Stir in the chopped tomatoes, pesto, stock and beans and bring to the boil. Lower the heat, cover and simmer gently for 25–30 minutes, until the vegetables are completely tender. Season with salt and black pepper to taste.

3 Heat the oil in a frying pan and fry the spinach for 2 minutes, or until wilted. Spoon the spinach into heated soup bowls, then ladle the soup over the spinach. Just before serving, drizzle with olive oil and sprinkle with ground black pepper.

seafood and coconut milk soup with garlic chives

THE LONG LIST OF INGREDIENTS in this Thai-inspired recipe could mislead you into thinking that this soup is complicated to make. In fact, it is very easy to put together.

Serves 4
600ml/1 pint/2½ cups fish stock
5 thin slices fresh galangal or fresh
   root ginger
2 lemon grass stalks, chopped
3 kaffir lime leaves, shredded
25g/1oz garlic chives (1 bunch)
15g/½oz fresh coriander (cilantro)
15ml/1 tbsp vegetable oil
4 shallots, chopped
400ml/14fl oz can coconut milk
30–45ml/2–3 tbsp Thai fish sauce
45–60ml/3–4 tbsp Thai green
   curry paste
450g/1lb uncooked large prawns
   (shrimp), peeled and deveined
450g/1lb prepared squid
a little lime juice (optional)
salt and ground black pepper
60ml/4 tbsp crisp fried shallot slices,
   to serve

1 Pour the fish stock into a large, heavy pan and add the slices of fresh galangal or root ginger, the chopped lemon grass stalks and about half of the shredded kaffir lime leaves.

NUTRITION NOTES

Per portion:	
Energy	394kcal/1651kJ
Protein	45.3g
Fat	18.8g
saturated fat	2.6g
Carbohydrate	10.4g
Fibre	0.8g
Calcium	225mg

2 Reserve a few garlic chives for the garnish, then snip the remainder. Add half the snipped garlic chives to the pan with the coriander stalks. Bring to the boil, reduce the heat and cover, then simmer gently for 20 minutes. Strain the stock.

3 Rinse the pan and add the oil and shallots. Cook for 5–10 minutes, until the shallots are just beginning to brown.

VARIATIONS
Instead of squid, you could add 400g/14oz firm white fish, such as monkfish or haddock, cut into small pieces, or 675g/1½lb fresh mussels.

4 Stir in the strained fish stock, the coconut milk, the remaining kaffir lime leaves and 30ml/2 tbsp of the fish sauce. Heat gently until simmering and cook over a low heat for about 5–10 minutes.

5 Stir in the Thai green curry paste and the peeled, deveined prawns, then cook for 3 minutes. Add the squid and cook for a further 2 minutes. Add the lime juice, if using, and season, adding more fish sauce to taste.

6 Chop the remaining coriander and add to the soup, with the rest of the garlic chives. Serve in warm bowls sprinkled with fried shallot slices.

fragrant thai fish soup

LIGHT AND AROMATIC – and with virtually no carbohydrate – this is a perfect lunch or dinner dish. It is an excellent source of low-fat protein and contains essential nutrients for good health.

Serves 3

1 litre/1¾ pints/4 cups fish stock
4 lemon grass stalks
3 limes
2 small fresh hot red chillies, seeded and thinly sliced
2cm/¾in piece fresh galangal, peeled and thinly sliced
6 coriander (cilantro) stalks, with leaves
2 kaffir lime leaves, coarsely chopped (optional)
350g/12oz monkfish fillet, skinned and cut into 2.5cm/1in pieces
15ml/1 tbsp rice vinegar
45ml/3 tbsp Thai fish sauce
30ml/2 tbsp chopped fresh coriander (cilantro) leaves, to garnish

1 Pour the stock into a large pan and bring to the boil. Slice the bulb ends of the lemon grass diagonally into 3mm/⅛in thick pieces. Peel off four wide strips of lime rind with a vegetable peeler, avoiding the white pith. Squeeze the limes and reserve the juice.

2 Add the lemon grass, lime rind, chillies, galangal and coriander stalks to the stock, with the kaffir lime leaves, if using. Simmer for 1–2 minutes.

3 Add the monkfish, vinegar, fish sauce and half the reserved lime juice. Simmer for 3 minutes, until the fish is just cooked.

4 Remove the coriander stalks from the pan and discard. Taste the broth and add more lime juice if necessary. Serve the soup very hot, sprinkled with the chopped coriander leaves.

VARIATION
Other fish or shellfish such as sole, prawns (shrimp), scallops or squid can be substituted for the monkfish.

NUTRITION NOTES

Per portion:

Energy	116Kcal/484kJ
Protein	25.8g
Fat	0.7g
saturated fat	0.2g
Carbohydrate	0.1g
Fibre	0g
Calcium	17.4mg

miso broth with tofu

THIS FLAVOURSOME BROTH is simple and highly nutritious. In Japan, it is traditionally eaten for breakfast, but it also makes a good appetizer, light lunch or supper.

Serves 4

1 bunch of spring onions (scallions) or
   5 baby leeks
15g/½oz fresh coriander (cilantro)
3 thin slices fresh root ginger
2 star anise
1 small dried red chilli
1.2 litres/2 pints/5 cups dashi or
   vegetable stock
225g/8oz pak choi (bok choy) or other
   Asian greens, thickly sliced
200g/7oz firm tofu, cut into 2.5cm/
   1in cubes
60ml/4 tbsp red miso
30–45ml/2–3 tbsp Japanese soy sauce
1 fresh red chilli, seeded and
   shredded (optional)

1 Cut the coarse green tops off the spring onions or baby leeks and slice the rest of the spring onions or leeks finely on the diagonal. Place the coarse green tops in a large pan with the stalks from the coriander, the fresh root ginger, star anise, dried chilli and dashi or vegetable stock.

2 Heat the mixture over a low heat until boiling, then lower the heat and simmer for about 10 minutes. Strain the broth, return it to the pan and reheat until simmering. Add the green portion of the sliced spring onions or leeks to the soup with the pak choi or Asian greens and tofu. Cook for 2 minutes.

3 In a small bowl, combine the miso with a little soup, then stir the mixture into the pan. Add soy sauce to taste.

4 Coarsely chop the coriander leaves and stir most of them into the soup with the white part of the spring onions or leeks. Cook for 1 minute, then ladle the soup into warmed bowls. Sprinkle with the remaining chopped coriander and the shredded fresh red chilli, if using, and serve immediately.

NUTRITION NOTES	
Per portion:	
Energy	72Kcal/300kJ
Protein	7.2g
Fat	3.1g
saturated fat	0.4g
Carbohydrate	4.2g
Fibre	3.4g
Calcium	374mg

hot and sour soup

THE HERBS, SPICES AND AROMATICS in this light and healthy soup provide a useful supply of nutrients and antioxidants to help promote good health.

Serves 6

225g/8oz unpeeled raw prawns (shrimp)
2 lemon grass stalks
1.5 litres/2½ pints/6¼ cups
    vegetable stock
4 kaffir lime leaves
2 slices peeled fresh root ginger
60ml/4 tbsp Thai fish sauce
60ml/4 tbsp fresh lime juice
2 garlic cloves, crushed
6 spring onions (scallions), chopped
1 fresh red chilli, seeded and cut into strips
115g/4oz/generous 1½ cups oyster
    mushrooms, sliced
fresh coriander (cilantro) leaves and kaffir
    lime slices, to garnish

2 Bring the stock and aromatics to the boil, then simmer for about 20 minutes. Strain into a large, clean pan. Discard the prawn shells, lime leaves and root ginger.

3 Add the Thai fish sauce, lime juice, garlic, spring onions, chilli and sliced oyster mushrooms to the stock. Bring the mixture to the boil, lower the heat and simmer gently for 5 minutes.

4 Add the peeled prawns to the broth and cook for 2–3 minutes. Serve immediately, garnished with fresh coriander leaves and slices of kaffir lime.

COOK'S TIP

Do not overcook the prawns or they will become tough and chewy and spoil the delicate nature of the soup.

1 Peel the prawns and set them aside. Put the shells in a large pan. Lightly crush the lemon grass and add the stalks to the pan with the stock, lime leaves and ginger.

NUTRITION NOTES

Per portion:	
Energy	34kcal/142kJ
Protein	7.2g
Fat	0.4g
saturated fat	0.1g
Carbohydrate	0.5g
Fibre	0.3g
Calcium	36mg

fish and egg-knot soup

TWISTS OF OMELETTE and steamed prawn balls add protein and substance to this light Asian soup. It is the perfect appetizer before a low-carbohydrate main course.

Serves 4

1 spring onion (scallion), finely shredded
800ml/1⅓ pints/3½ cups well-flavoured
   stock or dashi
5ml/1 tsp soy sauce
dash of sake or dry white wine
pinch of salt

For the prawn balls

200g/7oz/generous 1 cup large raw
   prawns (shrimp), peeled, thawed if frozen
65g/2½oz cod fillet, skinned
5ml/1 tsp egg white
5ml/1 tsp sake or dry white wine, plus
   a dash extra
25ml/1½ tbsp cornflour (cornstarch) or
   potato flour
2–3 drops soy sauce
pinch of salt

For the omelette

1 egg, beaten
dash of mirin
pinch of salt
oil, for cooking

1 To make the prawn balls, use a pin to remove the black vein running down the back of each prawn. Place the prawns, cod, egg white, sake or dry white wine, cornflour or potato flour, soy sauce and a pinch of salt in a food processor or blender and process to a thick, sticky paste.

2 Shape the fish mixture into four balls, place in a steaming basket and steam over a pan of vigorously boiling water for about 10 minutes.

3 Soak the shredded spring onion in iced water for about 5 minutes, until the shreds curl. Drain and set aside.

4 To make the omelette, combine the egg, mirin and salt. Heat a little oil in a frying pan and pour in the egg and mirin mixture, coating the pan evenly. When the omelette has set, turn it over and cook for 30 seconds. Slide out and leave to cool, then cut the omelette into strips and tie each in a knot.

5 Heat the stock or dashi, then add the soy sauce, wine and salt. Divide the prawn balls and egg-knots among four bowls and add the soup. Serve with the onion curls.

NUTRITION NOTES

Per portion:	
Energy	94kcal/392kJ
Protein	13.8g
Fat	2.3g
saturated fat	0.6g
Carbohydrate	5.3g
Fibre	0g
Calcium	54mg

appetizers

SET ANY MEAL OFF TO A GOOD start with these delicious, low-carbohydrate appetizers. However, try to avoid heavy, three-course meals in the evening – unless, of course, you are entertaining, in which case you should spoil yourself. There is no need to compromise on flavour with dishes such as figs with prosciutto and Roquefort or carpaccio with rocket, which could also be enjoyed as a light lunch. Other recipes in this chapter, including chicken satay with peanut sauce, and chilli egg rolls, make irresistible finger food at parties.

cheese and tomato soufflés

GUESTS ARE ALWAYS IMPRESSED by a home-made soufflé and this recipe for little individual ones is the ultimate in effortless entertaining. Just don't tell them you used a ready-made sauce.

1 Preheat the oven to 200°C/400°F/ Gas 6. Tip the cheese sauce into a bowl. Thinly slice the sun-dried tomatoes and add them to the sauce with 90g/ 3½oz/generous 1 cup of the Parmesan cheese and the egg yolks. Season well with salt and black pepper and stir until thoroughly combined.

2 Brush the base and sides of six 200ml/7fl oz/scant 1 cup ramekins or individual soufflé dishes with the oil, then divide about half of the remaining Parmesan cheese among the dishes. Coat the insides of the dishes with the cheese, tilting them until evenly covered. Tip out any excess cheese and set aside with the reserved cheese.

3 Whisk the egg whites in a clean, grease-free bowl until stiff. Use a large metal spoon to stir one-quarter of the egg whites into the sauce, stirring gently until evenly blended, then fold in the remaining egg whites.

4 Spoon the mixture into the prepared ramekins or soufflé dishes and sprinkle with the reserved cheese. Place the ramekins on a baking sheet and bake for about 15–18 minutes, or until the soufflé is well risen and golden. Serve immediately with a mixed green salad.

Serves 6

350g/12oz tub fresh cheese sauce
50g/2oz sun-dried tomatoes in olive oil, drained, plus 10ml/2 tsp of the oil
130g/4½oz/1½ cups grated Parmesan cheese
4 large (US extra large) eggs, separated
salt and ground black pepper

NUTRITION NOTES

Per portion:	
Energy	270kcal/1125kJ
Protein	16.7g
Fat	20.3g
saturated fat	9.6g
Carbohydrate	5.7g
Fibre	0.4g
Calcium	435mg

prawn, egg and avocado mousses

LIGHT AND CREAMY, WITH LOTS OF TEXTURE and a delicious combination of flavours, these little mousses are best served on the day you make them, but chill them well first.

Serves 6
olive oil, for greasing
11g/¼oz sachet gelatine
rind and juice of 1 lemon
60ml/4 tbsp good mayonnaise
60ml/4 tbsp chopped fresh dill
5ml/1 tsp anchovy essence (extract)
5ml/1 tsp Worcestershire sauce
4 eggs, hard boiled, peeled and
 finely chopped
175g/6oz/1 cup cooked, peeled
 prawns (shrimp), roughly chopped if large
1 large ripe but just firm avocado, peeled,
 stoned (pitted) and diced
250ml/8fl oz/1 cup double (heavy) or
 whipping cream, lightly whipped
2 egg whites
salt and ground black pepper
sprigs of dill, to garnish

2 Place the gelatine, lemon juice and 15ml/1 tbsp hot water in a small bowl, and place over a pan of hot water. Stir until the mixture becomes clear. Cool slightly, then blend in the lemon rind, mayonnaise, dill, anchovy essence and Worcestershire sauce.

3 Mix the chopped hard-boiled eggs, prawns and avocado in a medium bowl. Stir in the gelatine mixture, then fold in the whipped cream. Whisk the egg whites until holding soft peaks and fold into the mixture. Season to taste, then spoon into the ramekins and chill for about 4 hours. Garnish with sprigs of dill and serve.

VARIATION
For a good alternative to prawns, try smoked trout or cooked crab meat.

1 Lightly grease six small ramekins or soufflé dishes with olive oil, then wrap a piece of baking parchment tightly around the outside of each of the dishes to form a collar. Ensure that the paper comes well above the top of the dish, allowing plenty of room for the mousse to stand above the top of the dish. Secure the collars firmly with adhesive tape so that the paper will support the mousse as it sets. For more informal occasions, you could prepare one large soufflé dish and let your guests help themselves, rather than individual ramekins.

chilli egg rolls

THE TITLE OF THIS RECIPE could lead to some confusion. However, these are not Chinese egg rolls; they are wedges of a rolled Thai-flavoured omelette, perfect as finger food.

Serves 2

3 eggs, beaten
15ml/1 tbsp soy sauce
1 bunch garlic chives, thinly sliced
1–2 small fresh red or green chillies, seeded and finely chopped
small bunch fresh coriander (cilantro), chopped
pinch of granulated sugar
salt and ground black pepper
15ml/1 tbsp groundnut (peanut) oil

For the dipping sauce
60ml/4 tbsp light soy sauce
fresh lime juice, to taste

NUTRITION NOTES

Per portion:

Energy	218kcal/907kJ
Protein	11.4g
Fat	16.0g
saturated fat	4.0g
Carbohydrate	6.1g
Fibre	0
Calcium	67mg

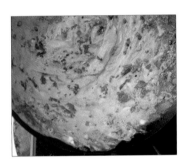

1 Make the dipping sauce. Pour the soy sauce into a bowl. Add a generous squeeze of lime juice. Taste and add more lime juice if needed.

2 Mix the eggs, soy sauce, chives, chillies and coriander. Add the sugar and season to taste. Heat the oil in a large frying pan, pour in the egg mixture and swirl the pan to make an omelette.

3 Cook for 1–2 minutes, until the omelette is just firm and the underside is turning golden. Slide it out on to a plate and roll up as though it were a pancake. Leave to cool completely.

4 When the omelette is cool, slice it diagonally in 1cm/½in pieces. Arrange the slices on a serving platter and serve with the bowl of dipping sauce.

COOK'S TIP
After preparing chillies, wash your hands thoroughly in warm, soapy water.

vegetable pancakes with tomato salsa

SPINACH AND EGG pancakes make a great start to a low-carbohydrate meal. Spinach is a valuable source of nutrients such as vitamin C, folic acid and iron.

Makes 10

225g/8oz spinach
1 small leek
a few sprigs of fresh coriander (cilantro) or parsley
3 large (US extra large) eggs
50g/2oz/½ cup plain (all-purpose) flour, sifted
oil, for frying
25g/1oz/⅓ cup freshly grated Parmesan cheese
salt, ground black pepper and freshly grated nutmeg

For the salsa

2 tomatoes, peeled and chopped
¼ fresh red chilli, finely chopped
2 pieces sun-dried tomato in oil, drained and chopped
1 small red onion, chopped
1 garlic clove, crushed
60ml/4 tbsp olive oil
30ml/2 tbsp sherry
2.5ml/½ tsp soft light brown sugar

COOK'S TIP
Try to find sun-ripened tomatoes for the salsa, as these have the best and sweetest flavour and are much superior to those ripened under glass.

1 Prepare the tomato salsa: place all the ingredients in a bowl and toss together to combine. Cover and leave to stand in a cool place for 2–3 hours.

2 To make the pancakes, finely shred or chop the spinach, leek and coriander or parsley. If you prefer, chop them in a food processor, but do not overprocess. Place the chopped vegetables in a bowl and beat in the eggs and seasoning. Blend in the flour and 30–45ml/2–3 tbsp water and leave to stand for 20 minutes.

3 To cook the pancakes, drop spoonfuls of the batter into a lightly oiled frying pan and cook until golden underneath. Using a fish slice (metal spatula), turn the pancakes over and cook briefly on the other side.

4 Carefully lift the pancakes out of the pan, drain on kitchen paper and keep warm while you cook the remaining mixture in the same way. Sprinkle the pancakes with grated Parmesan cheese and serve with the salsa.

NUTRITION NOTES	
Per portion:	
Energy	109kcal/456kJ
Protein	3.9g
Fat	8.7g
saturated fat	1.9g
Carbohydrate	3.0g
Fibre	0.9g
Calcium	71mg

roasted tomato and mozzarella with basil oil and mixed leaf salad

ROASTING THE TOMATOES IN OLIVE OIL adds a new dimension to this delicious dish and a superb sweetness to the tomatoes. Make the basil oil just before serving to retain its fresh flavour and vivid emerald-green colour.

Serves 4
olive oil, for brushing
6 large plum tomatoes
350g/12oz fresh mozzarella cheese, cut into 8–12 slices
fresh basil leaves, to garnish

For the basil oil
25 fresh basil leaves
60ml/4 tbsp extra virgin olive oil
1 garlic clove, crushed

For the salad
90g/3½oz/4 cups salad leaves
50g/2oz/2 cups mixed salad herbs, such as coriander (cilantro), basil and rocket (arugula)
25g/1oz/3 tbsp pumpkin seeds
25g/1oz/3 tbsp sunflower seeds

For the salad dressing
60ml/4tbsp extra virgin olive oil
15ml/1 tbsp balsamic vinegar
2.5ml/½ tsp Dijon mustard

NUTRITION NOTES

Per portion:	
Energy	642kcal/2673kJ
Protein	4.0g
Fat	57.5g
saturated fat	5.3g
Carbohydrate	5.4g
Fibre	2.6g
Calcium	28mg

1 Preheat the oven to 200°C/400°F/ Gas 6 and oil a large baking sheet. Cut the tomatoes in half lengthways and scoop out the seeds with a teaspoon. Place skin-side down on a baking sheet and roast for 20 minutes or until the tomatoes are tender and bubbling on top.

2 Meanwhile, make the basil oil. Place the basil leaves, olive oil and crushed garlic in a food processor and process until smooth. Transfer to a bowl and chill.

3 Put the salad leaves in a large bowl. Add the mixed salad herbs and toss lightly with your hands to mix.

4 Toast the seeds in a dry frying pan over a medium heat for 2 minutes, until golden, tossing them frequently. Leave to cool then sprinkle over the salad.

5 Combine the dressing ingredients in a screw-top jar. Shake until combined. Pour the dressing over the salad and toss. To reduce the energy and fat content, simply omit the salad dressing.

6 For each serving, place the tomato halves on top of 2 or 3 slices of mozzarella and drizzle over the basil oil. Season well, garnish with basil leaves and serve with the salad.

pink grapefruit and avocado salad

CREAMY AVOCADO AND ZESTY CITRUS FRUITS combine in this refreshing salad. Avocados turn brown quickly when exposed to the air, but the grapefruit juice will prevent this from occurring.

Serves 4
2 pink grapefruits
2 ripe avocados
30ml/2 tbsp chilli oil
90g/3½oz rocket (arugula)

1 Slice the top and bottom off one of the grapefruits, then cut off all of the peel and pith from around the side – the best way to do this is to cut down in wide strips. Working over a small bowl to catch the juices, carefully cut out the segments from between the membranes and place them in a separate bowl. Squeeze any juices remaining in the membranes into the bowl, then discard them. Repeat with the remaining grapefruit.

2 Halve, stone (pit) and peel both of the avocados. Slice the flesh and add it to the grapefruit segments. Whisk a pinch of salt into the grapefruit juice, followed by the chilli oil.

3 Pile the rocket leaves on to four plates and top with the grapefruit segments and avocado slices. Pour over the dressing and toss slightly with your hands, then serve immediately.

NUTRITION NOTES

Per portion:	
Energy	252kcal/1050kJ
Protein	4.1g
Fat	23.7g
saturated fat	3.0g
Carbohydrate	6.4g
Fibre	1.9g
Calcium	61mg

baked eggs with creamy leeks

THIS SIMPLE BUT ELEGANT APPETIZER is perfect for last-minute entertaining or quick dining. Garnish the baked eggs with crisp, freshly fried sage leaves and serve for a special meal.

Serves 4

15g/½oz/1 tbsp butter, plus extra
  for greasing
225g/8oz small leeks, thinly sliced
75–90ml/5–6 tbsp whipping cream
4 small-medium (US medium-large) eggs

1 Preheat the oven to 190°C/375°F/ Gas 5. Generously butter the base and sides of four small ramekins or individual soufflé dishes.

NUTRITION NOTES

Per portion:	
Energy	193kcal/800kJ
Protein	7.7g
Fat	16.4g
saturated fat	8.3g
Carbohydrate	4.0g
Fibre	1.7g
Calcium	76mg

2 Melt the butter in a frying pan and cook the leeks over a medium heat, stirring frequently, for 3–5 minutes, until softened and translucent, but not browned.

3 Add 45ml/3 tbsp of the cream and cook over a low heat for 5 minutes, until the leeks are very soft and the cream has thickened a little. Season to taste.

4 Place the ramekins in a small roasting pan and divide the cooked leeks among them. Break an egg into each, spoon over the remaining cream and season with salt and pepper.

5 Pour boiling water into the roasting pan to come about halfway up the sides of the ramekins. Transfer the pan to the preheated oven and bake for about 10 minutes, until just set. Serve piping hot.

leek terrine with red peppers

THIS PRESSED LEEK TERRINE is an impressive dish for dinner parties. It looks very pretty when sliced and served on individual plates with the dressing drizzled around the slices.

Serves 8

1.8kg/4lb slender leeks
4 large red (bell) peppers, halved and
   seeded
15ml/1 tbsp extra virgin olive oil
10ml/2 tsp balsamic vinegar
5ml/1 tsp ground roasted cumin seeds
salt and ground black pepper

For the dressing

120ml/4fl oz/½ cup extra virgin olive oil
1 garlic clove, bruised and peeled
5ml/1 tsp Dijon mustard
5ml/1 tsp soy sauce
15ml/1 tbsp balsamic vinegar
pinch of caster (superfine) sugar
2.5–5ml/½–1 tsp ground roasted
   cumin seeds
15–30ml/1–2 tbsp chopped mixed fresh
   basil and flat leaf parsley

1 Line a 23cm/9in long terrine or loaf tin (pan) with clear film (plastic wrap), leaving the ends overhanging the tin. Cut the leeks to the same length as the tin.

2 Cook the leeks in boiling salted water for about 5–7 minutes, until just tender. Drain thoroughly and allow to cool, then squeeze out as much water as possible from the leeks and leave them to drain on a clean dish towel – any excess water in the leeks will make the terrine too moist.

NUTRITION NOTES

Per portion:	
Energy	323kcal/1348kJ
Protein	7.1g
Fat	23.3g
saturated fat	3.2g
Carbohydrate	22.1g
Fibre	10.3g
Calcium	216mg

3 Grill (broil) the red peppers, skin-side up, until the skin blisters and blackens. Place in a bowl, cover and leave for 10 minutes. Peel the peppers and cut the flesh into long strips, then place them in a bowl and add the oil, balsamic vinegar and ground roasted cumin seeds. Season to taste with salt and pepper and toss well.

4 Layer the leeks and strips of red pepper in the lined tin, alternating the layers so that the white of the leeks in one row is covered by the green of the next row. Season the leeks with a little more salt and pepper.

5 Cover with the overhanging clear film. Top with a plate and weigh it down with heavy food cans or scale weights. Leave the terrine to chill for several hours or overnight if you have time.

6 To make the dressing, place the oil, garlic, mustard, soy sauce and balsamic vinegar in a jug (pitcher) and mix thoroughly. Season with salt and black pepper and add the caster sugar. Add ground roasted cumin seeds to taste and leave to stand for several hours. Discard the garlic and add the chopped basil and parsley to the dressing.

7 Unmould the terrine and cut it into thick slices. Put 1–2 slices on each plate, drizzle with dressing and serve.

COOK'S TIP

It is easier to slice the terrine if you leave the clear film on and use a sharp knife or an electric carving knife. Use a fish slice (metal spatula) to transfer the slices to plates, then remove the clear film.

mushrooms with garlic and chilli sauce

WHEN YOU ARE PLANNING a summer barbecue for friends and family, it can be tricky finding something really special for the vegetarians in the party. These tasty mushroom kebabs are ideal and will be enjoyed by non-vegetarians too.

Serves 4

12 large field (portabello), chestnut or oyster mushrooms or a mixture, cut in half
4 garlic cloves, coarsely chopped
6 coriander (cilantro) roots, coarsely chopped
15ml/1 tbsp granulated sugar
30ml/2 tbsp light soy sauce
ground black pepper

For the dipping sauce

15ml/1 tbsp granulated sugar
90ml/6 tbsp rice vinegar
5ml/1 tsp salt
1 garlic clove, crushed
1 small fresh red chilli, seeded and finely chopped

1 If using wooden skewers, soak eight of them in cold water for at least 30 minutes before making the kebabs. This will prevent them from burning over the barbecue or under the grill (broiler).

NUTRITION NOTES

Per portion:	
Energy	64kcal/266kJ
Protein	3.5g
Fat	1.0g
saturated fat	0.2g
Carbohydrate	10.0g
Fibre	4.7g
Calcium	16mg

2 Make the dipping sauce by heating the sugar, rice vinegar and salt in a small pan, stirring occasionally until the sugar and salt have dissolved. Add the garlic and chilli, pour into a serving dish and keep warm.

3 Thread three mushroom halves on to each skewer. Lay the filled skewers side by side in a shallow dish.

4 In a mortar or spice grinder pound or blend the garlic and coriander roots. Scrape into a bowl and mix with the sugar, soy sauce and a little pepper.

5 Brush the soy sauce mixture over the mushrooms and leave to marinate for 15 minutes. Prepare the barbecue or preheat the grill and cook the mushrooms for 2–3 minutes on each side. Serve with the dipping sauce.

COOK'S TIP

If you prefer extra spicy foods, try leaving the seeds in the red chillies, rather than removing them.

grilled spring onions and asparagus with prosciutto

THIS IS A GOOD CHOICE OF FIRST COURSE at the beginning of summer, when both spring onions and asparagus are at their best. The slight smokiness of the grilled vegetables goes very well with the sweetness of the air-dried ham.

Serves 4
about 24 plump spring onions (scallions)
500g/1¼lb asparagus
45–60ml/3–4 tbsp olive oil
20ml/4 tsp balsamic vinegar
8–12 slices prosciutto
50g/2oz Pecorino cheese
sea salt and ground black pepper
extra virgin olive oil, to serve

1 Trim the root, outer papery skin and the top off the spring onions.

2 Cut off and discard the woody ends of the asparagus and peel the bottom 7.5cm/3in of the spears.

3 Heat the grill (broiler). Toss the spring onions and asparagus in 30ml/2 tbsp olive oil. Place on two baking sheets and season well with sea salt and freshly ground black pepper.

4 Grill (broil) the asparagus for 5 minutes on each side, until just tender when tested with the tip of a sharp knife. Protect the tips with foil if they begin to char too much. Grill the spring onions for about 3–4 minutes on each side, until tinged a slightly golden colour. Brush both vegetables with a little more oil when you turn them.

5 Distribute the vegetables among four to six plates. Season with black pepper and drizzle over the vinegar. Lay two to three slices of ham on each plate and shave the Pecorino over the top. Provide extra olive oil for drizzling at the table.

COOK'S TIP
The spring onions could be cooked on a cast-iron ridged griddle pan. If it is more convenient, the asparagus can be roasted at 200°C/400°F/Gas 6 for 15 minutes instead of grilled.

NUTRITION NOTES

Per portion:	
Energy	236kcal/983kJ
Protein	3.8g
Fat	15.8g
saturated fat	1.4g
Carbohydrate	5.0g
Fibre	2.9g
Calcium	90mg

bacon-rolled enokitake mushrooms

THE JAPANESE NAME FOR THIS DISH is *obimaki enoki*. The strong, smoky flavour of the bacon complements the subtle flavour of the mushrooms. Small heaps of ground white pepper can be offered with these savouries, if you like.

Serves 4

450g/1lb fresh enokitake mushrooms
6 rindless smoked streaky (fatty) bacon
  rashers (strips)
4 lemon wedges

1 Cut off the root part of each enokitake cluster 2cm/¾in from the end. Do not separate the stems. Cut the bacon rashers in half lengthways.

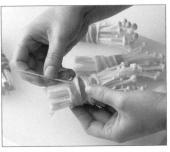

2 Divide the enokitake into 12 equal bunches. Take one bunch, then place the middle of the enokitake mushroom near the edge of one bacon rasher, with approximately 2.5–4cm/1–1½in of enokitake protruding at each end.

3 Carefully roll up the bunch of enokitake in the bacon. Tuck any straying short stems into the bacon and slide the bacon slightly upwards to cover about 4cm/1½in of the enokitake.

4 Secure the end of the bacon roll by skewering it with a cocktail stick (toothpick). Repeat using the remaining enokitake and bacon to make 11 more rolls. Preheat the grill (broiler) to high, and place the enokitake rolls on an oiled wire rack. Grill (broil) both sides until the bacon is crisp and golden and the enokitake mushrooms start to char. This should take about 10–13 minutes.

5 Remove the enokitake rolls and place on a chopping board. Using a knife and fork, chop each roll in half through the middle of the bacon belt. Arrange the top part of the enokitake roll standing upright, with the bottom part lying down next to it. Add a thin wedge of lemon to each portion and serve.

NUTRITION NOTES

Per portion:	
Energy	221kcal/916kJ
Protein	9.3g
Fat	20.5g
saturated fat	8.1g
Carbohydrate	0g
Fibre	3.6g
Calcium	8mg

figs with prosciutto and roquefort

FRESH FIGS ARE A DELICIOUS TREAT, whether you choose dark purple, yellowy green or green-skinned varieties. In this easy and stylish dish, soft ripe figs and clear honey balance the richness of the cured ham and cheese.

Serves 4

8 fresh figs
75g/3oz prosciutto
45ml/3 tbsp clear honey
75g/3oz Roquefort cheese

NUTRITION NOTES

Per portion:

Energy	200kcal/837kJ
Protein	11.0g
Fat	9.3g
saturated fat	4.4g
Carbohydrate	19.3g
Fibre	2.8g
Calcium	147mg

1 Preheat the grill (broiler). Quarter the figs and place on a foil-lined grill rack. Tear each slice of prosciutto into two or three pieces and crumple them up beside the figs. Brush the figs with 15ml/1 tbsp clear honey and grill (broil) until lightly browned.

2 Crumble the cheese and divide among four plates. Add the honey-grilled figs and ham and pour over any cooking juices caught on the foil. Drizzle the remaining honey over the figs, ham and cheese, and season with plenty of ground black pepper.

carpaccio with rocket

A VENETIAN DISH, carpaccio is named in honour of the Renaissance painter. In this fine Italian dish raw beef is lightly dressed with lemon juice and olive oil and is traditionally served with flakes of Parmesan cheese.

Serves 4

1 garlic clove
1½ lemons
50ml/2fl oz/¼ cup extra virgin olive oil
2 bunches rocket (arugula)
4 very thin slices of beef fillet
115g/4oz Parmesan cheese, shaved
salt and ground black pepper

1 Cut the garlic clove in half with a small sharp knife, then rub the cut side over the inside of a large glass bowl. Squeeze the lemons into the bowl, then gradually whisk in the extra virgin olive oil. Season with plenty of salt and freshly ground black pepper, then leave to stand for at least 15 minutes.

2 Carefully wash the rocket and tear off any thick stalks. Pat dry with kitchen paper. Arrange the rocket around the edge of a large serving platter or divide among four individual plates.

3 Place the sliced beef in the centre of the platter, and pour the sauce over it, spreading it evenly over the meat. Arrange the shaved Parmesan on top of the meat slices and serve immediately.

NUTRITION NOTES

Per portion:	
Energy	281kcal/1174kJ
Protein	17.6g
Fat	22.7g
saturated fat	7.5g
Carbohydrate	2.3g
Fibre	0.2g
Calcium	427mg

pork on lemon grass sticks

THIS SIMPLE RECIPE MAKES A substantial appetizer. The lemon grass sticks used to spear the pork not only add a distinctive, subtle flavour, but they look extremely attractive and make a good talking point.

Serves 4

300g/11oz minced (ground) pork
4 garlic cloves, crushed
4 fresh coriander (cilantro) roots, chopped
2.5ml/½ tsp granulated sugar
15ml/1 tbsp soy sauce
salt and ground black pepper
8 x 10cm/4in lengths of lemon grass stalks
sweet chilli sauce, to serve

1 Place the minced pork, crushed garlic cloves, chopped coriander roots, granulated sugar and soy sauce in a large bowl. Season to taste with salt and ground black pepper and mix well.

2 Divide into eight portions and mould each one into a ball. It may help to dampen your hands before shaping the mixture to prevent it from sticking.

NUTRITION NOTES

Per portion:

Energy	124kcal/520kJ
Protein	16.0g
Fat	5.5g
saturated fat	2.1g
Carbohydrate	2.6g
Fibre	0
Calcium	11mg

3 Stick a length of lemon grass halfway into each ball, then press the meat mixture around the lemon grass, shaping it like a chicken leg.

4 Cook the pork sticks under a hot grill (broiler) for approximately 3–4 minutes on each side, until just golden and cooked through. Serve alongside the sweet chilli sauce for dipping.

COOK'S TIP

Try making slimmer versions of these pork sticks to serve as a delicious party snack. They make a perfect canapé and can be passed around easily with the sweet chilli dipping sauce on the side. The mixture should be enough to make about 12 lemon grass sticks if you use it sparingly.

chicken satay with peanut sauce

THESE MINIATURE KEBABS ARE POPULAR all over South-east Asia, and they are especially delicious when cooked on a barbecue. The spicy peanut dipping sauce makes the perfect partner for the lightly marinated chicken.

Serves 4
4 skinless, boneless chicken breast portions

For the marinade
2 garlic cloves, crushed
2.5cm/1in piece fresh root ginger, finely grated
10ml/2 tsp Thai fish sauce (*nam pla*)
30ml/2 tbsp light soy sauce
15ml/1 tbsp clear honey

For the satay sauce
90ml/6 tbsp crunchy peanut butter
1 fresh red chilli, seeded and finely chopped
juice of 1 lime
60ml/4 tbsp coconut milk
salt

1 First, make the satay sauce. Put all the ingredients in a food processor or blender. Process until smooth, then add more salt or lime juice if necessary. Spoon the sauce into a bowl, cover with clear film (plastic wrap) and set aside.

2 Using a sharp knife, slice each chicken breast portion into four long strips. Put all the marinade ingredients in a large bowl and mix well, then add the chicken strips and toss together until thoroughly coated. Cover and leave for at least 30 minutes in the refrigerator to marinate. Meanwhile, soak 16 wooden satay sticks or kebab skewers in water, to prevent them from burning during cooking.

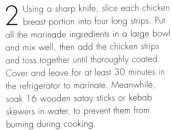

3 Preheat the grill (broiler) to high or prepare the barbecue. Drain the satay sticks or skewers. Drain the chicken strips. Thread one strip on to each satay stick or skewer. Grill (broil) for 3 minutes on each side, or until the chicken is golden brown and cooked through. Serve immediately with the satay sauce.

NUTRITION NOTES

Per portion:	
Energy	444kcal/1842kJ
Protein	27.3g
Fat	33.5g
saturated fat	9.5g
Carbohydrate	8.5g
Fibre	1.7g
Calcium	33mg

quail's eggs in aspic with prosciutto

THESE PRETTY LITTLE EGGS in jelly are easy to make and great for summer dining. They are excellent served with mixed salad leaves, which won't add to the total carbohydrate content.

4 Rinse 12 dariole moulds, but do not dry, then place the moulds on a tray. Cut each slice of ham in half and roll or fold so that they will fit into the moulds.

Makes 12

22g/1oz packet aspic powder
45ml/3 tbsp dry sherry
12 quail's eggs or other small eggs
6 slices prosciutto
12 fresh coriander (cilantro) leaves

NUTRITION NOTES

Per portion:

Energy	59kcal/246kJ
Protein	6.5g
Fat	3.3g
saturated fat	1.0g
Carbohydrate	0.1g
Fibre	0g
Calcium	18mg

1 To make the aspic jelly, follow the instructions on the packet, but replace 45ml/3 tbsp of the recommended quantity of water with the dry sherry to give it a greater depth of flavour.

2 Cover the bowl of aspic jelly with clear film (plastic wrap) and place in the refrigerator until it is just beginning to thicken, but do not let it become too thick or set.

3 Meanwhile, put the eggs in a pan of cold water and bring to the boil. Boil for 1½ minutes, then pour off the hot water and leave the eggs to stand in a bowl of cold water until completely cool. This way, the yolks should still be a little soft, but the eggs will be firm enough to peel.

5 Place a coriander leaf flat in the base of each dariole mould, then put a peeled egg on top. As the jelly begins to thicken, spoon in enough to nearly cover each egg, holding the egg steady. Put a slice of ham on each egg and spoon in the rest of the jelly to fill the moulds.

6 Transfer the tray of moulds to a cool place and leave for 3–4 hours until set and cold. When ready to serve, run a rounded knife blade around the sides of the dariole moulds to loosen. Dip the moulds into warm water and tap gently until they become loose. Invert the eggs on to small plates and serve immediately.

sautéed mussels with garlic and herbs

SHELLFISH IS ALWAYS a healthy choice as it is rich in valuable nutrients, such as B vitamins, zinc, iron and selenium, which are essential for good health. Mussels are a good source of protein and are low in fat and carbohydrate.

4 Pull the mussels apart and carefully remove the flesh from the shells. Pat the mussels dry on kitchen paper.

5 Heat the olive oil in a frying pan, add the mussels, and cook, stirring, for about 1 minute. Remove from the pan with a slotted spoon and set aside. Add the shallots and garlic to the pan and cook, covered, over a low heat for about 5 minutes, until the onions are soft and translucent, but not browned.

6 Remove the pan from the heat and stir in the chopped fresh parsley, paprika and chilli flakes. Return to the heat and stir in the cooked mussels. Heat through briefly, then place the lid on the pan and set aside for about 2 minutes before serving.

Serves 4

900g/2lb live mussels
1 lemon slice
45ml/3 tbsp olive oil
2 shallots, finely chopped
1 garlic clove, finely chopped
15ml/1 tbsp chopped fresh parsley
2.5ml/½ tsp paprika
1.5ml/¼ tsp dried chilli flakes

COOK'S TIP
Mussels are best cooked and eaten on the day of purchase. However, you can keep them in a large container of lightly salted water for a day.

1 Scrub the mussels and scrape off the beard. Discard any damaged specimens or any that do not close when tapped with the back of a knife.

2 Put the remaining mussels in a large pan, with 250ml/8fl oz/1 cup water and the lemon slice. Bring to the boil, cover tightly and cook over a high heat, shaking the pan occasionally, for about 4 minutes.

3 Remove the open mussels from the pan with a slotted spoon. Return the remaining mussels to the heat and cook for 1–2 minutes more. Remove any that open and discard those that remain closed.

NUTRITION NOTES

Per portion:

Energy	241kcal/1007kJ
Protein	27g
Fat	12.3g
saturated fat	2.0g
Carbohydrate	5.8g
Fibre	0.1g
Calcium	87mg

garlic prawns

THIS WONDERFUL, BUT SIMPLE dish with its aroma of garlic and hint of chilli takes only minutes to cook, so it is perfect for entertaining. Serve it for a dinner party and your guests will never guess that you are following a diet.

Serves 4

350–450g/12oz–1lb raw prawns (shrimp)
2 fresh red chillies
45ml/3 tbsp olive oil
3 garlic cloves, crushed
salt and ground black pepper

1 Remove the heads and shells from the prawns, leaving the tails intact. Remove the dark vein along the back of the prawns with a sharp knife or a pin.

2 Halve each chilli lengthways and discard the seeds. Heat the oil in a flameproof pan, suitable for serving.

3 Add the prawns, chillies and garlic to the pan and cook over a high heat for 3 minutes, stirring constantly until the prawns turn pink. Season and serve immediately.

VARIATIONS
• To add extra spice, stir in 10ml/ 2 tsp finely chopped fresh root ginger with the chillies and garlic.
• To make a light lunch, serve the prawns on a bed of colourful mixed salad leaves and fresh herbs, such as coriander (cilantro) or mint.
• For a special occasion, use lobster tails or crawfish instead of prawns.

NUTRITION NOTES

Per portion:

Energy	226kcal/944kJ
Protein	35g
Fat	9.4g
saturated fat	1.4g
Carbohydrate	0g
Fibre	0g
Calcium	44mg

ceviche with avocado salsa

THIS SIMPLE, NUTRITIOUS South American dish of marinated fish makes a delicious appetizer. Fish is a good low-fat source of protein, while olive oil and avocado provide healthy monounsaturated fats.

2 Meanwhile, make the salsa. Cut the avocado in half and scoop out the stone (pit) with the point of a knife. Peel and dice the flesh. Place in a bowl and add the tomatoes, lemon juice and olive oil and mix well. Cover with clear film (plastic wrap) and set aside in a cool place until required.

3 Season the fish with salt and sprinkle over the chillies. Drizzle with the olive oil. Toss the fish in the mixture, then replace the cover. Leave to marinate in the refrigerator for about 25 minutes more.

4 To serve, divide the salsa among six individual serving plates. Spoon on the ceviche, sprinkle with coriander leaves and serve immediately.

Serves 6

675g/1½lb halibut, sea bass or salmon
  fillets, skinned
juice of 3 limes
1–2 fresh red chillies, seeded and very
  finely chopped
15ml/1 tbsp olive oil
30ml/2 tbsp fresh coriander (cilantro) leaves
salt

For the salsa

1 ripe avocado
4 large firm tomatoes, peeled, seeded
  and diced
15ml/1 tbsp lemon juice
30ml/2 tbsp olive oil

1 Cut the fish into strips measuring about 5 x 1cm/2 x ½in. Lay these in a shallow, non-metallic dish and pour over the lime juice, turning the fish strips to coat them well. Cover and leave to stand for 1 hour.

NUTRITION NOTES

Per portion:	
Energy	234kcal/978kJ
Protein	25.3g
Fat	13.2g
saturated fat	2.5g
Carbohydrate	3.8g
Fibre	1.9g
Calcium	44mg

seared swordfish with citrus dressing

THE JAPANESE OFTEN TAKE RECIPES from other parts of the world and rework them in line with their traditions. This salad is a good example – fresh fish is sliced thinly and seared, then served with crisp salad vegetables and a tangy lime dressing.

Serves 4
75g/3oz mooli (daikon), peeled
50g/2oz carrot, peeled
1 cucumber
10ml/2 tsp vegetable oil
300g/11oz skinned fresh swordfish steak, cut against the grain
2 cartons mustard and cress
15ml/1 tbsp toasted sesame seeds

For the dressing
105ml/7 tbsp shoyu
105ml/7 tbsp water mixed with 5ml/1 tsp dashi-no-moto
30ml/2 tbsp toasted sesame oil
rind of ½ lime, shredded into strips
juice of ½ lime

1 Use a very sharp knife, mandolin or vegetable slicer with a julienne blade to make very thin (4cm/1½in long) strands of mooli, carrot and cucumber. Soak the mooli and carrot in iced water for about 5 minutes, then drain and chill.

NUTRITION NOTES

Per portion:

Energy	245kcal/1022kJ
Protein	20.6g
Fat	15.9g
saturated fat	1.3g
Carbohydrate	4.6g
Fibre	1.6g
Calcium	50mg

2 To make the dressing, mix together all the ingredients in a small bowl. Stir well, then chill thoroughly.

3 Heat the oil in a frying pan until smoking hot. Sear the fish for about 30 seconds on all sides. Immediately plunge it into cold water in a bowl to stop the cooking. Gently pat dry on kitchen paper and wipe off as much oil as possible.

4 Using a sharp knife, cut the swordfish steak in half lengthways before slicing it into 5mm/¼in thick pieces in the opposite direction, against the grain.

5 Arrange the fish slices in a ring on individual dinner plates. Mix together the vegetable strands, mustard and cress and sesame seeds. Fluff these up with your hands, then shape them into four spheres. Gently place each sphere in the centre of a plate, on top of the swordfish. Pour the dressing around the plate's edge and serve immediately.

COOK'S TIP
Dashi-no-moto are freeze-dried granules that are used to make a quick dashi stock. They are available from Japanese supermarkets and other specialist stores.

main course
salads

GENEROUS, LEAFY GREEN SALADS can easily be turned into a nutritious main meal with the addition of ingredients such as fish, tofu, nuts or meat. They are healthy and satisfying, offering essential fibre, nutrients and sustaining low-fat protein, which makes them perfect for a low-carbohydrate diet. All of the recipes in this chapter are simple to prepare, taste delicious and fit easily into your weekly menu and healthy eating plan. Try a simple warm duck salad with poached eggs or indulge in a Thai prawn salad with garlic dressing and frizzled shallots.

warm salad with poached eggs

SOFT POACHED EGGS, chilli oil, hot croûtons and cool, crisp salad leaves make a lively and unusual combination. This delicious salad will provide a sustaining lunch or supper.

3 Meanwhile, divide the salad leaves equally between two small plates.

4 Scatter the croutons over the mixed salad leaves. Wipe the frying pan clean with a piece of kitchen paper, then add the olive oil and heat gently. Add the crushed garlic and balsamic or sherry vinegar and cook over a high heat for about 1 minute, stirring occasionally. Pour the warm dressing over the salad leaves.

5 Remove the poached eggs from the pan with a slotted spoon, and pat them dry on kitchen paper. Place one egg on top of each plate of salad.

6 Top each plate of salad with thin shavings of fresh Parmesan cheese and season with ground black pepper, if using.

Serves 2

25ml/1½ tbsp chilli oil
1 slice wholegrain bread, crusts removed and cubed
2 eggs
115g/4oz mixed salad leaves
45ml/3 tbsp extra virgin olive oil
2 garlic cloves, crushed
15ml/1 tbsp balsamic or sherry vinegar
50g/2oz Parmesan cheese, shaved
ground black pepper (optional)

1 Heat the chilli oil in a frying pan. Add the cubes of bread and cook for 5 minutes, tossing the cubes occasionally, until they are crisp and golden. Remove from the pan and drain on a sheet of kitchen paper.

2 Bring a pan of water to a gentle boil. Break each egg into a jug (pitcher) and slide carefully into the water. Poach for 3–4 minutes, spooning water over the egg to ensure it cooks thoroughly.

NUTRITION NOTES

Per portion:

Energy	447kcal/1868kJ
Protein	20.7g
Fat	33.6g
saturated fat	9.7g
Carbohydrate	8.5g
Fibre	1.6g
Calcium	361mg

fried egg salad

CHILLIES AND EGGS MAY SEEM UNLIKELY PARTNERS, but they actually work well together. The peppery flavour of the watercress makes it the perfect foundation for this tasty salad.

Serves 2

15ml/1 tbsp groundnut (peanut) oil
1 garlic clove, thinly sliced
4 eggs
2 shallots, thinly sliced
2 small fresh red chillies, seeded and thinly sliced
½ small cucumber, finely diced
1cm/½ in piece fresh root ginger, peeled and grated
juice of 2 limes
30ml/2 tbsp soy sauce
5ml/1 tsp caster (superfine) sugar
small bunch coriander (cilantro)
bunch watercress, coarsely chopped

1 Heat the oil in a frying pan. Add the garlic and cook over a low heat until it starts to turn golden. Crack in the eggs. Break the yolks with a wooden spatula, then fry until the eggs are almost firm. Remove from the pan and set aside.

2 Mix the shallots, chillies, cucumber and ginger in a bowl. In a separate bowl, whisk the lime juice with the soy sauce and caster sugar. Pour this dressing over the vegetables and toss lightly.

3 Set aside a few coriander sprigs for the garnish. Chop the rest and add to the salad. Toss it again.

4 Reserve a few watercress sprigs and arrange the remainder on two serving plates. Cut the fried eggs into slices and divide them between the watercress mounds. Spoon the shallot mixture over them and serve, garnished with the reserved coriander and watercress.

NUTRITION NOTES

Per portion:

Energy	521kcal/2179kJ
Protein	36.2g
Fat	20.7g
saturated fat	4.9g
Carbohydrate	41.5g
Fibre	1.3g
Calcium	407mg

onion and aubergine salad with garlic and tahini dressing

THIS IS A DELICIOUSLY SMOKY SALAD that balances sweet and sharp flavours. Try serving it with some crisp lettuce leaves and sweet, ripe tomatoes for a light lunch.

4 Arrange the vegetables on a serving dish, sprinkle with the sumac, if using, and season with salt and pepper. Sprinkle with the remaining oil if they seem dry.

5 For the dressing, crush the garlic in a mortar with a pinch of salt and gradually work in the tahini, followed by the juice of 1 lemon and the water. Taste and add more lemon juice if you like. Thin with more water, if necessary, so that the dressing is fairly runny.

6 Drizzle the dressing over the salad and leave for 1 hour, then sprinkle with the chopped parsley and pine nuts. Serve immediately at room temperature.

Serves 6

3 aubergines (eggplant), cut into
   1cm/½in thick slices
675g/1½lb onions, thickly sliced
75–90ml/5–6 tbsp olive oil
5ml/1 tsp powdered sumac (optional)
45ml/3 tbsp roughly chopped flat
   leaf parsley
45ml/3 tbsp pine nuts, toasted
salt and ground black pepper

For the dressing

2 garlic cloves, crushed
150ml/¼ pint/⅔ cup light tahini
juice of 1–2 lemons
45–60ml/3–4 tbsp water

1 Place the aubergines on a rack or in a colander and sprinkle generously with salt. Leave for 45–60 minutes, then rinse thoroughly under cold running water and pat dry with kitchen paper.

2 Thread the onions on to skewers or place them in an oiled wire grill (broiler) cage.

3 Brush the aubergines and onions with 45ml/3 tbsp oil and grill for 6–8 minutes on each side. Brush with more oil when you turn the vegetables. They should be browned and soft when cooked. The onions may need longer than the aubergines.

NUTRITION NOTES

Per portion:	
Energy	358kcal/1504kJ
Protein	7.3g
Fat	31.1g
saturated fat	4.0g
Carbohydrate	16.6g
Fibre	7.3g
Calcium	156mg

grilled leek and courgette salad with feta and mint

SERVED ON CRISP, SWEET LETTUCE, this makes a delicious summery appetizer or main course. Try to obtain genuine ewe's milk feta for the best flavour and texture.

Serves 6

12 slender, baby leeks
6 small courgettes (zucchini)
90ml/6 tbsp extra virgin olive oil
finely shredded rind and juice of ½ lemon
1–2 garlic cloves, finely chopped
½ fresh red chilli, seeded and diced
pinch of caster (superfine) sugar (optional)
50g/2oz/½ cup black olives, stoned and
   roughly chopped
30ml/2 tbsp chopped fresh mint
150g/5oz feta cheese, sliced or crumbled
salt and ground black pepper
fresh mint leaves, to garnish

1 Bring a large pan of salted water to the boil. Add the leeks and cook for 2–3 minutes. Drain, refresh under cold water, then squeeze out any excess water and leave to drain.

2 Cut the courgettes in half lengthways. Place in a colander, adding 5ml/1 tsp salt to the layers, and leave to drain for about 45 minutes. Rinse and pat dry thoroughly on a piece of kitchen paper.

3 Heat the grill (broiler). Toss the leeks and courgettes in 30ml/2 tbsp oil. Grill (broil) the leeks for 2–3 minutes each side and the courgettes for about 5 minutes on each side. Cut the leeks into thin pieces and place them in a shallow dish with the grilled courgettes.

4 Place the remaining oil in a small bowl and whisk in the lemon rind, 15ml/ 1 tbsp lemon juice, the garlic, chilli and a pinch of sugar, if using. Season to taste with salt and ground black pepper. Add more lemon juice to taste.

5 Pour the dressing over the leeks and courgettes. Stir in the olives and mint, then set aside to marinate for a few hours, turning the vegetables once or twice. If the salad has been marinated in the fridge, remove it 30 minutes before serving and bring back to room temperature.

6 Add the crumbled feta cheese just before serving, and garnish with several fresh mint leaves.

NUTRITION NOTES

Per portion:

Energy	248kcal/1035kJ
Protein	6.7g
Fat	21.0g
saturated fat	5.1g
Carbohydrate	8.5g
Fibre	2.8g
Calcium	168mg

greek salad

THIS WONDERFULLY TANGY SALAD makes a perfect lunch or supper dish. The ingredients offer a range of nutrients, from vitamins C and E to monounsaturated fats and protein.

Serves 4

1 small cos or romaine lettuce, sliced
450g/1lb well-flavoured tomatoes,
    cut into eighths
1 cucumber, seeded and chopped
200g/7oz feta cheese, crumbled
4 spring onions (scallions), sliced
50g/2oz/½ cup black olives, pitted
    and halved

For the dressing

45ml/3 tbsp olive oil
25ml/1½ tbsp lemon juice
salt and ground black pepper

NUTRITION NOTES

Per portion:

Energy	240kcal/1002kJ
Protein	9.5g
Fat	20.4g
saturated fat	8.4g
Carbohydrate	5.4g
Fibre	2.3g
Calcium	210mg

1 Put the lettuce, tomatoes, cucumber, crumbled feta cheese, spring onions and olives in a large salad bowl.

2 For the dressing, whisk together the olive oil and lemon juice, then season. Pour over the salad, toss well and serve.

asparagus, bacon and leaf salad

THIS EXCELLENT SALAD makes an appetizing first course or light lunch. Frisée has feathery, curly, slightly bitter-tasting leaves and is a member of the chicory family.

Serves 4

500g/1¼lb medium asparagus spears
130g/4½oz thin-cut smoked back
(lean) bacon
250g/9oz frisée lettuce leaves or
mixed leaf salad
100ml/3½fl oz/scant ½ cup
French dressing

NUTRITION NOTES

Per portion:

Energy	192kcal/804kJ
Protein	11.6g
Fat	13.9g
saturated fat	2.4g
Carbohydrate	6.0g
Fibre	2.8g
Calcium	56mg

1 Trim off any tough ends from the asparagus and cut the spears into three, setting the tips aside. Heat 1cm/½in of water in a frying pan until simmering. Cook the spears for about 3 minutes, until almost tender, then add the tips and cook for 1 minute more. Drain and refresh under cold, running water.

2 Dry-fry the bacon until golden and crisp then set it aside to cool. Use scissors to snip it into pieces. Place the salad leaves in a bowl and add the bacon.

3 Add the cooked asparagus to the salad. Pour the dressing over and toss lightly, then serve immediately.

salad with omelette strips and bacon

CRISP BACON AND HERBY OMELETTE STRIPS add substance and protein to this light and tasty salad.

Serves 4

6 streaky (fatty) bacon rashers (strips),
   rinds removed and chopped
400g/14oz mixed salad leaves,
   including some distinctively flavoured
   leaves such as rocket (arugula),
   watercress and fresh herbs
2 eggs
2 spring onions (scallions), chopped
few sprigs of coriander (cilantro), chopped
25g/1oz/2 tbsp butter
60ml/4 tbsp olive oil
30ml/2 tbsp balsamic vinegar
salt and ground black pepper

1 Warm an omelette pan over a low heat. Add the chopped bacon and cook gently until the fat runs. Increase the heat to crisp the bacon, stirring frequently. When the bacon pieces are brown and crispy, remove from the heat and transfer to a hot dish to keep warm.

2 Place the salad leaves in a large bowl. In another bowl, beat the eggs with the chopped spring onions and coriander and season well with salt and pepper.

3 Melt the butter in the omelette pan and pour in the eggs. Cook for about 3 minutes to make an unfolded omelette. Cut into long strips and keep warm.

4 Add the oil, vinegar and seasoning to the pan and heat briefly. Sprinkle the bacon and omelette strips over the salad leaves, then pour over the dressing. Toss.

NUTRITION NOTES

Per portion:	
Energy	321kcal/1341kJ
Protein	13.4g
Fat	28.9g
saturated fat	9.0g
Carbohydrate	2.2g
Fibre	0.9g
Calcium	49mg

chilli salad omelettes with hummus

THESE DELICATE OMELETTES filled with healthy and nutritious salad make a refreshing low-carbohydrate lunch.

Serves 4

4 eggs
15ml/1 tbsp cornflour (cornstarch)
115g/4oz/1 cup shredded salad
   vegetables
60ml/4 tbsp chilli salad dressing
60–75ml/4–5 tbsp hummus
4 cooked bacon rashers (strips), chopped
salt and ground black pepper

NUTRITION NOTES

Per portion:	
Energy	358kcal/1498kJ
Protein	19.1g
Fat	29.1g
saturated fat	6.8g
Carbohydrate	6.2g
Fibre	0.8g
Calcium	54mg

1 Beat together the eggs, cornflour and 15ml/1 tbsp water. Heat a lightly oiled frying pan and pour a quarter of the mixture into the pan, tipping it to spread it out evenly. Cook the omelette gently. When cooked, remove from the pan, then make 3 more omelettes. Stack them between sheets of baking parchment, then chill.

2 When ready to serve, toss the shredded salad vegetables together with about 45ml/3 tbsp of the dressing.

3 Spread half of each omelette with hummus, top with the salad vegetables and chopped bacon and fold in half. Drizzle the rest of the dressing over the filled omelettes before serving.

aubergine salad with shrimp and egg

An appetizing and unusual salad that you will find yourself making over and over again for friends and family. Roasting the aubergines really brings out their rich, sweet flavour.

Serves 4

2 aubergines (eggplant)
15ml/1 tbsp vegetable oil
30ml/2 tbsp dried shrimp, soaked in warm
  water for 10 minutes
15ml/1 tbsp coarsely chopped garlic
1 hard-boiled egg, chopped
4 shallots, thinly sliced into rings
fresh coriander (cilantro) leaves and 2 fresh
  red chillies, seeded and sliced, to garnish

For the dressing

30ml/2 tbsp fresh lime juice
5ml/1 tsp palm sugar or light muscovado
  (brown) sugar
30ml/2 tbsp Thai fish sauce

1 Preheat the grill (broiler) to medium or preheat the oven to 180°C/350°F/Gas 4. Prick the aubergines several times with a skewer, then arrange on a baking sheet. Cook them under the grill for 30–40 minutes, or until they are charred and tender. Alternatively, roast them by placing them directly on the shelf of the oven for about 1 hour, turning them at least twice. Remove the aubergines and set aside until they are cool enough to handle.

VARIATION

For a special occasion, use salted duck's or quail's eggs, cut in half, instead of chopped hen's eggs.

2 Meanwhile, make the dressing. Put the lime juice, sugar and fish sauce into a small bowl. Whisk well with a fork or balloon whisk. Cover with clear film (plastic wrap) and set aside until required.

3 When the aubergines are cool enough to handle, peel off the skin and cut the flesh into medium slices.

4 Heat the oil in a frying pan. Drain the dried shrimp thoroughly and add them to the pan with the garlic. Cook over a medium heat for 3 minutes, until golden. Remove from the pan and set aside.

5 Arrange the aubergine slices on a serving dish. Top with the hard-boiled egg, shallots and dried shrimp mixture. Drizzle over the dressing and garnish with the coriander and red chillies.

NUTRITION NOTES

Per portion:	
Energy	146kcal/610kJ
Protein	7.7g
Fat	9.3g
saturated fat	1.2g
Carbohydrate	8.1g
Fibre	2.2g
Calcium	124mg

bean salad with tuna and red onion

THIS MAKES A GREAT LIGHT main meal, and is extremely nutritious. If you are really hungry, try serving it with a mixed green salad and some home-made garlic mayonnaise.

Serves 4

250g/9oz/1½ cups dried haricot (navy)
   or cannellini beans, soaked overnight
   in cold water
1 bay leaf
200–250g/7–9oz fine green beans, trimmed
1 large red onion, very thinly sliced
45ml/3 tbsp chopped fresh flat
   leaf parsley
200–250g/7–9oz good-quality canned
   tuna in olive oil, drained
200g/7oz cherry tomatoes, halved
salt and ground black pepper
a few onion rings, to garnish

For the dressing

90ml/6 tbsp extra virgin olive oil
15ml/1 tbsp tarragon vinegar
5ml/1 tbsp tarragon mustard
1 garlic clove, finely chopped
5ml/1 tsp grated lemon rind
a little lemon juice
pinch of caster (superfine) sugar (optional)

1 Drain the haricot or cannellini beans and bring them to the boil in a pan of fresh water with the bay leaf added. Boil rapidly for about 10 minutes, then reduce the heat and boil steadily for approximately 1–1½ hours, until tender (the cooking time will depend on the age of the dried beans). When cooked, drain the beans well and discard the bay leaf.

NUTRITION NOTES

Per portion:	
Energy	572kcals/2405kJ
Protein	28.9g
Fat	37.2g
saturated fat	5.6g
Carbohydrate	32.5g
Fibre	19.0g
Calcium	160mg

2 Meanwhile, place all the dressing ingredients apart from the lemon juice and sugar in a jug (pitcher) or bowl and whisk until mixed. Season to taste with salt, pepper, lemon juice and a pinch of caster sugar, if you like. Leave to stand.

3 Blanch the green beans in plenty of boiling water for 3–4 minutes. Drain, refresh under cold water and drain thoroughly again.

4 Place both types of beans in a bowl. Add half the dressing and toss to mix. Stir in the onion and half the chopped parsley, then season to taste.

5 Flake the tuna into large chunks and toss it into the beans with the tomatoes.

6 Arrange the salad on four plates. Drizzle the remaining dressing over the salad and scatter chopped parsley on top. Garnish with a few onion rings and serve immediately, at room temperature.

warm monkfish salad

GRIDDLED MONKFISH tossed with nutritious pine nuts and vitamin-rich baby spinach is a delicious combination that will make you forget you are on a diet.

Serves 4

2 monkfish fillets, each weighing about
    350g/12oz
25g/1oz/¼ cup pine nuts
15ml/1 tbsp olive oil
225g/8oz baby spinach leaves, washed
    and stalks removed
salt and ground black pepper

For the dressing

5ml/1 tsp Dijon mustard
5ml/1 tsp sherry vinegar
30ml/2 tbsp olive oil
1 garlic clove, crushed

VARIATION

Substitute salad leaves for the spinach if you like. Watercress and rocket (arugula) would be good alternatives.

1 Holding the knife at a slight angle, cut each monkfish fillet into 12 diagonal slices. Season lightly and set aside.

2 Heat a dry frying pan, put in the pine nuts and shake them over a low heat, until golden brown but not burned. Transfer to a plate and set aside.

3 To make the dressing, put the mustard, sherry vinegar, olive oil and garlic in a jug (pitcher) or small bowl and whisk thoroughly until smooth and creamy. Pour the dressing into a small pan, season to taste with salt and pepper and warm through over a low heat.

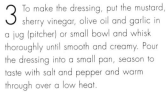

4 Heat the oil in a ridged griddle pan or frying pan until sizzling. Add the fish slices and sauté for about 20–30 seconds on each side.

5 Put the spinach leaves into a large bowl and pour over the warm salad dressing. Sprinkle on the toasted pine nuts, reserving a few, and toss together well. Divide the dressed spinach leaves among four serving plates and arrange the fish slices on top. Sprinkle over the reserved pine nuts and serve immediately.

NUTRITION NOTES

Per portion:	
Energy	222kcal/927kJ
Protein	29.9g
Fat	10.9g
saturated fat	1.3g
Carbohydrate	1.1g
Fibre	1.3g
Calcium	110mg

seafood salad

CRISP SALAD LEAVES and fresh shellfish are a tasty combination that fit perfectly within a diet because both are naturally low in carbohydrate. Vary the seafood depending on what is available.

Serves 6

450g/1lb live mussels, scrubbed
   and bearded
450g/1lb small clams, scrubbed
105ml/7 tbsp dry white wine
225g/8oz squid, cleaned
4 large scallops, with their corals
30ml/2 tbsp olive oil
2 garlic cloves, finely chopped
1 small dried red chilli, crumbled
225g/8oz cooked unpeeled
   prawns (shrimp)
6–8 large chicory (Belgian endive) leaves
6–8 radicchio leaves
15ml/1 tbsp chopped flat leaf parsley,
   to garnish

For the dressing

5ml/1 tsp Dijon mustard
30ml/2 tbsp white wine or cider vinegar
5ml/1 tsp lemon juice
75ml/5 tbsp extra virgin olive oil
salt and ground black pepper

1 Put the mussels and clams in a large pan and pour in the dry white wine. Cover tightly and cook over a high heat, shaking the pan occasionally, for about 4 minutes, until the shells have opened. Discard any that remain closed. Use a slotted spoon to transfer the shellfish to a bowl, then strain thoroughly and reserve the cooking liquid.

2 Cut the squid bodies into thin rings and chop the tentacles into bite-size pieces. Leave any small squid whole. Halve the scallops horizontally.

3 Heat the olive oil in a large frying pan. Add the chopped garlic, chilli, squid, scallops and their corals, and sauté gently over a low heat for about 2 minutes, until just cooked and tender. Lift the squid, scallops and corals out of the pan, reserving any oil that remains.

4 When the mussels and clams are cool, shell them, keeping 12 of each in the shell. Peel all but six of the prawns.

5 Strain the shellfish cooking liquid into a small pan, set over a high heat, bring to the boil and reduce by half. In a large bowl, combine all the mussels and clams with the squid and scallops, then add the prawns.

6 To make the dressing, whisk the Dijon mustard with the white wine or cider vinegar and lemon juice and season with salt and ground black pepper. Add the olive oil, whisk, then whisk in the cooking liquid and oil from the frying pan. Pour the dressing over the seafood mixture and toss lightly.

7 Arrange the salad leaves around the edge of a large serving dish and pile the seafood mixture into the centre of the dish. Sprinkle with the chopped parsley and serve immediately.

NUTRITION NOTES	
Per portion:	
Energy	252kcal/1053kJ
Protein	26.5g
Fat	13.5g
saturated fat	2.2g
Carbohydrate	3.9g
Fibre	0.1g
Calcium	106mg

anchovy and roasted pepper salad

SWEET PEPPERS, SALTY ANCHOVIES and plenty of garlic make an intensely flavoured salad that is delicious with meat, poultry or cheese. If you find canned anchovies too salty, you can reduce their saltiness by soaking them in milk first.

Serves 4

2 red, 2 orange and 2 yellow (bell) peppers, halved and seeded
50g/2oz can anchovies in olive oil
2 garlic cloves
45ml/3 tbsp balsamic vinegar

NUTRITION NOTES

Per portion:

Energy	74kcal/316kJ
Protein	5.5g
Fat	3.5g
saturated fat	0.6g
Carbohydrate	6.0g
Fibre	2.2g
Calcium	61mg

1 Preheat the oven to 200°C/400°F/ Gas 6. Place the peppers in a roasting pan and roast for 30–40 minutes. Transfer to a bowl and cover with clear film (plastic wrap).

2 When the peppers are cool, peel them and cut into strips. Drain the anchovies, reserving the oil. Halve the fillets lengthways.

3 Slice the garlic cloves as thinly as possible and place them in a large bowl. Stir in the olive oil, balsamic vinegar and a little ground black pepper. Add the sliced peppers and anchovy fillets and use a spoon or fork to fold the ingredients together. Cover with clear film and chill until ready to serve.

leek salad with anchovy and egg

CHOPPED HARD-BOILED EGGS and cooked leeks are a classic combination in many French-style salads. This one makes a tasty main dish, which is perfect for lunch or served with a simple tomato salad as a light dinner.

Serves 4
675g/1½lb thin or baby leeks, trimmed
2 large or 3 medium eggs
50g/2oz good-quality anchovy fillets in
   olive oil, drained
15g/½oz flat leaf parsley, chopped
a few black olives, stoned (optional)
salt and ground black pepper

For the dressing
5ml/1 tsp Dijon mustard
15ml/1 tbsp tarragon vinegar
75ml/5 tbsp olive oil
30ml/2 tbsp double (heavy) cream
1 small shallot, very finely chopped
pinch of caster (superfine) sugar (optional)

1 Add a pinch of salt to a pan of water and bring to the boil. Plunge the leeks into the boiling water and cook for 3–4 minutes. Drain, plunge into cold water, then drain again. Squeeze out any excess water, then pat dry with kitchen paper.

2 Place the eggs in a pan of cold water, bring to the boil and cook for 6–7 minutes. Drain, plunge into cold water, then shell and roughly chop the eggs.

3 To make the dressing, whisk the Dijon mustard with the tarragon vinegar. Gradually whisk in the olive oil, followed by the double cream. Stir in the shallot, then season to taste with salt, pepper and a pinch of caster sugar, if you like.

4 Leave the leeks whole or thickly slice them, then place in a serving dish. Pour most of the dressing over them and stir to mix. Leave for at least 1 hour, or until ready to serve.

5 Arrange the anchovies on the leeks, then scatter the eggs and parsley over the top. Drizzle with the remaining dressing, season with black pepper and dot with a few olives, if using. Serve immediately.

NUTRITION NOTES

Per portion:

Energy	356kcal/1483kJ
Protein	11.2g
Fat	29.5g
saturated fat	6.6g
Carbohydrate	12.0g
Fibre	5.5g
Calcium	172mg

COOK'S TIP
Make sure the leeks are thoroughly drained and squeezed of excess water otherwise the excess liquid will dilute the intense flavour of the mustard dressing and spoil the dish.

thai prawn salad with garlic dressing and frizzled shallots

IN THIS INTENSELY FLAVOURED SALAD, sweet prawns and juicy mango are partnered with a sweet-sour garlic dressing and the fiery taste of fresh chilli. The crisp, frizzled shallots are a traditional addition to many Thai salads.

Serves 6

675g/1½lb medium-size raw prawns (shrimp), shelled and deveined with tails on
finely shredded rind of 1 lime
½ fresh red chilli, seeded and finely chopped
30ml/2 tbsp olive oil, plus extra for brushing
1 ripe but firm mango
2 carrots, cut into long thin shreds
10cm/4in piece cucumber, sliced
1 small red onion, halved and thinly sliced
a few sprigs of fresh coriander (cilantro)
a few sprigs of fresh mint
45ml/3 tbsp roasted peanuts, roughly chopped
4 large shallots, thinly sliced and fried until crisp in 30ml/2 tbsp peanut oil
salt and ground black pepper

For the dressing

1 large garlic clove, chopped
10–15ml/2–3 tsp caster (superfine) sugar
juice of 2 limes
15–30ml/1–2 tbsp Thai fish sauce
1 red chilli, seeded
5–10ml/1–2 tsp light rice vinegar

NUTRITION NOTES

Per portion:	
Energy	266kcal/1118kJ
Protein	19.2g
Fat	14.4g
saturated fat	2.2g
Carbohydrate	15.8g
Fibre	3.5g
Calcium	148mg

1 Place the prawns in a bowl and add the lime rind and chilli. Season with salt and pepper and spoon the oil over them. Leave to marinate for 30–40 minutes.

2 For the dressing, place the garlic in a mortar with 10ml/2 tsp caster sugar and pound until smooth, then work in the juice of 1½ limes and 15ml/1 tbsp of the Thai fish sauce.

3 Transfer the dressing to a jug (pitcher). Finely chop half the chilli. and add it to the dressing. Taste the dressing then add more sugar, lime juice, fish sauce and rice vinegar to taste.

4 Peel and stone the mango, then cut it into very fine strips.

5 Toss together the mango, carrots, cucumber and onion, and half the dressing. Arrange the salad on individual plates or in bowls.

6 Heat a ridged, cast-iron griddle pan or heavy frying pan until very hot. Brush with a little oil, then sear the prawns for 2–3 minutes on each side, until they turn pink and are patched with brown on the outside. Arrange the prawns on the salads.

7 Sprinkle the remaining dressing over the salads and scatter the sprigs of coriander and mint over. Finely shred the remaining chilli and sprinkle it over the salads with the peanuts and crisp-fried shallots. Serve immediately.

COOK'S TIP
To devein prawns, make a shallow cut down the back of the prawn, lift out the thin, black vein, then rinse thoroughly under cold, running water.

salad niçoise

THIS CLASSIC FRENCH SALAD makes a simple yet unbeatable meal. It offers the perfect combination of low-carbohydrate salad vegetables and healthy oily fish.

Serves 4

115g/4oz green beans, trimmed and halved
115g/4oz mixed salad leaves
½ small cucumber, sliced
4 ripe tomatoes, quartered
1 tuna steak, weighing about 175g/6oz
olive oil, for brushing
50g/2oz can anchovies, drained and
   halved lengthways
4 eggs, hard boiled, shelled and quartered
½ bunch small radishes, trimmed
50g/2oz/½ cup small black olives
salt and ground black pepper

For the dressing
90ml/6 tbsp extra virgin olive oil
2 garlic cloves, crushed
15ml/1 tbsp white wine vinegar

1 To make the dressing, whisk all the ingredients together and season to taste.

2 Cook the beans in boiling water for 2 minutes, until just tender, then drain. In a large shallow bowl, combine the salad leaves, sliced cucumber, tomatoes and beans.

3 Preheat the grill (broiler). Brush the tuna with olive oil and season. Grill (broil) for 3–4 minutes on each side until cooked through. Leave to cool, then flake.

4 Sprinkle the flaked tuna, anchovies, quartered eggs, radishes and olives over the salad. Pour over the dressing and toss lightly to combine, then serve.

NUTRITION NOTES

Per portion:

Energy	355kcal/1483kJ
Protein	21.4g
Fat	28.3g
saturated fat	4.8g
Carbohydrate	4.2g
Fibre	2.3g
Calcium	109mg

crab salad with capers

COMBINING TANGY CITRUS JUICE, sweet peppers and crab offers a powerhouse of valuable nutrients including vitamin C, B vitamins, zinc, potassium and betacarotene.

Serves 4

white and brown meat from 4 small dressed
    fresh crabs, about 450g/1lb
1 small red (bell) pepper, seeded
    and finely chopped
1 small red onion, finely chopped
30ml/2 tbsp drained capers
30ml/2 tbsp chopped fresh
    coriander (cilantro)
grated rind and juice of 2 lemons
Tabasco sauce
40g/1½oz rocket (arugula) leaves
30ml/2 tbsp sunflower oil
15ml/1 tbsp fresh lime juice
salt and ground black pepper
lemon rind strips, to garnish

1 Put the crab meat, red pepper, onion, capers and coriander in a bowl. Add the lemon rind and juice and toss gently to mix. Season to taste with Tabasco sauce, salt and ground black pepper.

2 Wash the rocket leaves and pat dry. Divide among four plates. Mix the oil and lime juice in a small bowl. Dress the leaves, then pile the crab salad on top and serve garnished with strips of lemon rind.

NUTRITION NOTES

Per portion:

Energy	156kcal/652kJ
Protein	21.3g
Fat	6.3g
saturated fat	0.8g
Carbohydrate	3.9g
Fibre	1.1g
Calcium	159mg

scented fish salad

FOR A TASTE OF THE FAR EAST, try this delicious fish salad scented with coconut, fruit and warm Thai spices. Try to find a pitaya or dragon fruit – the flesh is sweet and refreshing, with a slightly acidic melon-like flavour that goes well with fish.

Serves 4

350g/12oz fillet of red mullet, sea bream or snapper
1 cos or romaine lettuce
1 papaya or mango, peeled and sliced
1 pitaya, peeled and sliced
1 large ripe tomato, cut into wedges
½ cucumber, peeled and cut into batons
3 spring onions (scallions), sliced
salt

For the marinade

5ml/1 tsp coriander seeds
5ml/1 tsp fennel seeds
2.5ml/½ tsp cumin seeds
5ml/1 tsp caster (superfine) sugar
2.5ml/½ tsp hot chilli sauce
30ml/2 tbsp garlic oil

For the dressing

15ml/1 tbsp creamed coconut
   (60ml/4 tbsp coconut cream)
pinch of salt
45ml/3 tbsp boiling water
60ml/4 tbsp groundnut (peanut) oil
finely grated rind and juice of 1 lime
1 fresh red chilli, seeded and
   finely chopped
5ml/1 tsp granulated sugar
45ml/3 tbsp chopped fresh
   coriander (cilantro)

NUTRITION NOTES

Per portion:

Energy	227kcal/955kJ
Protein	18.0g
Fat	10.0g
saturated fat	1.1g
Carbohydrate	16.3g
Fibre	2.3g
Calcium	100mg

1 Cut the fish fillets into fairly thin, even strips, removing any stray bones wtih your fingers. Set aside on a plate.

2 Make the marinade. Put the coriander, fennel and cumin seeds in a mortar. Add the sugar and crush with a pestle. Stir in the chilli sauce and garlic oil, then add salt to taste and mix to a smooth paste.

3 Spread the paste over the fish strips, cover with clear film (plastic wrap) and leave to marinate in a cool place for at least 20 minutes.

4 Make the dressing. Place the creamed coconut and salt in a screw-top jar. Stir in the boiling water. Add the groundnut oil, lime rind and juice, chopped chilli, sugar and coriander. Shake well.

5 Wash and dry the lettuce leaves. Place in a bowl and add the sliced papaya or mango, pitaya, tomato, cucumber and spring onions. Pour in the dressing and toss well to coat.

6 Heat a large non-stick frying pan, add the fish and cook for 5 minutes, turning once. Add the cooked fish to the salad, toss lightly and serve immediately.

COOK'S TIP

If planning ahead, you can leave the fish in its marinade for up to 8 hours in the refrigerator. The dressing can also be made in advance, but do not add the fresh coriander (cilantro) until the last minute and shake vigorously again before pouring it over the salad.

warm chicken and tomato salad

THIS SIMPLE, WARM SALAD combines pan-fried chicken breasts, cherry tomatoes and fresh baby spinach with a light, nutty dressing. Serve it for lunch on a cool autumn day.

Serves 4

45ml/3 tbsp olive oil
30ml/2 tbsp hazelnut oil
15ml/1 tbsp white wine vinegar
1 garlic clove, crushed
15ml/1 tbsp chopped fresh mixed herbs
225g/8oz baby spinach leaves
250g/9oz cherry tomatoes, halved
1 bunch spring onions (scallions), chopped
2 skinless chicken breast portions,
　cut into thin strips
salt and ground black pepper

VARIATIONS

Instead of chicken, try using beef steak, pork fillet or even salmon fillet.

1 First make the dressing: place 30ml/ 2 tbsp of the olive oil, the hazelnut oil, vinegar, garlic and chopped herbs in a small bowl or jug (pitcher) and whisk together until thoroughly mixed. Set aside.

2 Trim any long stalks from the baby spinach leaves, then place in a large serving bowl with the halved cherry tomatoes and chopped spring onions, and gently toss together to mix.

3 Heat the remaining olive oil in a frying pan, and stir-fry the chicken strips over a high heat for about 7–10 minutes, until they are cooked through. The chicken should be tender and lightly browned.

4 Arrange the cooked chicken pieces over the mixed salad. Give the dressing a quick whisk to make sure the ingredients are well mixed, then drizzle it over the salad, to taste. Season with salt and ground black pepper, toss lightly with your hands and serve immediately.

NUTRITION NOTES

Per portion:	
Energy	265kcal/1111kJ
Protein	14.8g
Fat	20.9g
saturated fat	3.1g
Carbohydrate	5.3g
Fibre	2.6g
Calcium	85mg

citrus chicken salad

THIS ATTRACTIVE, ZESTY SALAD offers a delicious combination of healthy raw vegetables, lean, grilled chicken and oranges and limes, which are rich in vitamin C.

Serves 6

6 skinless chicken breast portions
4 oranges
5ml/1 tsp Dijon mustard
15ml/3 tsp clear honey
60ml/4 tbsp extra virgin olive oil
300g/11oz/2¾ cups finely shredded
    white cabbage
300g/11oz carrots, peeled and
    thinly sliced
2 spring onions (scallions),
    thinly sliced
2 celery sticks, cut into thin batons
30ml/2 tbsp chopped fresh tarragon
2 limes
salt and ground black pepper

1 Place the chicken under a preheated grill (broiler) and cook for 5 minutes on each side, or until it is cooked through and golden brown. Leave to cool.

2 Peel two of the oranges, cutting off all pith, then cut out the segments and set aside. Grate the rind and squeeze the juice from one of the remaining oranges and place in a bowl.

3 Stir the mustard, 5ml/1 tsp of the honey, the oil and seasoning into the orange juice. Mix in the cabbage, carrots, spring onions and celery, then leave to stand for 10 minutes.

4 Meanwhile, squeeze the juice from the remaining orange and mix it with the remaining honey and tarragon. Peel and segment the limes and lightly mix the segments into the dressing with the reserved orange segments and seasoning to taste.

5 Slice the chicken and stir into the dressing with the oranges and limes. Divide the vegetables among six plates, add the chicken, then serve.

NUTRITION NOTES

Per portion:	
Energy	303kcal/1226kJ
Protein	48.8g
Fat	10.7g
saturated fat	1.9g
Carbohydrate	2.8g
Fibre	1.2g
Calcium	40mg

warm duck salad with poached eggs

GRILLED DUCK COOKED ON skewers looks and tastes wonderful in this spectacular salad. It makes the ideal choice for a special meal that won't ruin your healthy eating plan.

Serves 4

3 skinless duck breast portions,
   thinly sliced
30ml/2 tbsp soy sauce
30ml/2 tbsp balsamic vinegar
30ml/2 tbsp groundnut (peanut) oil
1 shallot, finely chopped
115g/4oz/1½ cups chanterelle mushrooms
4 eggs
50g/2oz mixed salad leaves
salt and ground black pepper
30ml/2 tbsp extra virgin olive oil,
   to serve

1 Put the duck in a shallow dish and toss with the soy sauce and balsamic vinegar. Cover and chill for 30 minutes. Meanwhile, soak 12 bamboo skewers (about 13cm/5in long) in water to help prevent them from burning during cooking.

2 Preheat the grill (broiler). Thread the marinated duck slices on to the skewers, pleating them neatly.

3 Place the skewers on a grill pan and cook for 3–5 minutes, then turn the skewers and cook for a further 3 minutes, or until the duck is golden brown.

4 Meanwhile, heat the groundnut oil in a frying pan and cook the chopped shallot until softened. Add the mushrooms and cook over a high heat for 5 minutes, stirring occasionally.

5 While the chanterelles are cooking, half fill a frying pan with water, add a little salt and heat until simmering. Break the eggs one at a time into a cup, then gently tip into the water. Poach the eggs gently for about 3 minutes, or until the whites are set. Use a slotted spoon to transfer the eggs to a warm plate, pat dry with kitchen paper, then trim off any untidy white.

6 Arrange the salad leaves on four plates, then add the chanterelles and skewered duck. Place the eggs on the salad. Drizzle with olive oil and season with pepper, then serve immediately.

NUTRITION NOTES

Per portion:	
Energy	321kcal/1341kJ
Protein	36.5g
Fat	19.4g
saturated fat	3.9g
Carbohydrate	0.2g
Fibre	0.1g
Calcium	45mg

spiced quail and mushroom salad

A WARM SALAD of grilled quail, walnuts, mushrooms and salad leaves is perfect for a hearty autumn or winter meal. It is warming and tasty yet contains barely any carbohydrate.

Serves 4
8 quail breast portions
5ml/1 tsp paprika
salt and ground black pepper

For the salad
25g/1oz/2 tbsp butter
75g/3oz/generous 1 cup chanterelle
   mushrooms, sliced if large
25g/1oz/3 tbsp walnut halves, toasted
30ml/2 tbsp walnut oil
30ml/2 tbsp olive oil
45ml/3 tbsp balsamic vinegar
115g/4oz mixed salad leaves

1 Preheat the grill (broiler). Arrange the quail breast portions on the grill rack, skin sides up. Sprinkle with half the paprika and a little salt.

2 Grill (broil) the breast portions for 3 minutes, then turn over and sprinkle with the remaining paprika and a little salt. Grill for a further 3 minutes, or until cooked through. Transfer the quail portions to a warmed dish, cover with foil and leave to stand while preparing the salad.

3 Heat the butter in a frying pan until foaming and cook the chanterelles for about 3 minutes, or until just beginning to soften. Add the walnuts and heat through. Remove from the heat.

4 Meanwhile, make the dressing, whisk the oils with the balsamic vinegar, then season and set aside.

5 Using a sharp knife, slice the cooked quail portions thinly and arrange them on four individual serving plates with the warmed chanterelle mushrooms and walnuts and mixed salad leaves. Drizzle the oil and vinegar dressing over the salad and serve immediately while still warm.

NUTRITION NOTES

Per portion:

Energy	353kcal/1391kJ
Protein	42.9g
Fat	19.8g
saturated fat	5.7g
Carbohydrate	0.7g
Fibre	0.6g
Calcium	23mg

warm chorizo and spinach salad

IN THIS HEARTY WARM SALAD, spinach has sufficient flavour to compete with the spiciness of the chorizo. Try using a flavoured olive oil as well – rosemary, garlic or chilli oil would be perfect.

Serves 4

225g/8oz baby spinach leaves
45ml/3 tbsp extra virgin olive oil
150g/5oz chorizo sausage, very
  thinly sliced
30ml/2 tbsp sherry vinegar

NUTRITION NOTES

Per portion:

Energy	287kcal/1200kJ
Protein	11.0g
Fat	25.8g
saturated fat	7.0g
Carbohydrate	2.8g
Fibre	1.3g
Calcium	57mg

1 Discard any tough stalks from the baby spinach leaves. Pour the oil into a large frying pan and add the sliced chorizo sausage. Cook gently for 3 minutes, until the sausage slices start to shrivel slightly and turn a darker colour.

2 Add the spinach leaves and remove the pan from the heat. Toss the spinach in the warm oil until it just starts to wilt. Add the sherry vinegar and a little seasoning. Toss the ingredients briefly, then serve immediately, while still warm.

thai beef salad

THIS QUICK AND HEALTHY traditional Thai dish provides a good source of vitamin C, folic acid, iron, calcium, potassium, zinc and the health-giving phytochemical lycopene.

Serves 6

675g/1½lb fillet (beef tenderloin) or
   rump (round) steak
30ml/2 tbsp olive oil
2 small mild red chillies, seeded
   and sliced
225g/8oz/3¼ cups shiitake
   mushrooms, sliced

For the dressing

3 spring onions (scallions), finely chopped
2 garlic cloves, finely chopped
juice of 1 lime
15–30ml/1–2 tbsp Thai fish sauce
   or oyster sauce, to taste
30ml/2 tbsp chopped fresh
   coriander (cilantro)

To serve

1 cos or romaine lettuce, torn into strips
175g/6oz cherry tomatoes, halved
5cm/2in piece cucumber, peeled, halved
   and thinly sliced

NUTRITION NOTES

Per portion:	
Energy	332kcal/1387kJ
Protein	40.4g
Fat	18.2g
saturated fat	4.5g
Carbohydrate	2.1g
Fibre	1.6g
Calcium	106mg

1 Preheat the grill (broiler) until hot, then cook the steak for 2–4 minutes on each side depending on how well done you like your steak. Leave to stand and firm up for at least 15 minutes.

2 Use a very sharp knife to slice the meat as thinly as possible and place the slices in a bowl.

3 Heat the olive oil in a small frying pan. Add the red chillies and mushrooms and cook for 5 minutes, stirring occasionally. Turn off the heat and add the grilled steak slices to the pan, then stir well to coat the beef slices in the chilli and mushroom mixture.

4 Stir all the ingredients for the dressing together, then pour it over the meat mixture and toss gently. Arrange the salad ingredients on a serving plate. Spoon the steak mixture in the centre and sprinkle the sesame seeds over. Serve immediately.

meat,
poultry and game

HOT MEALS ARE AN ESSENTIAL PART of most people's weekly menu, but they don't have to be a danger zone of high-carbohydrate comfort food. Eat meat and poultry regularly for essential and filling proteins and fats. Whatever your taste, from hot and spicy to subtle and delicate, there is a perfect dish here, from skewered lamb with coriander yogurt to curried pork with pickled garlic, and chicken with Serrano ham. For optimum nutrition, always serve these dishes with a large mixed-leaf salad or a low-carbohydrate vegetable dish.

steak with warm tomato salsa

A REFRESHING, TANGY SALSA of tomatoes, spring onions and balsamic vinegar makes a colourful topping for chunky, pan-fried steaks. Serve with a mixed leaf salad and mustard dressing.

Serves 2

2 rump (round) steaks, about 2cm/¾in thick
3 large plum tomatoes
2 spring onions (scallions)
30ml/2 tbsp balsamic vinegar

NUTRITION NOTES

Per portion:	
Energy	502kcal/2105kJ
Protein	47g
Fat	33.5g
saturated fat	7.8g
Carbohydrate	3.0g
Fibre	1.4g
Calcium	35mg

1 Trim any fat from the steaks, then season on both sides. Heat a non-stick frying pan and cook the steaks for 3 minutes on each side for medium-rare. Cook for longer if you like your steak well-cooked.

2 Meanwhile, put the plum tomatoes in a heatproof bowl, cover with boiling water and leave for about 1–2 minutes, until the skins start to split. Drain and carefully peel the tomatoes, then halve them and scoop out the seeds with a spoon. Roughly chop the tomato flesh and thinly slice the spring onions.

3 Transfer the steaks to plates and keep warm. Add the vegetables, balsamic vinegar, 30ml/2 tbsp water and a little seasoning to the cooking juices in the pan and stir briefly until warm, scraping up any meat residue, which will add extra flavour. Spoon the warm tomato salsa over the steaks and serve immediately.

green beef curry with thai aubergines

THIS IS A VERY QUICK CURRY so be sure to use the best quality meat you can find. Sirloin is recommended, but tender rump steak could be used instead.

Serves 4

450g/1lb beef sirloin
15ml/1 tbsp vegetable oil
45ml/3 tbsp Thai green curry paste
600ml/1 pint/2½ cups coconut milk
4 kaffir lime leaves, torn
15–30ml/1–2 tbsp Thai fish sauce
5ml/1 tsp palm sugar or light muscovado
  (brown) sugar
150g/5oz small Thai aubergines
  (eggplants), halved
a small handful of fresh Thai basil
2 fresh green chillies, to garnish

1 Trim off any excess fat from the beef. Using a sharp knife, cut it into long, thin strips. This is easiest to do if it is well chilled. Set it aside.

2 Heat the oil in a large, heavy pan or wok. Add the curry paste and cook for 1–2 minutes, until it is fragrant.

3 Stir in half the coconut milk, a little at a time. Cook, stirring frequently, for about 5–6 minutes, until an oily sheen appears on the surface of the liquid.

4 Add the beef to the pan with the kaffir lime leaves, Thai fish sauce, palm or muscovado sugar and aubergine halves. Cook for 2–3 minutes, then stir in the remaining coconut milk.

5 Bring back to a simmer and cook until the meat and aubergines are tender. Stir in the Thai basil just before serving. Finely shred the green chillies and use to garnish the curry.

NUTRITION NOTES

Per portion:

Energy	431kcal/1792kJ
Protein	20.5g
Fat	33.4g
saturated fat	11.8g
Carbohydrate	12.5g
Fibre	1.3g
Calcium	62mg

COOK'S TIP

To make the green curry paste, put 15 fresh green chillies, 2 chopped lemon grass stalks, 3 sliced shallots, 2 garlic cloves, 15ml/1 tbsp chopped galangal, 4 chopped kaffir lime leaves, 2.5ml/½ tsp grated kaffir lime rind, 5ml/1 tsp chopped coriander (cilantro) root, 6 black peppercorns, 5ml/1 tsp each roasted coriander and cumin seeds, 15ml/1 tbsp granulated sugar, 5ml/1 tsp salt and 5ml/1 tsp shrimp paste into a food processor and process until smooth. Gradually add 30ml/2 tbsp vegetable oil, processing after each addition.

stir-fried beef and mushrooms with garlic and black beans

THIS CLASSIC CHINESE DISH is low in fat and offers a good supply of minerals needed for optimum health, including zinc and iron. Serve with steamed vegetables such as broccoli.

Serves 4

30ml/2 tbsp dark soy sauce
30ml/2 tbsp Chinese rice wine
10ml/2 tsp cornflour (cornstarch)
10ml/2 tsp sesame oil
450g/1lb fillet (beef tenderloin) or rump (round) steak, trimmed of fat
12 dried shiitake mushrooms
25ml/1½ tbsp salted black beans
5ml/1 tsp caster (superfine) sugar
60ml/4 tbsp groundnut (peanut) oil
4 garlic cloves, thinly sliced
2.5cm/1in piece fresh root ginger, cut into fine strips
200g/7oz open cap mushrooms, sliced
1 bunch spring onions (scallions), sliced diagonally
1 fresh red chilli, seeded and shredded
salt and ground black pepper

1 In a large bowl, mix together half the dark soy sauce, half the Chinese rice wine, half the cornflour and all of the sesame oil with 15ml/1 tbsp fresh cold water until smooth and thoroughly combined. Add a generous pinch of salt and ground black pepper.

NUTRITION NOTES

Per portion:	
Energy	169kcal/706kJ
Protein	26.1g
Fat	6.8g
saturated fat	2.2g
Carbohydrate	0.9g
Fibre	0.4g
Calcium	31mg

2 Cut the beef into very thin slices, no more than 5mm/¼in thick. Add the slices to the cornflour mixture and rub the mixture into the beef with your fingers. Set aside for 30 minutes.

3 Meanwhile, pour boiling water over the dried mushrooms and leave to soak for about 25 minutes. Drain thoroughly, reserving 45ml/3 tbsp of the soaking water. Remove and discard the stalks and cut the caps in half.

4 Mash the salted black beans with the caster sugar. In another bowl, combine the remaining cornflour, soy sauce and Chinese rice wine.

5 Heat the oil in a wok, then stir-fry the beef for about 30–45 seconds, until just brown. Transfer it to a plate and set aside. Pour off some oil to leave about 45ml/3 tbsp in the wok.

6 Add the garlic and ginger to the wok, stir-fry for 1 minute, then add all the mushrooms and stir-fry for 2 minutes. Set aside a few tablespoons of the green part of the spring onions, then add the rest to the wok. Add the black beans and stir-fry for 1–2 minutes. Stir in the beef, then add the shiitake soaking water. Stir in the cornflour mixture and simmer until the sauce thickens. Sprinkle the chilli and reserved spring onions over the beef and serve.

steak béarnaise

BÉARNAISE IS A CREAMY EGG and butter sauce flavoured with tarragon. It is a classic accompaniment for griddled, grilled or pan-fried steak. Roasted vegetables are the ideal accompaniment.

Serves 4

4 sirloin steaks, each weighing about 225g/8oz, trimmed
15ml/1 tbsp sunflower oil (optional)
salt and ground black pepper

For the Béarnaise sauce
45ml/3 tbsp white wine vinegar
6 black peppercorns
1 bay leaf
1 shallot, finely chopped
2 fresh tarragon sprigs
2 egg yolks
100g/3½oz/scant ½ cup unsalted (sweet) butter, diced, at room temperature
15ml/1 tbsp chopped fresh tarragon
freshly ground white pepper

1 Put the white wine vinegar, black peppercorns, bay leaf, shallot and tarragon sprigs in a small pan and simmer until reduced to 30ml/2 tbsp. Strain the vinegar through a fine sieve.

NUTRITION NOTES

Per portion:	
Energy	681kcal/2839kJ
Protein	71.0g
Fat	44.0g
saturated fat	20.7g
Carbohydrate	0.3g
Fibre	0.1g
Calcium	34mg

2 Beat the egg yolks with salt and freshly ground white pepper in a small, heatproof bowl. Stand the bowl over a pan of very gently simmering water, then thoroughly beat the strained vinegar into the yolks.

3 Gradually beat in the butter, one piece at a time, allowing each addition to melt before adding the next. Do not allow the water to heat beyond a gentle simmer, otherwise the sauce will overheat and curdle.

4 While cooking the sauce, heat a large frying pan, griddle pan or grill (broiler) until very hot.

5 Beat the chopped fresh tarragon into the sauce and remove the pan from the heat. The sauce should now be smooth, thick and very glossy.

6 Cover the surface of the sauce with clear film (plastic wrap) or dampened baking parchment (to prevent a skin from forming) and leave over the pan of hot water (still off the heat) to keep hot.

7 Season the steaks with salt and plenty of ground black pepper.

8 A pan is not usually oiled before cooking steak, but if it is essential to grease the pan, add only the minimum oil. Cook the steaks for 2–4 minutes on each side. The cooking time depends on the thickness of the steaks and the extent to which you want to cook them. As a guide, 2–4 minutes will give a medium-rare result.

9 Serve the steaks on warmed plates. Peel the clear film or dampened baking parchment off the sauce and stir it lightly, then spoon it over the steaks.

skewered lamb with coriander yogurt

YOU COULD ALSO MAKE THESE KEBABS using diced lean beef or pork. For extra colour alternate the cubes of meat with chunks of red, orange or yellow pepper, wedges of lemon or onions.

Serves 6
900g/2lb lean boneless lamb
1 large onion, grated
3 bay leaves
5 thyme or rosemary sprigs
grated rind and juice of 1 lemon
2.5ml/½ tsp caster (superfine) sugar
75ml/5 tbsp olive oil
salt and ground black pepper
sprigs of rosemary, to garnish
lemon wedges, to serve

For the coriander yogurt
150ml/¼ pint/⅔ cup natural (plain) yogurt
15ml/1 tbsp chopped fresh mint
15ml/1 tbsp chopped fresh
   coriander (cilantro)
10ml/2 tsp grated onion

1 To make the coriander yogurt, put the yogurt, mint, coriander and grated onion in a bowl and mix well to combine. Transfer the coriander yogurt to a small serving dish and chill until ready to serve.

2 To make the kebabs, cut the lamb into small chunks and put in a bowl. In a separate bowl, combine the grated onion, bay leaves, thyme or rosemary sprigs, lemon rind and juice, sugar and olive oil, then add salt and ground black pepper and pour over the lamb.

3 Mix thoroughly to make sure the lamb is well coated. Cover with clear film (plastic wrap) and leave to marinate in the refrigerator for several hours or overnight.

4 Drain the meat and thread on to skewers. Arrange on a grill (broiler) rack with the lemon wedges and grill for about 10 minutes until browned, turning occasionally. Transfer to a plate and garnish with rosemary. Serve with coriander yogurt.

NUTRITION NOTES	
Per portion:	
Energy	536kcal/2240kJ
Protein	47.7g
Fat	35.3g
saturated fat	10.9g
Carbohydrate	6.9g
Fibre	0.8g
Calcium	91mg

barbecue-cooked lamb steaks with red pepper salsa

DELICIOUS, JUICY STEAKS are rich in B vitamins, zinc and iron. Lamb steaks cut across the leg are a healthy option as they are relatively lean.

3 Cook the marinated steaks over a hot barbecue or under a pre-heated grill (broiler), if you prefer. Cook for 2–5 minutes on each side, depending on how well done you want the meat.

4 While the lamb steaks are cooking, quickly prepare the salsa. Place the roasted red peppers, chopped garlic, chives and remaining olive oil in a small bowl and stir well to combine.

5 When the lamb steaks are cooked, serve them immediately with the salsa, either spooned on to the plate or served separately. Garnish the steaks with lettuce and sprigs of flat leaf parsley.

Serves 6

6 lamb steaks
about 15g/½oz fresh rosemary leaves
3 garlic cloves, 2 sliced and
   1 finely chopped
90ml/6 tbsp olive oil
200g/7oz red (bell) peppers, roasted,
   peeled, seeded and chopped
15ml/1 tbsp chopped chives
salt and ground black pepper
lettuce and fresh flat leaf parsley, to garnish

1 Place the lamb steaks in a shallow dish in a single layer and season with salt and ground black pepper. Sprinkle the rosemary leaves and slices of garlic over the meat, then drizzle over 60ml/4 tbsp of the olive oil.

2 Cover the dish with clear film (plastic wrap) and place in the refrigerator to marinate until ready to cook. The steaks can be left to marinate for up to 24 hours.

NUTRITION NOTES

Per portion:

Energy	275kcal/1149kJ
Protein	30.5g
Fat	16.2g
saturated fat	6.3g
Carbohydrate	1.7g
Fibre	0.4g
Calcium	20mg

lamb pot-roast with tomatoes, green beans and onions

THIS SLOW-BRAISED DISH of lamb and tomatoes, spiced with cinnamon and stewed with green beans, has a Greek influence. It is also good made with courgettes instead of beans.

Serves 8

1kg/2¼lb lamb on the bone
8 garlic cloves, chopped
2.5–5ml/½–1 tsp ground cumin
45ml/3 tbsp olive oil
juice of 1 lemon
2 onions, thinly sliced
about 500ml/17fl oz/2¼ cups lamb, beef
    or vegetable stock
75–90ml/5–6 tbsp tomato purée (paste)
1 cinnamon stick
2–3 large pinches of ground allspice or
    ground cloves
15–30ml/1–2 tbsp sugar
400g/14oz/scant 3 cups runner (green)
    beans, cut into 2.5cm/1in lengths
salt and ground black pepper
chopped fresh parsley, to garnish

1 Preheat the oven to 160°C/325°F/Gas 3. Coat the joint of lamb with the chopped garlic, cumin, olive oil, lemon juice, salt and pepper.

2 Heat a flameproof casserole. Sear the lamb on all sides. Add the onions and pour the stock over the meat to cover. Stir in the tomato purée, spices and sugar. Cover and cook in the oven for 2–3 hours.

3 Remove the casserole from the oven and pour the stock into a pan. Move the onions to the side of the dish and return to the oven, uncovered, for 20 minutes.

NUTRITION NOTES

Per portion:	
Energy	242kcal/1018kJ
Protein	24.8g
Fat	12.0g
saturated fat	3.8g
Carbohydrate	9.2g
Fibre	1.9g
Calcium	41mg

4 Meanwhile, add the beans to the stock and cook until tender. Slice the meat and serve with the pan juices, onions and beans. Garnish with parsley.

italian sausages with cannellini beans

VARIATIONS ON THE THEME of sausage and bean stew are found in most countries as an inexpensive, easy and hearty peasant dish. This is a meal in itself, but you could serve it with fresh, steamed green vegetables, such as broccoli or spinach.

Serves 4

15ml/1 tbsp sunflower oil
12 Italian spicy fresh pork sausages
50g/2oz pancetta, chopped
2 onions, quartered
2 garlic cloves, crushed
1 red (bell) pepper, halved, seeded and sliced
2 x 400g/14oz cans chopped tomatoes
400g/14oz can cannellini beans, drained and rinsed
salt and ground black pepper

NUTRITION NOTES

Per portion:	
Energy	551kcal/2298kJ
Protein	22.1g
Fat	38.1g
saturated fat	13.0g
Carbohydrate	30.8g
Fibre	7.0g
Calcium	108mg

1 Pour the oil into a flameproof casserole and add the sausages and pancetta. Cook over a medium heat for about 10 minutes, turning the sausages and pancetta occasionally, or until the pancetta is crispy and the sausages are golden brown. Be careful to moderate the heat – if it is too fierce the sausages will burst.

2 When cooked, use a slotted spoon to remove the sausages and pancetta from the casserole. Set aside.

3 Discard any excess fat and add the onions and crushed garlic. Cook for about 5 minutes over a high heat, stirring frequently. Add the sliced pepper and cook for 2–3 minutes.

4 Return the sausages and pancetta to the casserole and stir in the chopped tomatoes and cannellini beans. Cover and simmer for about 20 minutes, stirring occasionally. Season to taste.

VARIATION

Try using beef or lamb sausages in place of pork, substitute chopped leeks for the onions and add a finely chopped and seeded red chilli along with the pepper.

curried pork with pickled garlic

THIS VERY RICH CURRY is best accompanied by a light vegetable dish. It could serve four if served with a vegetable curry. Most Asian stores sell pickled garlic and it is well worth investing in a jar as the taste is sweet and delicious.

2 Heat the oil in a wok or large, heavy frying pan and cook the garlic over a low to medium heat until golden brown. Do not let it burn, otherwise it will have an unpleasant bitter taste. Add the curry paste and stir it in well.

3 Add the coconut cream and stir until the liquid begins to reduce and thicken. Stir in the pork slices and cook for about 2 minutes more, until the pork is cooked through.

4 Add the chopped ginger, vegetable or chicken stock, fish sauce, sugar and ground turmeric, stirring constantly, then add the lemon juice and pickled garlic. Spoon into individual serving bowls, garnish with thin strips of lemon and lime rind, and serve immediately.

Serves 2

130g/4½oz lean pork steaks
30ml/2 tbsp vegetable oil
1 garlic clove, crushed
15ml/1 tbsp Thai red curry paste
130ml/4½fl oz/generous ½ cup coconut cream
2.5cm/1in piece fresh root ginger, finely chopped
30ml/2 tbsp vegetable or chicken stock
30ml/2 tbsp Thai fish sauce (nam pla)
5ml/1 tsp granulated sugar
2.5ml/½ tsp ground turmeric
10ml/2 tsp lemon juice
4 pickled garlic cloves, finely chopped
strips of lemon and lime rind, to garnish

1 Place the pork steaks in the freezer for 30–40 minutes, until firm, then, using a sharp knife, cut the meat into fine slivers, trimming off any excess fat.

NUTRITION NOTES

Per portion:

Energy	544kcal/2268kJ
Protein	20.1g
Fat	45g
saturated fat	23g
Carbohydrate	19g
Fibre	0.5g
Calcium	15mg

stir-fried pork with dried shrimp

DRIED SHRIMP ARE A COMMON ingredient in many Asian cuisines. Their flavour is strong but, rather than overpowering a dish, they simply give a delicious savoury taste.

2 Heat the oil in a wok or frying pan and cook the garlic until golden brown, but be careful not to let it burn. Add the pork and stir-fry for about 4 minutes, until just cooked through.

Serves 4

250g/9oz pork fillet (tenderloin)
30ml/2 tbsp vegetable oil
2 garlic cloves, finely chopped
45ml/3 tbsp dried shrimp
10ml/2 tsp dried shrimp paste or 5mm/
   ¼in piece from block of shrimp paste
30ml/2 tbsp soy sauce
juice of 1 lime
15ml/1 tbsp palm sugar or light
   muscovado (brown) sugar
1 small fresh red or green chilli, seeded
   and finely chopped
4 pak choi (bok choy) or 450g/1lb spring
   greens (collards), shredded

1 Place the pork in the freezer for about 30 minutes, until firm. Remove from the freezer, then, using a sharp knife, cut it into thin slices.

NUTRITION NOTES

Per portion:

Energy	227kcal/949kJ
Protein	22.0g
Fat	12.6g
saturated fat	2.7g
Carbohydrate	6.6g
Fibre	3.7g
Calcium	241mg

3 Add the dried shrimp, then stir in the shrimp paste with the soy sauce, lime juice and sugar. Add the chopped chilli and shredded pak choi or spring greens and toss over the heat until the vegetables are just beginning to wilt.

4 Transfer the stir-fry to warm individual bowls and serve immediately.

COOK'S TIP
When using a wok, the oil should be very hot before you start cooking.

pork and pineapple coconut curry

THE HEAT OF THIS CURRY balances out its sweetness to make a smooth and fragrant dish. It takes very little time to cook, so is ideal for a quick supper or a midweek family meal.

Serves 4

400ml/14fl oz can or carton
  coconut milk
10ml/2 tsp Thai red curry paste
400g/14oz pork loin steaks, trimmed
  and thinly sliced
15ml/1 tbsp Thai fish sauce (*nam pla*)
5ml/1 tsp palm sugar or light muscovado
  (brown) sugar
15ml/1 tbsp tamarind juice, made by
  mixing tamarind paste with warm water
2 kaffir lime leaves, torn
½ medium pineapple, peeled and chopped
1 fresh red chilli, seeded and sliced

1 Pour the coconut milk into a bowl and let it settle, so that the cream rises to the surface. Scoop the cream into a measuring jug (cup). You should have about 250ml/8fl oz/1 cup. If necessary, add a little of the coconut milk.

2 Pour the coconut cream into a large pan and bring it to the boil.

3 Reduce the heat and simmer the coconut cream for about 10 minutes, until the cream separates, stirring frequently to prevent it from sticking to the base of the pan and scorching. Add the red curry paste and stir until well mixed. Cook, stirring occasionally, for about 4 minutes, until the paste is fragrant.

4 Add the sliced pork and stir in the fish sauce, sugar and tamarind juice. Cook, stirring constantly, for 1–2 minutes, until the sugar has dissolved and the pork is no longer pink.

5 Add the remaining coconut milk and the lime leaves. Bring to the boil, then stir in the pineapple. Reduce the heat and simmer for 3 minutes, or until the pork is cooked. Sprinkle over the chilli and serve.

NUTRITION NOTES

Per portion:	
Energy	223kcal/936kJ
Protein	22.0g
Fat	8.2g
saturated fat	3.0g
Carbohydrate	16.0g
Fibre	1.0g
Calcium	55mg

red chicken curry with bamboo shoots

BAMBOO SHOOTS have a lovely crunchy texture. It is quite acceptable to use canned shoots, as fresh bamboo is not readily available in the West. Canned whole bamboo shoots are crisper and of better quality than sliced shoots.

Serves 6

1 litre/1¾ pints/4 cups coconut milk
450g/1lb skinless chicken breast
  portions, diced
30ml/2 tbsp Thai fish sauce
15ml/1 tbsp granulated sugar
1–2 drained canned bamboo shoots,
  total weight about 225g/8oz, rinsed
  and sliced
5 kaffir lime leaves, torn
salt and ground black pepper
sliced fresh red chillies and kaffir lime
  leaves, to garnish

For the red curry paste
5ml/1 tsp coriander seeds
2.5ml/½ tsp cumin seeds
12–15 fresh red chillies, seeded and
  coarsely chopped
4 shallots, thinly sliced
2 garlic cloves, chopped
15ml/1 tbsp chopped fresh galangal
2 lemon grass stalks, chopped
3 kaffir lime leaves, chopped
4 fresh coriander (cilantro) roots
10 black peppercorns
good pinch of ground cinnamon
5ml/1 tsp ground turmeric
2.5ml/½ tsp shrimp paste
5ml/1 tsp salt
30ml/2 tbsp vegetable oil

NUTRITION NOTES

Per portion:

Energy	350kcal/1473kJ
Protein	28.9g
Fat	14.0g
saturated fat	2.4g
Carbohydrate	25.8g
Fibre	0.5g
Calcium	151mg

1 Make the curry paste. Dry-fry the coriander seeds and cumin seeds for 1–2 minutes, then put in a mortar or food processor with all the remaining ingredients except the vegetable oil. Pound with a pestle or process to a smooth paste.

2 Add the vegetable oil, a little at a time, mixing or processing well after each addition. Transfer to a screw-top jar, put on the lid and store in the refrigerator until ready to use.

3 Pour half of the coconut milk into a large, heavy pan. Bring to the boil over a medium heat and simmer gently until the coconut milk has separated. Stir the milk constantly with a wooden spatula to prevent it from sticking to the base of the pan and scorching.

4 Stir in 30ml/2 tbsp of the red curry paste and cook the mixture, stirring constantly, for 2–3 minutes, until the curry paste is thoroughly incorporated. The remaining red curry paste can be stored in the closed jar in the refrigerator for up to 3 months.

5 Add the diced chicken, fish sauce and sugar to the pan. Stir well, then lower the heat and cook gently for 5–6 minutes, stirring until the chicken changes colour and is cooked through. Take care that the curry does not stick to the base of the pan.

6 Pour the remaining coconut milk into the pan, then add the sliced bamboo shoots and torn lime leaves. Bring back to the boil over a medium heat, stirring constantly to prevent the mixture from sticking to the pan, then taste and add salt and pepper if necessary.

7 To serve, spoon the curry into a warmed serving dish and garnish with the sliced chillies and lime leaves.

VARIATION

Instead of bamboo shoots, try using straw mushrooms, available in cans from Asian stores and large supermarkets.

devilled chicken

GRILLING IS A VERY HEALTHY way of cooking meat, and these spicy chicken skewers are a good source of protein. Serve them with a crisp leaf salad for a nutritious main meal.

Serves 4

60ml/4 tbsp olive oil
finely grated rind and juice of 1 lemon
2 garlic cloves, finely chopped
10ml/2 tsp finely chopped or crumbled
  dried red chillies
12 skinless, boneless chicken thighs, each
  cut into 3 or 4 pieces
salt and ground black pepper
flat leaf parsley leaves, to garnish
lemon wedges, to serve

COOK'S TIP

These skewers are great for barbecues. Cook for about 8 minutes, until the chicken is done, turning frequently.

1 In a shallow dish, combine the oil, lemon rind and juice, garlic, dried chillies and seasoning. Add the chicken pieces and turn to coat. Cover and place in the refrigerator for at least 4 hours, or overnight.

2 When ready to cook, thread the chicken on to eight oiled skewers and cook under a pre-heated grill (broiler) for 6–8 minutes, turning frequently. Garnish with parsley and serve with lemon wedges.

NUTRITION NOTES

Per portion:	
Energy	301kcal/1258kJ
Protein	18.7g
Fat	25.2g
saturated fat	5.5g
Carbohydrate	0g
Fibre	0g
Calcium	24mg

chicken with tarragon cream

THE ANISEED-LIKE FLAVOUR of tarragon has a particular affinity with chicken, especially in creamy sauces such as the one in this French bistro-style dish. Serve with seasonal vegetables.

NUTRITION NOTES

Per portion:
Energy	580kcal/2406kJ
Protein	26.4g
Fat	49.0g
saturated fat	24.4g
Carbohydrate	2.5g
Fibre	0.9g
Calcium	58mg

Serves 4

30ml/2 tbsp light olive oil
4 chicken supremes, each weighing
　about 250g/9oz
3 shallots, finely chopped
2 garlic cloves, finely chopped
115g/4oz/1½ cups wild mushrooms (such
　as chanterelles or ceps) or shiitake
　mushrooms, halved
150ml/¼ pint/⅔ cup dry white wine
300ml/½ pint/1¼ cups double (heavy) cream
15g/½oz mixed fresh tarragon and flat
　leaf parsley, chopped
salt and ground black pepper
sprigs of fresh tarragon and flat leaf
　parsley, to garnish

1 Heat the olive oil in a frying pan and add the chicken, skin-side down. Cook for 10 minutes, turning the chicken twice, until it is a golden brown colour.

2 Reduce the heat and gently cook the chicken pieces for 10 minutes more, turning occasionally. Use a draining spoon to remove the chicken from the pan and set aside.

3 Add the shallots and garlic to the pan and cook gently, stirring, until the shallots are softened but not browned. Increase the heat, add the mushrooms and stir-fry for 2 minutes, or until the mushrooms just start to colour.

4 Replace the chicken, nestling the pieces down into the other ingredients, and then pour in the white wine. Simmer for about 5–10 minutes, or until most of the wine has evaporated.

5 Add the cream and gently move the ingredients around in the pan to mix in the cream. Simmer for 10 minutes, or until the sauce has thickened. Stir the chopped herbs into the sauce with seasoning to taste. Arrange the chicken on warm plates and spoon the sauce over. Garnish with sprigs of tarragon and flat leaf parsley.

VARIATION
Chicken breast portions could be used in place of the chicken supremes.

chicken with serrano ham

LEAN CHICKEN IS AN IDEAL CHOICE for anyone following a low-carbohydrate diet. For a well-balanced meal serve with a large mixed green leaf and herb salad.

Serves 4
4 skinless, boneless chicken breast portions
4 slices Serrano ham
40g/1½oz/3 tbsp butter
30ml/2 tbsp chopped capers
30ml/2 tbsp fresh thyme leaves
1 large lemon, cut lengthways into 8 slices
a few small fresh thyme sprigs
salt and ground black pepper

COOK'S TIP
This dish is just as good with other thinly sliced cured ham, such as prosciutto, in place of the Serrano ham.

1 Preheat the oven to 200°C/400°F/ Gas 6. Wrap each chicken breast portion loosely in clear film (plastic wrap) and beat with a rolling pin until flattened. Unwrap the chicken breast portions and arrange in a single layer in a large, shallow ovenproof dish. Top each piece of chicken with a slice of Serrano ham.

2 In a bowl, beat the butter with the capers, thyme and seasoning. Divide the butter into quarters and shape neat portions, then place on each ham-topped chicken breast portion. Arrange two lemon slices on the butter and sprinkle with thyme sprigs. Bake for 25 minutes, or until the chicken is cooked through.

3 Transfer the chicken portions to a warmed serving platter or four plates and spoon the piquant, buttery juices over the top. Serve immediately, removing the lemon slices first, if you prefer.

NUTRITION NOTES

Per portion:	
Energy	352kcal/1471kJ
Protein	52.7g
Fat	15.7g
saturated fat	8.5g
Carbohydrate	0g
Fibre	0g
Calcium	11mg

griddled chicken with tomato salsa

THIS AROMATIC DISH is a great way to enjoy the flavour, colour and health benefits of fresh ingredients. For the best result, marinate the chicken overnight.

Serves 4

4 skinless, boneless chicken breast portions, about 175g/6oz each
30ml/2 tbsp fresh lemon juice
30ml/2 tbsp olive oil
10ml/2 tsp ground cumin
10ml/2 tsp dried oregano
15ml/1 tbsp coarsely ground black pepper

For the salsa

1 green chilli
450g/1lb plum tomatoes, seeded and chopped
3 spring onions (scallions), chopped
15ml/1 tbsp chopped fresh parsley
30ml/2 tbsp chopped fresh coriander (cilantro)
30ml/2 tbsp fresh lemon juice
45ml/3 tbsp olive oil

4 Chop the chilli very finely and place in a bowl. Add the seeded and chopped tomatoes, the chopped spring onions, chopped fresh parsley and coriander, lemon juice and olive oil and mix well. Set aside until ready to serve.

NUTRITION NOTES

Per portion:

Energy	338kcal/1420kJ
Protein	25.9g
Fat	23.9g
saturated fat	4.4g
Carbohydrate	4.8g
Fibre	2.2g
Calcium	50mg

5 Remove the chicken from the marinade. Heat a ridged griddle pan. Add the chicken fillets and cook on one side until browned, for about 3 minutes. Turn over and cook for a further 4 minutes. Serve with the tomato salsa.

1 With a meat mallet, pound the chicken between two sheets of clear film (plastic wrap) until thin.

2 In a shallow dish, combine the lemon juice, oil, cumin, oregano and pepper. Add the chicken, cover and leave to marinate for at least 2 hours.

3 To make the salsa, char the chilli skin over a gas flame or under the grill (broiler). Leave to cool, then carefully rub off the charred skin.

stir-fried chicken with basil and chilli

THIS QUICK AND EASY chicken dish is alive with the flavours of Thai cuisine. Thai basil, which is sometimes known as holy basil, has a unique, pungent flavour that is both spicy and sharp. Deep-frying the leaves adds another dimension to this dish.

Serves 6

45ml/3 tbsp vegetable oil

4 garlic cloves, thinly sliced

2–4 fresh red chillies, seeded and finely chopped

450g/1lb skinless, boneless chicken breast portions, cut into bitesize pieces

45ml/3 tbsp Thai fish sauce

10ml/2 tsp dark soy sauce

5ml/1 tsp granulated sugar

10–12 fresh Thai basil leaves

2 fresh red chillies, seeded and finely chopped, and about 20 deep-fried Thai basil leaves, to garnish

2 Add the pieces of chicken to the wok or pan, in batches if necessary, and stir-fry until the chicken changes colour.

3 Stir in the fish sauce, soy sauce and sugar. Continue to stir-fry the mixture for 3–4 minutes, or until the chicken is fully cooked and golden brown.

4 Stir in the fresh Thai basil leaves. Spoon the mixture on to a warm platter, or into individual dishes. Garnish with the chopped chillies and deep-fried Thai basil and serve immediately.

COOK'S TIP

To deep-fry Thai basil leaves, first make sure that the leaves are completely dry. Heat vegetable or groundnut (peanut) oil in a wok or deep-fryer to 190°C/ 375°F or until a cube of bread, added to the oil, browns in about 45 seconds. Add the leaves and deep-fry them briefly until they are crisp and translucent – this will take only about 30–40 seconds. Lift out the leaves using a slotted spoon and leave them to drain on kitchen paper before using.

1 Heat the oil in a wok or frying pan. Add the garlic and chillies and stir-fry over a medium heat for 1–2 minutes until the garlic is golden. Take care not to let the garlic burn, otherwise it will taste bitter.

NUTRITION NOTES

Per portion:

Energy	271kcal/1130kJ
Protein	25.1g
Fat	16.3g
saturated fat	2.8g
Carbohydrate	5.0g
Fibre	0.2g
Calcium	25mg

duck and sesame stir-fry

THIS RECIPE IS TRADITIONALLY intended for game birds, as farmed duck would usually have too much fat. Use wild duck if you can get it, or even partridge, pheasant or pigeon. If you do use farmed duck, you should remove the skin and fat layer.

Serves 4

250g/9oz wild duck breast portions
15ml/1 tbsp sesame oil
15ml/1 tbsp vegetable oil
4 garlic cloves, finely sliced
2.5ml/½ tsp dried chilli flakes
15ml/1 tbsp Thai fish sauce
15ml/1 tbsp light soy sauce
120ml/4fl oz/½ cup water
1 head broccoli, cut into small florets
coriander (cilantro) and 15ml/1 tbsp
    toasted sesame seeds, to garnish

VARIATIONS
Pak choi (bok choy) or Chinese flowering cabbage can be used instead of broccoli.

1 Cut the duck into bitesize pieces. Heat the oils in a wok or large, heavy frying pan and stir-fry the garlic over a medium heat until it is golden brown – do not let it burn. Add the duck pieces to the pan and stir-fry for a further 2 minutes, until the meat begins to brown.

2 Stir in the chilli flakes, fish sauce, soy sauce and water. Add the broccoli and continue to stir-fry for about 2 minutes, until the duck is just cooked through.

3 Serve on warmed plates, garnished with coriander and sesame seeds.

NUTRITION NOTES

Per portion:	
Energy	173kcal/721kJ
Protein	15.0g
Fat	10.9g
saturated fat	1.2g
Carbohydrate	3.2g
Fibre	1.8g
Calcium	57mg

duck with plum sauce

THIS IS AN UPDATED VERSION of an old English dish, which was traditionally served in the late summer and early autumn when Victoria plums are beautifully ripe.

NUTRITION NOTES

Per portion:

Energy	190kcal/804kJ
Protein	25.1g
Fat	5.8g
saturated fat	1.6g
Carbohydrate	10.3g
Fibre	2.4g
Calcium	41mg

3 Pour away all but 30ml/2 tbsp of the duck fat, then stir-fry the onion for about 5 minutes, or until softened. Add the plums and cook for a further 5 minutes, stirring frequently. Add the redcurrant jelly and mix well.

4 Replace the duck portions and simmer gently for a further 5 minutes, or until the duck is thoroughly reheated. Season to taste with salt and ground black pepper before serving.

Serves 4

4 duck quarters
1 large red onion, finely chopped
500g/1¼lb ripe plums, stoned (pitted) and quartered
30ml/2 tbsp redcurrant jelly
salt and ground black pepper

1 Prick the duck skin all over to release the fat during cooking, then place the portions in a frying pan, skinside down.

2 Cook the duck pieces over a medium heat for 10 minutes on each side, or until golden brown and cooked right through. Remove the duck from the frying pan using a draining spoon, and keep warm.

COOK'S TIP

The plums used in this dish must be very ripe, otherwise the mixture will be dry and the sauce extremely tart.

VARIATIONS

If you cannot find a red onion, use a white onion instead. Fine-cut orange marmalade makes a delicious tangy alternative to the redcurrant jelly.

buffalo steaks with horseradish cream

THE FLAVOUR OF BUFFALO is very like that of beef so, not surprisingly, it goes extremely well with horseradish cream – one of the classic beef accompaniments.

Serves 4

4 buffalo steaks, each weighing
   about 150g/5oz
25g/1oz/2 tbsp butter
15ml/1 tbsp sunflower oil
salt and ground black pepper
a few whole chives, to garnish
mixed salad leaves, to serve

For the horseradish cream

15ml/1 tbsp freshly grated horseradish
   (or to taste)
115g/4oz/½ cup crème fraîche
15ml/1 tbsp fresh chopped chives

1 Season the steaks on both sides with salt and plenty of ground black pepper. Heat the butter and oil in a large frying pan until sizzling. Add the steaks and cook for 3–4 minutes on each side, turning once.

2 Meanwhile, mix the horseradish, crème fraîche and chopped chives in a small bowl. Serve the steaks with a dollop of horseradish cream, garnished with chives and accompanied by a mixed leaf salad.

NUTRITION NOTES

Per portion:	
Energy	340kcal/1412kJ
Protein	31.5g
Fat	22.4g
saturated fat	12.0g
Carbohydrate	1.2g
Fibre	0.3g
Calcium	24mg

fish
and shellfish

FISH AND SHELLFISH CONTAIN essential vitamins and minerals, which are important in any diet. A huge variety of seafood is now available in supermarkets, and it is incredibly easy to cook. Among the healthiest and tastiest ways to prepare fish are to steam it or wrap a fillet in paper and bake in the oven – none of the nutrients will be lost if the fish is cooked like this. Prepare steamed lettuce-wrapped sole for a quick midweek meal, impress your guests with a baked whole salmon with watercress sauce or treat yourself to halibut with sauce vierge.

salmon with leeks and peppers

ATTRACTIVE PAPER PARCELS OF FISH are as healthy as they are tasty. The fish and vegetables cook in their own juices, allowing them to retain all their valuable nutrients.

4 When the vegetable mixture is cool, divide it equally among the parchment or foil and top with a portion of salmon.

5 Drizzle each portion of fish with a little sesame oil and sprinkle with the remaining chives and the chopped fennel fronds. Season with a little more salt and ground black pepper.

6 Fold the baking parchment or foil over to enclose the fish, rolling and twisting the edges together to seal the parcels.

7 Place the parcels on a baking sheet and bake for 15–20 minutes, or until the parcels are puffed up and, if made with parchment, lightly browned. Carefully transfer the parcels to six warmed plates and serve immediately, still wrapped in baking parchment or foil.

Serves 6

25ml/1½ tbsp groundnut (peanut) oil
2 yellow (bell) peppers, seeded and thinly sliced
4cm/1½in fresh root ginger, peeled and finely shredded
1 large fennel bulb, thinly sliced, fronds chopped and reserved
1 fresh green chilli, seeded and finely shredded
2 large leeks, cut into 10cm/4in lengths and shredded lengthways
30ml/2 tbsp chopped fresh chives
10ml/2 tsp light soy sauce
6 portions salmon fillet, each weighing about 150–175g/5–6oz, skinned
10ml/2 tsp toasted sesame oil
salt and ground black pepper

1 Heat the oil in a large non-stick frying pan. Add the yellow peppers, ginger and fennel bulb and cook, stirring occasionally, for 5–6 minutes, until they are softened, but not browned.

2 Add the fresh green chilli and leeks to the pan and cook, stirring occasionally, for about 3 minutes. Stir in half the chopped chives and the soy sauce and season to taste with a little salt and freshly ground black pepper. Set the vegetable mixture aside to cool slightly.

3 Meanwhile, preheat the oven to 190°C/375°F/Gas 5. Cut six 35cm/14in rounds of baking parchment or foil and set aside.

NUTRITION NOTES

Per portion:	
Energy	325kcal/1358kJ
Protein	31.6g
Fat	20.5g
saturated fat	3.4g
Carbohydrate	4.0g
Fibre	2.1g
Calcium	48mg

steamed lettuce-wrapped sole

COOKING FOOD IN STEAM is extremely healthy as it helps to retain the nutrients that can be lost by other cooking methods. It also gives wonderfully succulent results.

Serves 4

2 large sole fillets, skinned
15ml/1 tbsp sesame seeds
15ml/1 tbsp sunflower or groundnut
   (peanut) oil
2.5cm/1in piece fresh root ginger,
   peeled and grated
3 garlic cloves, finely chopped
15ml/1 tbsp soy sauce or Thai fish sauce
juice of 1 lemon
2 spring onions (scallions), thinly sliced
8 large soft lettuce leaves
12 large live mussels, scrubbed
   and bearded
salt and ground black pepper
sesame oil, for drizzling (optional)

1 Cut the sole fillets in half lengthways. Season with salt and ground black pepper, then set aside.

2 Heat a dry frying pan until hot. Toast the sesame seeds lightly, until golden brown, then set aside.

3 Heat the sunflower or groundnut oil in the frying pan. Add the ginger and garlic and cook, stirring, until lightly coloured but not browned; stir in the soy sauce or Thai fish sauce, lemon juice and spring onions. Remove the pan from the heat and stir in the toasted sesame seeds.

4 Lay the pieces of fish on baking parchment, skinned side up; spread each evenly with the ginger mixture. Roll up each piece, starting at the tail end and place the rolls on a baking sheet.

5 Bring a pan of water, over which the steamer will fit, to the boil. Plunge the lettuce leaves into the boiling water and immediately lift them out. Lay them out flat on kitchen paper and pat dry.

6 Tightly wrap each sole parcel in two lettuce leaves, making sure they are very secure. Arrange the fish parcels in the steamer basket, cover and steam over simmering water for 8 minutes.

7 Add the mussels to the steamer and steam for 2–4 minutes, until they open. Discard any that remain closed. Put the parcels on four plates and garnish with the mussels. Serve drizzled with oil, if you like.

NUTRITION NOTES

Per portion:

Energy	136kcal/568kJ
Protein	17.4g
Fat	7.1g
saturated fat	1.0g
Carbohydrate	0.6g
Fibre	0.3g
Calcium	47mg

roasted cod with fresh tomato sauce

REALLY FRESH COD FILLETS have a sweet, delicate flavour and pure white flaky flesh. Served with an aromatic fresh tomato sauce, they make a delicious and nutritious meal.

Serves 4
350g/12oz ripe plum tomatoes
75ml/5 tbsp olive oil
2.5ml/½ tsp sugar
2 strips of pared orange rind
1 fresh thyme sprig
6 fresh basil leaves
900g/2lb fresh cod fillet, skin on
salt and ground black pepper
steamed green beans, to serve

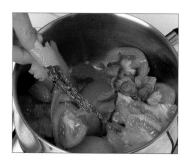

NUTRITION NOTES

Per portion:

Energy	354kcal/1492kJ
Protein	40.0g
Fat	20.3g
saturated fat	2.9g
Carbohydrate	3.0g
Fibre	1.3g
Calcium	48mg

1 Preheat the oven to 230°C/450°F/ Gas 8. Using a small, sharp knife, roughly chop the plum tomatoes, leaving their skins on, and set aside.

2 Heat 15ml/1 tbsp of the olive oil in a heavy pan, add the tomatoes, sugar, orange rind, thyme and basil, and simmer for 5 minutes, until the tomatoes are soft.

3 Press the tomato mixture through a fine sieve (strainer), discarding the solids that remain in the sieve. Pour into a small pan and heat gently.

4 Scale the cod fillet and cut on the diagonal into 4 pieces. Season well.

5 Heat the remaining oil in a heavy frying pan and fry the cod, skin side down, until the skin is crisp. Place the fish on a greased baking sheet, skin side up, and roast in the oven for 8–10 minutes, until cooked through. Serve the fish on top of the steamed green beans with the fresh tomato sauce.

VARIATIONS
Try haddock, pollock, coley or any other firm white fish instead of the cod.

grilled halibut with sauce vierge

TOMATOES, CAPERS, ANCHOVIES, herbs and fresh lemon make a vibrant sauce that is perfect for halibut, but it is so versatile that it will suit any thick white fish fillets.

Serves 4
105ml/7 tbsp olive oil
2.5ml/½ tsp fennel seeds
2.5ml/½ tsp celery seeds
5ml/1 tsp mixed peppercorns
5ml/1 tsp fresh thyme leaves, chopped
5ml/1 tsp fresh rosemary leaves, chopped
5ml/1 tsp fresh oregano or marjoram
   leaves, chopped
675–800g/1½–1¾lb middle cut of
   halibut, about 3cm/1¼in thick, cut
   into four pieces
coarse sea salt
shredded lettuce and lemon wedges,
   to serve

For the sauce
2 tomatoes
105ml/7 tbsp extra virgin olive oil
juice of 1 lemon
1 garlic clove, finely chopped
5ml/1 tsp small capers
2 drained canned anchovy fillets, chopped
5ml/1 tsp chopped fresh chives
15ml/1 tbsp shredded fresh
   basil leaves
15ml/1 tbsp chopped fresh chervil

1 For the sauce, plunge the tomatoes into boiling water for about 30 seconds or until the skins split, then refresh them in cold water. Peel off the skins, remove the seeds with a teaspoon and finely dice the flesh. Set aside.

2 Heat a ridged griddle or preheat the grill (broiler) to high. Brush the griddle or grill pan with a little of the olive oil.

VARIATIONS
Try turbot, brill or John Dory, or even humbler fish, such as cod or haddock, with this tangy sauce.

3 Meanwhile, mix the fennel and celery seeds with the peppercorns in a mortar. Crush with a pestle, and then stir in sea salt to taste. Spoon the mixture into a large, flat dish and stir in the herbs and the remaining olive oil.

NUTRITION NOTES

Per portion:	
Energy	653kcal/2742kJ
Protein	32.5g
Fat	57.5g
saturated fat	8.0g
Carbohydrate	1.3g
Fibre	0.4g
Calcium	47mg

4 Add the halibut pieces to the olive oil and herb mixture, turning them to coat thoroughly, then arrange them on the oiled griddle or grill pan with the dark skin uppermost. Cook for approximately 7 minutes, turning once, or until the fish is completely cooked through and the skin is nicely browned.

5 Combine all the sauce ingredients, except for the fresh herbs, in a pan and heat gently until warm but not hot. Gradually stir in the chives, basil leaves and fresh chervil.

6 Place the halibut on four plates and spoon the sauce over the fish. Serve with the lettuce and lemon wedges.

grilled sea bass with fennel

THIS IS AN IMPRESSIVE DISH that is perfect for entertaining. Guests will never guess that this opulent dish is part of a successful healthy-eating, weight-loss diet.

Serves 8

1 sea bass, weighing 1.8–2kg/4–4½lb
60ml/4 tbsp olive oil
10–15ml/2–3 tsp fennel seeds
2 large fennel bulbs, trimmed and thinly
  sliced (reserve any fronds)
60ml/4 tbsp Pernod
salt and ground black pepper

NUTRITION NOTES

Per portion:

Energy	308kcal/1287kJ
Protein	37.1g
Fat	15.3g
saturated fat	2.9g
Carbohydrate	3.2g
Fibre	0.9g
Calcium	44mg

3 Preheat the grill (broiler). Put the slices of fennel in a flameproof dish or on the grill rack and brush with a little olive oil. Cook for 4 minutes on each side until just tender. Transfer the fennel to a serving plate and set aside while you grill (broil) the fish.

4 Place the fish on the grill rack and position about 10–14cm/4–5½in away from the heat. Grill for 12 minutes on each side, brushing with oil occasionally during cooking.

1 With a sharp knife, make 3–4 deep cuts in both sides of the fish. Brush the fish with olive oil and season with salt and plenty of ground black pepper.

5 Transfer the fish to the serving platter, placing it on top of the grilled fennel. Sprinkle over any reserved fennel fronds.

2 Sprinkle the fennel seeds in the cavity and into the cuts on both sides of the fish. Set aside while you cook the fennel.

6 Heat the Pernod in a small pan, ignite it and pour it, flaming, over the fish. Serve immediately.

chinese-style steamed trout

TROUT IS RICH IN ESSENTIAL fatty acids, which are vital for good health. Serve this dish with a low-carbohydrate vegetable dish, such as stir-fried spring greens, for a satisfying meal.

Serves 6

2 trout, each weighing about
   675–800g/1½–1¾lb
25ml/1½ tbsp salted black beans
2.5ml/½ tsp sugar
30ml/2 tbsp finely shredded fresh
   root ginger
4 garlic cloves, thinly sliced
30ml/2 tbsp Chinese rice wine or
   dry sherry
30ml/2 tbsp light soy sauce
4–6 spring onions (scallions), finely
   shredded or sliced diagonally
45ml/3 tbsp groundnut (peanut) oil
10ml/2 tsp sesame oil

1 Wash the trout inside and out under cold running water, then pat the fish dry on a sheet of kitchen paper. Using a sharp knife, carefully slash 3–4 deep crosses on each side of each fish.

2 Place half the black beans and the sugar in a small bowl and mash together with the back of a fork. Stir in the remaining whole beans.

3 Place a little ginger and garlic inside the cavity of each fish, then lay them on a plate or dish that will fit inside a large steamer. Rub the bean mixture into the fish, working it into the slashes, then sprinkle the remaining ginger and garlic over the top. Cover with clear film (plastic wrap) and place the fish in the refrigerator for at least 30 minutes.

4 Remove the fish from the refrigerator and place the steamer over a pan of boiling water. Sprinkle the rice wine or sherry and half the soy sauce over the fish and place the plate of fish inside the steamer. Steam for 15–20 minutes, or until the fish is just cooked and the flesh flakes easily when tested with a fork.

5 Using a fish slice (metal spatula), carefully lift the fish on to a warmed serving dish. Sprinkle the fish with the remaining soy sauce and then sprinkle with the shredded or sliced spring onions.

6 In a small pan, heat the groundnut oil until very hot and smoking, then trickle it over the spring onions and fish. Lightly sprinkle the sesame oil over the fish and serve immediately.

NUTRITION NOTES	
Per portion:	
Energy	378kcal/1580kJ
Protein	52.4g
Fat	18.7g
saturated fat	3.5g
Carbohydrate	0.2g
Fibre	0.1g
Calcium	51mg

baked salmon with watercress sauce

THIS PRETTY DISH IS PERFECT for parties or buffet-style meals. Baking the salmon in foil produces a result similar to poaching fish, while decorating the fish with thin slices of cucumber conceals any flesh that may look ragged after skinning.

Serves 8

2–3kg/4½–6¾lb salmon, cleaned with head and tail left on
3–5 spring onions (scallions), thinly sliced
1 lemon, thinly sliced
1 cucumber, thinly sliced
salt and ground black pepper
fresh dill sprigs, to garnish
lemon wedges, to serve

For the watercress sauce

3 garlic cloves, chopped
200g/7oz watercress leaves, finely chopped
40g/1½oz fresh tarragon, finely chopped
300g/11oz low-fat mayonnaise
15–30ml/1–2 tbsp freshly squeezed lemon juice
100g/3½oz/scant ½ cup unsalted (sweet) butter

1 Preheat the oven to 180°C/350°F/ Gas 4. Rinse the salmon and lay it on a large piece of foil. Stuff the fish with the sliced spring onions and layer the lemon slices inside and around the fish, then sprinkle with plenty of salt and ground black pepper.

2 Loosely fold the foil around the fish and fold the edges over to seal the package. Place the foil-wrapped fish in the preheated oven and bake for 1 hour.

3 Remove the fish from the oven and leave to stand, still wrapped in the foil, for 15 minutes, then unwrap the parcel and leave the fish to cool.

4 When the fish is cool, carefully lift it on to a large plate, still covered with lemon slices. Cover the fish with clear film (plastic wrap) and chill for several hours.

5 Before serving, discard the lemon slices around the fish. Using a blunt knife to lift up the edge of the skin, carefully peel the skin away from the flesh. Try to avoid tearing the flesh, and pull out any fins at the same time.

6 Arrange the cucumber slices in overlapping rows along the length of the fish, to resemble large fish scales.

7 To make the sauce, put the garlic, watercress, tarragon, mayonnaise and lemon juice in a food processor or blender, and process to combine.

8 Melt the unsalted butter, then add to the watercress mixture a little at a time, processing until the butter has been incorporated and the sauce is thick, smooth and glossy. Pour into a bowl, cover and chill before serving. Serve the fish, garnished with fresh dill sprigs, with the sauce and plenty of lemon wedges.

NUTRITION NOTES

Per portion:	
Energy	679kcal/2821kJ
Protein	47.3g
Fat	52.0g
saturated fat	14.6g
Carbohydrate	5.3g
Fibre	1.1g
Calcium	140mg

COOK'S TIP

Do not prepare the sauce more than a few hours ahead of serving as the watercress will discolour the sauce.

hake au poivre with red pepper relish

FIRM, WHITE HAKE is ideal for this tasty dish. The red pepper relish, with hints of anchovy and garlic, complements it perfectly, without overwhelming the delicate flavour of the hake.

4 Pour the contents of the pan into a food processor or a blender and whizz to a coarse purée. Transfer to a bowl and season to taste with salt and ground black pepper. Stir in the capers, balsamic vinegar and shredded basil leaves. Keep the relish hot.

5 Heat the olive oil in a frying pan, add the hake steaks and fry them, in batches if necessary, for about 5 minutes on each side, turning them once or twice with a fish slice (metal spatula) until they are just cooked through.

6 Place the fish on individual plates and spoon a little red pepper relish on to each plate. Garnish with basil leaves and a little extra balsamic vinegar. Serve the rest of the relish separately.

Serves 4

30–45ml/2–3 tbsp mixed peppercorns
  (black, white, pink and green)
4 hake steaks, about 175g/6oz each
30ml/2 tbsp olive oil
sea salt and ground black pepper

For the relish

2 red (bell) peppers
15ml/1 tbsp olive oil
2 garlic cloves, chopped
4 ripe tomatoes, peeled, seeded
  and quartered
4 drained canned anchovy fillets,
  roughly chopped
5ml/1 tsp capers
15ml/1 tbsp balsamic vinegar, plus a little
  extra to serve
12 fresh basil leaves, shredded, plus a few
  extra to garnish

1 Put the peppercorns in a mortar and crush them coarsely with a pestle. Alternatively, put them in a plastic bag and crush them with a rolling pin.

2 Season the hake fillets with salt, then coat them on both sides with the crushed peppercorns. Set the coated fish steaks aside while you make the relish.

3 Cut the red peppers in half lengthways, remove the core and seeds from each and cut the flesh into 1cm/½in wide strips. Heat the olive oil in a wok or shallow pan with a lid. Add the peppers and cook for about 5 minutes, or until they are slightly softened. Stir in the chopped garlic, tomatoes and anchovies, then cover the pan and simmer for about 20 minutes, until the peppers are very soft.

NUTRITION NOTES	
Per portion:	
Energy	284kcal/1200kJ
Protein	32.5g
Fat	16.2g
saturated fat	2.2g
Carbohydrate	2.6g
Fibre	1.0g
Calcium	36mg

scallops with fennel and bacon

THIS IMPRESSIVE DISH IS A DELICIOUS combination of succulent scallops and crispy bacon, served on a bed of tender fennel and melting mascarpone cheese – irresistible.

Serves 2

2 small fennel bulbs
130g/4½oz/generous ½ cup
  mascarpone cheese
8 large scallops, shelled
75g/3oz thin smoked streaky (fatty)
  bacon rashers (strips)

NUTRITION NOTES

Per portion:

Energy	658kcal/2744kJ
Protein	57.5g
Fat	46.2g
saturated fat	25.5g
Carbohydrate	3.3g
Fibre	2.2g
Calcium	287mg

1 Trim, halve and slice the fennel bulbs thinly, chopping any feathery tops and reserving them to be used as a garnish. Bring a large pan of water to the boil and blanch the fennel slices for about 3 minutes, or until soft and tender. Drain well and set aside.

2 Preheat the grill (broiler) to medium. Place the fennel in a shallow flameproof dish and season. Dot with the mascarpone and grill (broil) for about 5 minutes, until the cheese has melted and the fennel is lightly browned.

3 Meanwhile, pat the scallops dry with kitchen paper. Cook the bacon in a frying pan, until crisp and golden, turning once. Drain and keep warm. Fry the scallops in the bacon fat for 1–2 minutes on each side, until cooked through.

4 Transfer the fennel to serving plates and crumble or snip the bacon into bitesize pieces over the top. Pile the scallops on the bacon and sprinkle with any reserved fennel tops.

seared tuna steaks with tomato salsa

FRESH AND FRUITY tomato salsa provides a delicious boost of vitamins to accompany the health-promoting omega-3 fatty acids that can be found in fresh tuna fish.

Serves 4

4 tuna steaks, each weighing about
   175–200g/6–7oz
30ml/2 tbsp extra virgin olive oil
5ml/1 tsp cumin seeds, toasted
grated rind and juice of 1 lime
pinch of dried red chilli flakes
1 small red onion, finely chopped
200g/7oz cherry tomatoes, chopped
1 avocado, peeled, stoned (pitted)
   and chopped
2 kiwi fruit, peeled and chopped
1 fresh red chilli, seeded and chopped
15g/½oz fresh coriander (cilantro), chopped
6 fresh mint sprigs, leaves only, chopped
5–10ml/1–2 tsp Thai fish sauce (*nam pla*)
salt and ground black pepper
lime wedges and fresh coriander (cilantro)
   sprigs, to garnish

1 Place the tuna steaks on a glass or ceramic plate and drizzle over the extra virgin olive oil. Sprinkle the steaks with half the toasted cumin seeds, salt, ground black pepper, half the lime rind and the dried chilli flakes. Set aside and leave to stand for about 30 minutes.

2 Meanwhile, make the salsa. Combine the onion, tomatoes, avocado, kiwi fruit, chilli, coriander and mint in a bowl. Add the remaining cumin seeds and lime rind and half the lime juice. Stir in Thai fish sauce to taste. Cover with clear film (plastic wrap) and set aside for about 20 minutes, then taste and add more Thai fish sauce and lime juice, if necessary.

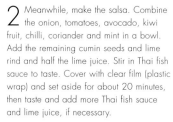

3 Heat a ridged, cast-iron griddle pan until very hot. Carefully lay the tuna steaks in the pan and cook for 2 minutes on each side for rare tuna or a little longer for a medium result.

4 Transfer the tuna steaks to four warmed serving plates and garnish with lime wedges and fresh coriander sprigs. Spoon on the tomato salsa, or transfer it to a serving bowl and offer it separately.

NUTRITION NOTES	
Per portion:	
Energy	419kcal/1751kJ
Protein	48.7g
Fat	22.9g
saturated fat	5.1g
Carbohydrate	4.9g
Fibre	2.3g
Calcium	49mg

warm swordfish and peppery salad

ROBUST SWORDFISH teamed with peppery salad makes a healthy meal that's perfect for any occasion, whether it's part of a low-carbohydrate eating plan or a sophisticated dinner.

2 Heat a ridged griddle pan or the grill (broiler) until very hot. Remove the fish steaks from the marinade and pat dry with kitchen paper.

3 Place the fish steaks in the griddle pan or under the grill (broiler) and cook for 2 minutes on each side until the swordfish is opaque and just cooked through.

4 Meanwhile, remove the stems from the rocket leaves and put the leaves in a large bowl. Season with salt and pepper. Drizzle over the remaining olive oil and toss well to combine. Shave the Pecorino cheese over the top of the salad leaves.

5 Place the swordfish steaks on four individual plates and arrange a little pile of salad on each steak. Serve immediately, while still warm.

Serves 4

4 swordfish steaks, 150g/5oz each
75ml/5 tbsp extra virgin olive oil
juice of 1 lemon
30ml/2 tbsp finely chopped parsley
115g/4oz rocket (arugula) leaves
115g/4oz Pecorino cheese
salt and ground black pepper

1 Lay the swordfish steaks in a shallow dish. In a small jug (pitcher) or bowl, mix about 60ml/4 tbsp of the olive oil with the lemon juice. Pour the mixture over the fish. Season with salt and ground black pepper, sprinkle on the finely chopped parsley and turn the fish to coat well. Cover with clear film (plastic wrap) and leave to marinate for at least 10 minutes.

NUTRITION NOTES

Per portion:	
Energy	451kcal/1885kJ
Protein	43.6g
Fat	30.5g
saturated fat	9.5g
Carbohydrate	0.5g
Fibre	0.6g
Calcium	400mg

paper-wrapped and steamed red snapper with asparagus

THIS JAPANESE RECIPE uses an origami packet to seal in the flavours of asparagus, spring onions and lime. You could make a simpler version by folding the baking parchment in half lengthways and double folding the three open edges to seal.

Serves 4
4 small red snapper fillets, no larger than
   18 x 6cm/7 x 2½in each
8 asparagus spears, trimmed of any
   tough ends
4 spring onions (scallions)
60ml/4 tbsp sake
rind of ½ lime, cut in thin strips
½ lime, thinly sliced
salt
5ml/1 tsp shoyu, to serve (optional)

1 Lightly sprinkle the red snapper fillets with salt and chill for 20 minutes. Preheat the oven to 180°C/350°F/Gas 4.

2 To make the parcels, cut out rectangles of baking parchment measuring about 38 x 30cm/15 x 12in. Use two rectangles for each fillet. Lay them out flat, fold up one-third of the rectangle and turn back 1cm/½in from one end to make a flap.

COOK'S TIP
Shoyu is Japanese soy sauce, and is quite diffeent from Chinese varieties. Find it in Japanese food stores.

3 Fold 1cm/½in in from the other end to make another flap. Fold the top edge down to fold over the first flap, and interlock the two flaps to form a long rectangle.

4 At each end, fold the top corners down diagonally, then fold the bottom corners up to meet the opposite folded edge to make a triangle. Press flat. Repeat to make four parcels.

5 Cut 2.5cm/1in from the tip of the asparagus. Slice the asparagus stems and spring onions diagonally into ovals. Par-boil the tips for 1 minute in lightly salted water and drain. Set aside.

6 Carefully open the parcels and place the spring onion and asparagus slices inside. Sprinkle with salt, top with the fish, add more salt and some sake, then add the strips of lime rind. Refold the parcels.

7 Pour hot water into a deep roasting pan, fitted with a wire rack, to 1cm/½in below the rack. Place the parcels on the rack and cook for 20 minutes.

8 Transfer the parcels to plates. Unfold both triangular ends and lift open the middle a little. Insert a slice of lime and place two asparagus tips on top. Add a little shoyu before serving, if you like.

NUTRITION NOTES

Per portion:	
Energy	162kcal/682kJ
Protein	29.3g
Fat	3.2g
saturated fat	1.0g
Carbohydrate	2.3g
Fibre	1.0g
Calcium	87mg

crab and tofu stir-fry

FOR A YEAR-ROUND LIGHT MEAL, this speedy stir-fry is the ideal choice. Crab meat has a very strong flavour so you need only a little bit. You could use the canned variety if fresh crab meat is unavailable, making this a very economical dish.

Serves 2

250g/9oz silken tofu
60ml/4 tbsp vegetable oil
2 garlic cloves, finely chopped
115g/4oz white crab meat
130g/4½oz/generous 1 cup baby corn, halved lengthways
2 spring onions (scallions), chopped
1 fresh red chilli, seeded and finely chopped
30ml/2 tbsp soy sauce
15ml/1 tbsp Thai fish sauce (*nam pla*)
5ml/1 tsp palm sugar or light muscovado (brown) sugar
juice of 1 lime
small bunch fresh coriander (cilantro), chopped, to garnish
lime wedges, to serve

1 Using a sharp knife, cut the silken tofu into 1cm/½in cubes.

2 Heat the oil in a wok or large, heavy frying pan. Add the tofu cubes and stir-fry until golden. Remove the tofu with a slotted spoon and set aside.

3 Add the garlic to the wok or pan and stir-fry until golden. Add the crab meat, tofu, corn, spring onions, chilli, soy sauce, fish sauce and sugar. Cook, stirring constantly, until the vegetables are just tender. Stir in the lime juice, sprinkle with coriander and serve with lime wedges.

NUTRITION NOTES	
Per portion:	
Energy	545kcal/2269kJ
Protein	24.9g
Fat	38.0g
saturated fat	4.2g
Carbohydrate	26.3g
Fibre	3.2g
Calcium	104mg

fish curry with shallots and lemon grass

THIS IS A THIN FISH CURRY made with salmon fillets. It has wonderfully strong, aromatic flavours. Originally from northern Thailand, it should ideally be served in small bowls with soup spoons to help scoop up the delicious sauce.

Serves 4

450g/1lb salmon fillets
500ml/17fl oz/2¼ cups vegetable stock
4 shallots, finely chopped
2 garlic cloves, finely chopped
2.5cm/1in piece fresh root ginger,
    finely chopped
1 lemon grass stalk, finely chopped
2.5ml/½ tsp dried chilli flakes
15ml/1 tbsp Thai fish sauce (*nam pla*)
5ml/1 tsp palm sugar or light muscovado
    (brown) sugar

NUTRITION NOTES	
Per portion:	
Energy	229kcal/956kJ
Protein	21.7g
Fat	13.6g
saturated fat	3.4g
Carbohydrate	5.1g
Fibre	0.3g
Calcium	38mg

1 Place the salmon fillets in the freezer for about 30–40 minutes to firm up the flesh slightly. Remove and discard the skin, then use a sharp knife to cut the fish into 2.5cm/1in cubes, removing any stray bones as you do so.

2 Pour the vegetable stock into a pan and bring it slowly to the boil. Add the chopped shallots, garlic, ginger, lemon grass, dried chilli flakes, fish sauce and sugar. Bring back to the boil, stir well to ensure the ingredients are thoroughly mixed, then reduce the heat and simmer gently for about 15 minutes.

3 Add the fish pieces, bring back to the boil, then turn off the heat. Leave the curry to stand for 10–15 minutes, then serve in small bowls.

fresh tuna and tomato stew

THIS DELICIOUSLY SIMPLE Italian recipe relies on good basic ingredients: fresh fish, ripe tomatoes and mixed herbs. Serve with a crisp green salad for a healthy, satisfying meal.

Serves 4

12 baby (pearl) onions, peeled
900g/2lb ripe tomatoes
675g/1½lb tuna
45ml/3 tbsp olive oil
2 garlic cloves, crushed
45ml/3 tbsp chopped fresh herbs
2 bay leaves
2.5ml/½ tsp caster (superfine) sugar
30ml/2 tbsp sun-dried tomato purée (paste)
150ml/¼ pint/⅔ cup dry white wine
salt and ground black pepper
baby courgettes (zucchini) and fresh
  herbs, to garnish

1 Leave the onions whole and cook in a pan of boiling water for 4–5 minutes until softened. Drain. Plunge the tomatoes into boiling water for 30 seconds, then refresh in cold water. Peel and chop roughly.

2 Cut the tuna into 2.5cm/1in chunks. Heat the oil in a large frying or sauté pan and quickly fry the tuna until the surface has browned. Remove with a slotted spoon and set aside.

VARIATION
Two large mackerel could be used instead of tuna. Lay the whole fish over the sauce and cook, covered with a lid, until the mackerel is cooked through.

3 Stir in the garlic, tomatoes, chopped herbs, bay leaves, sugar, tomato purée and white wine, and bring to the boil, breaking up the tomatoes with a wooden spoon. Add the onions.

4 Reduce the heat and simmer the sauce gently for 5 minutes. Return the fish to the pan and cook for a further 5 minutes. Season, and serve hot, garnished with baby courgettes and fresh herbs.

NUTRITION NOTES

Per portion:

Energy	381kcal/1589kJ
Protein	42.7g
Fat	19.6g
saturated fat	3.8g
Carbohydrate	13.0g
Fibre	4.2g
Calcium	77mg

pan-steamed mussels with thai herbs

LIKE SO MANY Thai dishes, these mussels are extremely easy to prepare and ready in minutes. The lemon grass stalks and kaffir lime leaves add a refreshing tang to the fresh mussels.

Serves 4

1kg/2¼lb fresh mussels
2 lemon grass stalks, finely chopped
4 shallots, chopped
4 kaffir lime leaves, coarsely torn
2 fresh red chillies, sliced
15ml/1 tbsp Thai fish sauce (*nam pla*)
30ml/2 tbsp fresh lime juice
thinly sliced spring onions (scallions),
   to garnish

1 Clean the mussels by pulling off the beards and scrubbing the shells well. Discard any mussels that are broken or which are open and do not close when tapped sharply.

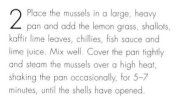

2 Place the mussels in a large, heavy pan and add the lemon grass, shallots, kaffir lime leaves, chillies, fish sauce and lime juice. Mix well. Cover the pan tightly and steam the mussels over a high heat, shaking the pan occasionally, for 5–7 minutes, until the shells have opened.

COOK'S TIP
Mussels are available all year round and are relatively cheap. Buy slightly more than you think you will need to allow for wastage. Store fresh mussels in the refrigerator and eat within one day of purchase.

3 Using a slotted spoon, transfer the cooked mussels to a warmed serving dish or individual bowls. Discard any mussels that have failed to open.

4 Garnish the mussels with the thinly sliced spring onions. Serve immediately in deep bowls, with small side plates for the empty shells.

NUTRITION NOTES

Per portion:	
Energy	83kcal/353kJ
Protein	14.0g
Fat	1.8g
saturated fat	0.3g
Carbohydrate	2.8g
Fibre	0.4g
Calcium	25mg

vegetarian
dishes

IT IS IMPORTANT TO make sure you eat enough protein if you are a vegetarian on a low-carbohydrate diet. Nutritious meals based around lentils, beans, nuts, eggs and tofu are essential, and make sure you eat plenty of fresh green vegetables to obtain the recommended daily allowance of essential vitamins and minerals. Substantial and filling meals include creamy lemon Puy lentils or mixed bean and aubergine tagine with mint yogurt. For a delicious light lunch, try aromatic tofu and green bean red curry.

chinese omelette parcels

STIR-FRIED FRESH VEGETABLES cooked in a tasty black bean sauce make a really unusual yet remarkably good omelette filling, for a quick low-carb lunch.

4 Beat the eggs lightly and season well with salt and ground black pepper. Heat a little of the remaining groundnut oil in a small frying pan and add a quarter of the beaten egg. Swirl the egg until it covers the base of the pan, then sprinkle over a quarter of the reserved coriander leaves. Cook until set, then carefully turn out on to a plate and keep warm in the oven while you make three more omelettes, adding a little more oil when necessary.

5 Spoon the vegetable stir-fry on to the omelettes and roll up. Cut in half crossways and serve garnished with coriander leaves and chilli.

COOK'S TIP
Black bean sauce is available in jars or cans from most large supermarkets.

NUTRITION NOTES

Per portion:	
Energy	184kcal/767kJ
Protein	9.7g
Fat	13.1g
saturated fat	3.1g
Carbohydrate	5.5g
Fibre	3.1g
Calcium	127mg

Serves 4

130g/4½oz broccoli, cut into small florets
30ml/2 tbsp groundnut (peanut) oil
1cm/½in piece of fresh root ginger, finely grated
1 large garlic clove, crushed
2 red chillies, seeded and thinly sliced
4 spring onions (scallions), sliced diagonally
175g/6oz/3 cups pak choi (bok choy), shredded
50g/2oz/2 cups fresh coriander (cilantro) leaves, plus extra to garnish
115g/4oz/2 cups beansprouts
45ml/3 tbsp black bean sauce
4 eggs
salt and ground black pepper

1 Blanch the broccoli in salted, boiling water for 2 minutes, drain well, then refresh under cold running water.

2 Meanwhile, heat 15ml/1 tbsp oil in a frying pan or wok. Add the ginger, garlic and half the chilli and stir-fry for 1 minute. Add the spring onions, broccoli and pak choi and stir-fry for 2 minutes, tossing the vegetables to prevent them sticking.

3 Chop three-quarters of the coriander and add to the frying pan or wok. Add the beansprouts and stir-fry for 1 minute, then add the black bean sauce and heat through for 1 minute more. Remove the pan from the heat and keep warm.

creamy lemon puy lentils

WHOLESOME LENTILS contain slowly absorbed carbohydrates that provide energy but avoid an exaggerated insulin response, which can be caused by quickly absorbed carbohydrates.

Serves 6

250g/9oz/generous 1 cup Puy lentils
1 bay leaf
30ml/2 tbsp olive oil
4 spring onions (scallions), sliced
2 large garlic cloves, chopped
15ml/1 tbsp Dijon mustard
finely grated rind and juice of 1 large lemon
4 plum tomatoes, seeded and diced
6 eggs
60ml/4 tbsp crème fraîche
salt and ground black pepper
30ml/2 tbsp chopped fresh flat leaf
    parsley, to garnish

1 Put the Puy lentils and bay leaf in a large pan, cover with cold water, and slowly bring to the boil. Reduce the heat and simmer, partially covered, for about 25 minutes, or until the lentils are tender. Stir the lentils occasionally and add more water, if necessary. Drain.

2 Heat the oil in a frying pan and cook the spring onions and garlic for about 1 minute or until softened. Add the Dijon mustard, lemon rind and juice, and mix.

3 Stir the tomatoes and seasoning into the onion mixture, then cook gently for 1–2 minutes until the tomatoes are heated through, but still retain their shape. Add a little water if the mixture becomes too dry.

4 Meanwhile, poach the eggs in a pan of lightly salted barely simmering water for 4 minutes, adding them one at a time.

5 Gently stir the lentils and crème fraiche into the tomato mixture, remove and discard the bay leaf, then heat through for 1 minute. Divide the mixture among six serving plates. Top each portion with a poached egg, and sprinkle with parsley. Serve immediately.

NUTRITION NOTES

Per portion:	
Energy	232kcal/969kJ
Protein	14.9g
Fat	10.2g
saturated fat	2.9g
Carbohydrate	21.7g
Fibre	4.1g
Calcium	62mg

roasted garlic and aubergine custards with red pepper dressing

THESE ELEGANT LITTLE MOULDS make a rather splendid main course for a special dinner. Serve steamed broccoli or a green salad as an accompaniment.

Serves 6
2 large heads of garlic
6–7 fresh thyme sprigs
60ml/4 tbsp extra virgin olive oil, plus
extra for greasing
350g/12oz aubergines (eggplant), cut into
1cm/½in dice
2 large red (bell) peppers, halved and seeded
pinch of saffron strands
300ml/½ pint/1¼ cups whipping cream
2 large (US extra large) eggs
pinch of caster (superfine) sugar
30ml/2 tbsp shredded fresh basil leaves
salt and ground black pepper

For the dressing
90ml/6 tbsp extra virgin olive oil
15–25ml/1–1½ tbsp balsamic vinegar
pinch of caster (superfine) sugar
115g/4oz tomatoes, peeled, seeded
and finely diced
½ small red onion, finely chopped
generous pinch of ground toasted
cumin seeds
handful of fresh basil leaves

1 Preheat the oven to 190°C/375°F/ Gas 5. Place the garlic on a piece of foil with the thyme sprigs and sprinkle with 15ml/1 tbsp of the olive oil. Wrap the foil around the garlic, place in a roasting pan and roast for 35–45 minutes, or until the garlic is soft. Cool slightly. Reduce the oven temperature to 180°C/350°F/Gas 4.

2 Meanwhile, heat the remaining olive oil in a heavy pan. Add the diced aubergines and fry over a medium heat, stirring frequently, for about 5–8 minutes, until the aubergine pieces are soft, browned and cooked through.

3 Grill (broil) the peppers, skin sides up, until they are black. Place the peppers in a bowl, cover and leave for 10 minutes.

4 When the peppers are cool enough to handle, peel and dice them. Soak the saffron strands in 15ml/1 tbsp hot water for about 10 minutes.

5 Unwrap the roasted garlic and pop it out of its skin into a blender or food processor. Discard the thyme sprigs. Add the oil from cooking, the cream and eggs to the garlic. Process until smooth. Add the soaked saffron with its liquid and season well with salt, pepper and a pinch of sugar. Stir in half the red pepper and the basil.

6 Lightly grease six large ovenproof ramekins (about 200–250ml/7–8fl oz/ 1 cup capacity) and line the base of each with a circle of non-stick baking parchment. Grease the parchment.

7 Divide the aubergines among the dishes. Pour the egg mixture into the ramekins, then place them in a roasting pan. Cover each dish with foil and make a little hole in the centre of the foil to allow steam to escape. Pour hot water into the pan to come halfway up the outsides of the ramekins. Bake for 25–30 minutes, until the custards are just set in the centre.

8 Make the dressing while the custards are cooking. Whisk the oil and vinegar with salt, pepper and a pinch of sugar. Stir in the tomatoes, red onion, remaining red pepper and cumin. Set aside a few basil leaves for garnishing, then chop the rest and add to the dressing.

9 Leave the custards to cool for about 5 minutes, then turn them out on to warmed serving plates. Spoon the dressing around the custards and garnish each with the reserved fresh basil leaves.

NUTRITION NOTES	
Per portion:	
Energy	450kcal/1876kJ
Protein	4.3g
Fat	44.5g
saturated fat	14.6g
Carbohydrate	8.7g
Fibre	2.0g
Calcium	62mg

lentil and nut loaf

FOR CHRISTMAS OR A special celebration, serve this with all the trimmings, including a vegetarian gravy. Garnish with fresh cranberries and flat leaf parsley for a really festive effect.

Serves 6

115g/4oz/½ cup red lentils
115g/4oz/1 cup hazelnuts
115g/4oz/1 cup walnuts
1 large carrot
2 celery sticks
1 large onion
115g/4oz/1½ cups mushrooms
50g/2oz/¼ cup butter, plus extra
 for greasing
10ml/2 tsp mild curry powder
30ml/2 tbsp tomato ketchup
30ml/2 tbsp vegetarian Worcestershire sauce
1 egg, beaten
10ml/2 tsp salt
60ml/4 tbsp chopped fresh parsley
150ml/¼ pint/⅔ cup water

1 Cover the lentils with cold water and soak for 1 hour. Grind the nuts in a food processor, then place them in a large bowl. Coarsely chop the carrot, celery, onion and mushrooms, add to the food processor and process until finely chopped.

NUTRITION NOTES

Per portion:

Energy	326kcal/1356kJ
Protein	10.1g
Fat	25.0g
saturated fat	6.0g
Carbohydrate	16.1g
Fibre	5.7g
Calcium	62mg

2 Heat the butter in a large pan. Add the vegetables and fry gently over a low heat, stirring occasionally, for 5 minutes. Stir in the curry powder and cook for 1 minute more. Remove from the heat and set aside to cool.

3 Drain the lentils and stir them into the ground nuts. Add the vegetables, ketchup, vegetarian Worcestershire sauce, egg, salt, chopped parsley and water.

4 Preheat the oven to 190°C/375°F/ Gas 5. Grease a 1kg/2¼lb loaf tin (pan) and line with baking parchment or foil. Press the mixture into the tin.

5 Bake for 1–1¼ hours, until just firm, covering the top with foil if it starts to burn. Leave to stand for 15 minutes, turn out and peel off the paper.

baked peppers with egg and lentils

THESE OVEN-BAKED, STUFFED peppers make a delicious appetizer or an excellent light meal for vegetarians, as well as a tasty side dish for grilled fish or pork chops.

Serves 4

75g/3oz/½ cup Puy lentils
2.5ml/½ tsp ground turmeric
2.5ml/½ tsp ground coriander
2.5ml/½ tsp paprika
450ml/¾ pint/1¾ cups vegetable stock
2 large (bell) peppers, halved and seeded
a little olive oil
15ml/1 tbsp chopped fresh mint
4 eggs
salt and ground black pepper
sprigs of coriander (cilantro), to garnish

1 Put the Puy lentils in a large pan with the turmeric, coriander, paprika and vegetable stock. Bring to the boil, stirring occasionally, and simmer for 30–40 minutes. If the lentils start to dry out, add some more water during cooking.

2 Brush the peppers lightly with a little olive oil and place them close together on a large non-stick baking tray, skin side down. Stir the chopped fresh mint into the lentils, then fill the halved peppers with the lentil mixture. Preheat the oven to 190°C/375°F/Gas 5.

NUTRITION NOTES

Per portion:	
Energy	172kcal/720kJ
Protein	11.8g
Fat	8.5g
saturated fat	2.1g
Carbohydrate	12.0g
Fibre	3.0g
Calcium	41mg

3 Crack the eggs, one at a time, into a small jug (pitcher) and pour into the middle of each stuffed pepper. Stir the white into the lentils and sprinkle with salt and ground black pepper. Bake for about 10 minutes or until the egg white is just set. Garnish with sprigs of coriander and serve.

roasted ratatouille moussaka

BASED ON THE CLASSIC Greek dish, this moussaka really has a taste of the Mediterranean. Roasting brings out the deep rich flavours of the vegetables, which give a colourful contrast to the light and mouth-watering egg and cheese topping.

Serves 6

2 red (bell) peppers, seeded and cut into large chunks
2 yellow (bell) peppers, seeded and cut into large chunks
2 aubergines (eggplants), cut into large chunks
3 courgettes (zucchini), thickly sliced
45ml/3 tbsp olive oil
3 garlic cloves, crushed
400g/14oz can chopped tomatoes
30ml/2 tbsp sun-dried tomato purée (paste)
45ml/3 tbsp chopped fresh basil or
    15ml/1 tbsp dried basil
15ml/1 tbsp balsamic vinegar
1.5ml/¼ tsp soft light brown sugar
salt and ground black pepper
basil leaves, to garnish

For the topping

25g/1oz/2 tbsp butter
25g/1oz/¼ cup plain (all-purpose) flour
300ml/½ pint/1¼ cups milk
1.5ml/¼ tsp freshly grated nutmeg
250g/9oz ricotta cheese
3 eggs, beaten
25g/1oz/⅓ cup freshly grated
    Parmesan cheese

1 Preheat the oven to 230°C/450°F/ Gas 8. Arrange the peppers, aubergines and courgettes in a large roasting pan. Season well with salt and black pepper.

2 Mix together the oil and crushed garlic cloves and pour this mixture over the vegetables. Shake the roasting pan to ensure the vegetables are thoroughly coated in the garlic mixture.

3 Roast in the oven for about 15–20 minutes until slightly charred, lightly tossing the vegetables once during cooking. Remove the pan from the oven and set aside. Reduce the oven temperature to 200°C/400°F/Gas 6.

4 Put the chopped tomatoes, sun-dried tomato purée, fresh or dried basil, balsamic vinegar and brown sugar in a large, heavy pan and heat to boiling point. Reduce the heat and simmer, uncovered, for about 10–15 minutes until thickened, stirring occasionally. Season with salt and freshly ground black pepper to taste.

5 Carefully transfer the roasted vegetables into the pan of warm tomato sauce. Mix well, coating the vegetables thoroughly in the tomato sauce. Spoon into an ovenproof serving dish.

VARIATION
Try making this recipe in individual dishes – reduce the baking time to 25 minutes.

6 To make the topping, melt the butter in a large pan over a gentle heat. Stir in the flour and cook for 1 minute. Pour in the milk, stirring constantly, then whisk until blended. Add the nutmeg and continue whisking over a gentle heat until thickened. Cook, stirring, for a further 2 minutes, then remove from the heat and allow to cool.

7 Mix in the ricotta cheese and beaten eggs thoroughly. Season to taste with salt and plenty of black pepper.

8 Level the surface of the roasted vegetable mixture with the back of a spoon. Spoon the moussaka topping over the vegetables and sprinkle with the Parmesan cheese. Bake for 30–35 minutes until the topping is golden brown. Serve immediately, garnished with basil leaves.

NUTRITION NOTES

Per portion:	
Energy	444kcal/1863kJ
Protein	21.7g
Fat	29.8g
saturated fat	11.3g
Carbohydrate	24.3g
Fibre	5.0g
Calcium	260mg

lemony okra and tomato tagine

IN THIS SPICY VEGETABLE DISH, the heat of the chilli is offset by the refreshing flavour of lemon juice. Based on a Moroccan recipe, this is ideal as a light main course with a side salad.

Serves 4

350g/12oz okra
5–6 tomatoes
2 small onions
2 garlic cloves, crushed
1 fresh green chilli, seeded
5ml/1 tsp paprika
small handful of fresh coriander (cilantro),
    plus extra to garnish
30ml/2 tbsp sunflower oil
juice of 1 lemon

1 Trim the okra and then cut them into 1cm/½in lengths. Set aside.

2 Cut the tomatoes in half and scoop out the seeds with a teaspoon. Chop the fleah coarsely and set aside.

3 Coarsely chop one of the onions and place it in a food processor or blender with the crushed garlic, green chilli, paprika, fresh coriander and 60ml/4 tbsp water. Process to a smooth paste.

4 Heat the sunflower oil in a large pan. Thinly slice the second onion and cook gently in the oil for about 5–6 minutes, or until soft and golden brown. Transfer the cooked onion slices to a plate with a slotted spoon.

5 Reduce the heat and pour in the onion and coriander mixture. Cook for 1–2 minutes, stirring frequently, and then add the okra pieces, chopped tomatoes, lemon juice and about 120ml/4fl oz/½ cup water. Stir well to mix, cover tightly, and simmer gently over a low heat for about 15 minutes, or until the okra is tender.

6 Transfer to a large warmed serving dish, sprinkle with the fried onion rings, garnish with fresh coriander and serve immediately.

NUTRITION NOTES

Per portion:	
Energy	106kcal/438kJ
Protein	2.9g
Fat	7.5g
saturated fat	1.0g
Carbohydrate	6.5g
Fibre	2.9g
Calcium	83mg

cheese-topped roast baby vegetables

THIS IS A SIMPLE WAY of serving deliciously tender baby vegetables. Roasting them really brings out their sweet flavour, and the addition of cheese makes this a substantial meal.

Serves 4

1kg/2¼lb mixed baby vegetables, such as aubergines (eggplants), onions or shallots, courgettes (zucchini), corn cobs and mushrooms
1 red (bell) pepper, seeded and cut into large pieces
1–2 garlic cloves, finely chopped
15–30ml/1–2 tbsp olive oil
30ml/2 tbsp chopped fresh mixed herbs
225g/8oz cherry tomatoes
115g/4oz/1 cup coarsely grated mozzarella cheese
salt and ground black pepper
black olives, to serve (optional)

1 Preheat the oven to 220°C/425°F/ Gas 7. Cut the mixed baby vegetables in half lengthways.

NUTRITION NOTES	
Per portion:	
Energy	281kcal/1176kJ
Protein	5.6g
Fat	16.5g
saturated fat	1.4g
Carbohydrate	21.5g
Fibre	6.4g
Calcium	54mg

2 Place the halved baby vegetables and pepper pieces in an ovenproof dish with the garlic and plenty of salt and ground black pepper. Drizzle with the oil and toss the vegetables to coat them. Bake for 20 minutes, or until the vegetables are tinged brown at the edges.

3 Remove from the oven and stir in the chopped fresh mixed herbs. Sprinkle the cherry tomatoes over the surface and top with the coarsely grated mozzarella cheese. Return to the oven and bake for 5–10 minutes more until the cheese has melted and is bubbling. Serve immediately with black olives, if you like.

VARIATION
Use 2–3 sprigs of fresh rosemary instead of chopped fresh mixed herbs.

mixed bean and aubergine tagine with mint yogurt

IN THIS TRADITIONAL-STYLE, hearty Moroccan dish, the mixed beans and aubergine provide both texture and flavour, which are enhanced by the herbs and chillies.

Serves 4

115g/4oz/generous ½ cup dried red
   kidney beans, soaked overnight in cold
   water and drained
115g/4oz/generous ½ cup dried
   black-eyed beans (peas) or cannellini
   beans, soaked overnight in cold water
   and drained
600ml/1 pint/2½ cups water
2 bay leaves
2 celery sticks, each cut into 4 batons
75ml/5 tbsp olive oil
1 aubergine (eggplant), about 350g/
   12oz, cut into chunks
1 onion, thinly sliced
3 garlic cloves, crushed
1–2 fresh red chillies, seeded and chopped
30ml/2 tbsp tomato purée (paste)
5ml/1 tsp paprika
2 large tomatoes, roughly chopped
300ml/½ pint/1¼ cups vegetable stock
15ml/1 tbsp each chopped fresh mint,
   parsley and coriander (cilantro)
salt and ground black pepper
fresh herb sprigs, to garnish

For the mint yogurt
150ml/¼ pint/⅔ cup natural (plain) yogurt
30ml/2 tbsp chopped fresh mint
2 spring onions (scallions), chopped

NUTRITION NOTES	
Per portion:	
Energy	413kcal/1742kJ
Protein	17.4g
Fat	20.2g
saturated fat	2.9g
Carbohydrate	41.2g
Fibre	10.8g
Calcium	192mg

1 Place the soaked and drained kidney beans in a large pan of unsalted boiling water. Bring back to the boil and boil rapidly for 10 minutes, then drain. Place the soaked and drained black-eyed or cannellini beans in a separate large pan of boiling unsalted water and boil rapidly for 10 minutes, then drain.

2 Place the 600ml/1 pint/2½ cups of water in a large tagine or casserole, and add the bay leaves, celery and beans. Cover and place in an unheated oven. Set the oven to 190°C/375°F/Gas 5. Cook for 1–1½ hours or until the beans are tender, then drain.

3 Heat 60ml/4 tbsp of the oil in a large frying pan or cast-iron tagine base. Add the aubergine chunks and cook, stirring, for 4–5 minutes, until evenly browned. Remove and set aside.

4 Add the remaining oil to the tagine base or frying pan, then add the sliced onion and cook, stirring, for about 4–5 minutes, until softened. Add the crushed garlic and chopped red chillies and cook for a further 5 minutes, stirring frequently, until the onion is golden.

5 Reset the oven temperature to 160°C/325°F/Gas 3. Add the tomato purée and paprika to the onion mixture and cook for 1–2 minutes. Add the tomatoes, aubergine, beans and stock, then season to taste.

6 Cover the tagine base with the lid or, if using a frying pan, transfer the contents to a clay tagine or casserole. Place in the oven and cook for 1 hour.

7 Meanwhile, mix together the yogurt, mint and spring onions. Just before serving, add the fresh mint, parsley and coriander to the tagine and lightly mix through the vegetables. Garnish with fresh herb sprigs and serve with the mint yogurt.

pan-fried tofu with caramelized sauce

TOFU IS OFTEN USED AS a nutritious meat substitute for vegetarians. This traditional dish was created by Chinese Buddhist monks, who invented many delicious and filling protein dishes from tofu and other soya bean products.

Serves 4

2 x 285g/10¼oz packets tofu blocks
4 garlic cloves
10ml/2 tsp vegetable oil
50g/2oz/¼ cup butter, cut into
    5 equal pieces
watercress or rocket (arugula), to garnish

For the marinade

4 spring onions (scallions)
60ml/4 tbsp sake
60ml/4 tbsp shoyu or soy sauce
60ml/4 tbsp mirin (sweet cooking sake)

1 Unpack the tofu blocks and discard the liquid, then wrap in three layers of kitchen paper. Put a large plate or wooden chopping board on top as a weight and leave for 30 minutes to allow time for the excess liquid to be absorbed by the paper. This process makes the tofu firmer and, when cooked, it will crisp on the outside.

2 To make the marinade, chop the spring onions finely. Mix with the other ingredients in a wide, shallow bowl. Leave for 15 minutes.

3 Slice the garlic very thinly. Heat the oil in a frying pan and fry the garlic for a few moments until golden. Turn the chips frequently to prevent sticking and burning. Scoop them out on to kitchen paper. Reserve the oil in the pan.

4 Unwrap the tofu. Slice one block horizontally in half, then cut each half into four pieces. Repeat with the other block. Soak in the marinade for 15 minutes.

5 Take out the tofu and wipe off the excess marinade with kitchen paper. Reserve the marinade.

6 Reheat the oil in the frying pan and add one piece of butter. When the oil starts sizzling, reduce the heat to medium and add the pieces of tofu one by one.

7 Cover the pan and cook until the edge of the tofu is browned and quite firm, approximately 5–8 minutes on each side.

8 Pour the marinade into the pan. Cook for 2 minutes, or until the spring onions are soft. Remove the tofu and arrange four pieces on each plate. Pour over the marinade and spring onion mixture and top with a piece of butter. Sprinkle with the garlic chips and garnish with watercress.

NUTRITION NOTES	
Per portion:	
Energy	233kcal/966kJ
Protein	12.0g
Fat	16.6g
saturated fat	7.0g
Carbohydrate	9.1g
Fibre	1.2g
Calcium	93mg

tofu and green bean red curry

THIS IS ONE OF THOSE versatile recipes that should be in every cook's repertoire. This version uses green beans, but other types of vegetable work equally well. The tofu takes on the flavour of the spice paste and also boosts the nutritional value.

2 Add the red curry paste, fish sauce and sugar to the coconut milk. Mix thoroughly, then add the mushrooms. Stir and cook for 1 minute.

Serves 4

600ml/1 pint/2½ cups canned coconut milk
15ml/1 tbsp Thai red curry paste
45ml/3 tbsp Thai fish sauce (nam pla)
10ml/2 tsp palm sugar or light muscovado (brown) sugar
225g/8oz/3¼ cups button (white) mushrooms
115g/4oz/scant 1 cup green beans, trimmed
175g/6oz firm tofu, rinsed, drained and cut in 2cm/¾in cubes
4 kaffir lime leaves, torn
2 fresh red chillies, seeded and sliced
fresh coriander (cilantro) leaves, to garnish

1 Pour about one-third of the coconut milk into a wok or pan. Cook gently until it starts to separate and an oily sheen appears on the surface.

NUTRITION NOTES

Per portion:	
Energy	105kcal/438kJ
Protein	6.0g
Fat	3.1g
saturated fat	0.6g
Carbohydrate	12.8g
Fibre	2.4g
Calcium	75mg

3 Stir in the remaining coconut milk. Bring back to the boil, then add the green beans and tofu cubes. Simmer gently for 4–5 minutes more.

4 Stir in the kaffir lime leaves and sliced red chillies. Spoon the curry into a serving dish, garnish with the coriander leaves and serve immediately.

COOK'S TIP
Fresh tofu can be kept in plenty of water in the refrigerator for up to three days, if the water is changed daily.

balti stir-fried vegetables with cashews

THIS VERSATILE STIR-FRY recipe will accommodate most combinations of vegetables so feel free to experiment. The cashew nuts add a delicious crunch to the dish.

2 Heat the oil in a wok and stir-fry the curry leaves, cumin seeds and dried chillies for 1 minute.

3 Add the vegetables and nuts and toss them over the heat for 3–4 minutes. Add the salt and lemon juice and stir-fry for about 2 minutes more, until the vegetables are crisp-tender.

4 Transfer to a warm dish and serve garnished with mint leaves.

Serves 4
2 carrots
1 red (bell) pepper, seeded
1 green (bell) pepper, seeded
2 courgettes (zucchini)
115g/4oz green beans, halved
1 bunch of spring onions (scallions)
15ml/1 tbsp extra virgin olive oil
4–6 curry leaves
2.5ml/½ tsp cumin seeds
4 dried red chillies
10–12 cashew nuts
5ml/1 tsp salt
30ml/2 tbsp lemon juice
fresh mint leaves, to garnish

1 Cut the carrots, peppers and courgettes into matchsticks, halve the beans and chop the spring onions. Set aside.

NUTRITION NOTES

Per portion:

Energy	100kcal/420kJ
Protein	3.1g
Fat	5.7g
saturated fat	0.8g
Carbohydrate	9.1g
Fibre	3.2g
Calcium	92mg

COOK'S TIP
When making stir-fries, it is a good idea to use a non-stick wok to minimize the amount of oil needed. However, it cannot be heated to the same high temperature as a conventional wok.

aromatic chickpea and spinach curry

HIGH IN FIBRE, this hearty, warming curry tastes great and boosts vitality with essential vitamins. Serve it with spicy mango chutney and a cooling mint raita.

Serves 4

15ml/1 tbsp sunflower oil
1 large onion, finely chopped
2 garlic cloves, crushed
2.5cm/1in piece of fresh root ginger,
  finely chopped
1 green chilli, seeded and finely chopped
30ml/2 tbsp medium curry paste
10ml/2 tsp ground cumin
5ml/1 tsp ground turmeric
225g/8oz can chopped tomatoes
1 green or red (bell) pepper, seeded
  and chopped
300ml/½ pint/1¼ cups vegetable stock
15ml/1 tbsp tomato purée (paste)
450g/1lb fresh spinach
425g/15oz can chickpeas, drained
45ml/3 tbsp chopped fresh coriander
  (cilantro)
5ml/1 tsp garam masala (optional)
salt

1 Heat the sunflower oil in a large, heavy pan and cook the chopped onion, crushed garlic, root ginger and chilli over a gentle heat for about 5 minutes, or until the onion has softened, but not browned. Stir in the medium curry paste, mix thoroughly and cook for 1 minute, then stir in the ground cumin and turmeric. Stir over a low heat for 1 minute more.

2 Add the tomatoes and pepper and stir to coat with the spice mixture. Pour in the stock and stir in the tomato purée. Bring to the boil, lower the heat, cover and simmer for 15 minutes.

3 Remove any coarse stalks from the spinach, then rinse the leaves thoroughly, drain them and tear into large pieces. Add them to the pan, in batches, adding a handful more as each batch cooks down and wilts.

4 Stir in the chickpeas, cover and cook gently for 5 minutes more. Add the fresh chopped coriander, season with salt to taste and stir well. Spoon into a warmed bowl and sprinkle with the garam masala, if using. Serve immediately.

NUTRITION NOTES

Per portion:

Energy	253kcal/1064kJ
Protein	13.3g
Fat	11.1g
saturated fat	1.6g
Carbohydrate	26.9g
Fibre	9.1g
Calcium	200mg

salads
and side dishes

EATING PLENTY OF VEGETABLES is an essential part of any healthy diet, and having a good proportion of them raw, as salads, ensures they keep the maximum nutritional value. All vegetables contain carbohydrate but some contain far more than others and some are absorbed more gradually, which helps to maintain steady blood sugar levels. Starchy vegetables, such as potatoes and yams, are strictly off limits, but any other vegetables are good choices for side dishes or salads. Try crisp pak choi with lime dressing or a nutritious beetroot and red onion salad.

mixed green leaf and herb salad

THIS FLAVOURFUL SALAD makes an ideal side dish that goes well with meat and fish. You could turn it into a more substantial dish for a light lunch by trying one of the variations.

Serves 4

15g/½oz/½ cup mixed fresh herbs, such as chervil, tarragon (use sparingly), dill, basil, marjoram (use sparingly), flat leaf parsley, mint, sorrel, fennel and coriander (cilantro)

350g/12oz mixed salad leaves, such as rocket (arugula), radicchio, chicory (Belgian endive), watercress, frisée, baby spinach, oakleaf lettuce and dandelion

For the dressing

50ml/2fl oz/¼ cup extra virgin olive oil
15ml/1 tbsp cider vinegar
salt and ground black pepper

1 Wash and dry the herbs and salad leaves in a salad spinner, or use two clean, dry dishtowels to pat them dry.

2 To make the dressing, blend together the olive oil and cider vinegar in a small bowl and season with salt and ground black pepper to taste.

3 Place the mixed herbs and salad leaves in a large salad bowl. Just before serving, pour over the dressing and toss thoroughly to mix well, using your hands. Serve immediately.

VARIATIONS

To make a more substantial salad for a light lunch or supper, try adding some of the following ingredients:
• Baby broad (fava) beans, cooked, sliced artichoke hearts and quartered hard-boiled eggs
• Cooked chickpeas, asparagus tips and pitted green olives.

NUTRITION NOTES

Per portion:
Energy	111kcal/463kJ
Protein	0.7g
Fat	11.4g
saturated fat	1.7g
Carbohydrate	1.5g
Fibre	0.8g
Calcium	25mg

spinach and roast garlic salad

SPINACH OFFERS A GOOD supply of vitamin C, folates and potassium, and garlic is reputed to have many health-giving properties and is a natural anti-viral and anti-bacterial agent.

Serves 4

12 garlic cloves, unpeeled
60ml/4 tbsp extra virgin olive oil
450g/1lb baby spinach leaves
50g/2oz/½ cup pine nuts, lightly toasted
juice of ½ lemon
salt and ground black pepper

1 Preheat the oven to 190°C/375°F/ Gas 5. Place the unpeeled garlic cloves in a small roasting pan, drizzle over 30ml/ 2 tbsp of the olive oil and toss to coat. Bake for about 15 minutes until slightly charred.

2 Place the garlic cloves, still in their skins, in a salad bowl. Add the spinach, pine nuts, lemon juice and remaining olive oil. Toss well and season with salt and ground black pepper. Serve immediately, gently squeezing the softened garlic purée out of the skins to eat.

NUTRITION NOTES

Per portion:

Energy	222kcal/927kJ
Protein	5.7g
Fat	20.5g
saturated fat	2.4g
Carbohydrate	3.9g
Fibre	3.0g
Calcium	194mg

COOK'S TIPS

• When spinach is served raw in a salad, the leaves need to be young and tender. Wash them well, drain and pat them dry with kitchen paper.
• Don't worry about the large amount of garlic used in this salad. Roasting subdues garlic's pungent flavour and it will become sweet and subtle, while retaining its health-giving properties.

pak choi with lime dressing

THE COCONUT DRESSING for this dish is traditionally made using Thai fish sauce, but mushroom sauce is a suitable vegetarian alternative. Beware, this is a fiery dish!

Serves 4
30ml/2 tbsp oil
3 fresh red chillies, cut into thin strips
4 garlic cloves, thinly sliced
6 spring onions (scallions), sliced
   diagonally
2 pak choi (bok choy), shredded
15ml/1 tbsp crushed peanuts

For the dressing
30ml/2 tbsp fresh lime juice
15–30ml/1–2 tbsp Thai fish sauce
   (*nam pla*)
250ml/8fl oz/1 cup coconut milk

2 Heat the oil in a wok and stir-fry the chillies for 2–3 minutes, until crisp. Transfer to a plate using a slotted spoon. Add the garlic to the wok and stir-fry for 30–60 seconds, until golden brown. Transfer to the plate.

3 Stir-fry the white parts of the spring onions for about 2–3 minutes, then add the green parts and stir-fry for 1 minute more. Transfer to the plate.

4 Bring a large pan of lightly salted water to the boil and add the pak choi. Stir twice, then drain immediately.

5 Place the pak choi in a large bowl, add the dressing and toss to mix. Spoon into a large serving bowl and sprinkle with the crushed peanuts and the stir-fried chilli mixture. Serve warm or cold.

1 Make the dressing. Put the lime juice and fish sauce in a bowl and mix well, then gradually whisk in the coconut milk until thoroughly combined.

NUTRITION NOTES	
Per portion:	
Energy	134kcal/564kJ
Protein	3.1g
Fat	9.6g
saturated fat	1.4g
Carbohydrate	8.8g
Fibre	1.8g
Calcium	81mg

thai fruit and vegetable salad

THIS UNUSUAL FRUIT SALAD is perfect alongside a spicy main course. In Thailand, it is traditionally served as a cooler to counteract the heat of chillies in other dishes.

Serves 6

1 small pineapple
1 small mango, peeled and sliced
1 green apple, cored and sliced
6 rambutans or lychees, peeled and stoned (pitted)
115g/4oz/1 cup green beans, trimmed and halved
1 red onion, sliced
1 small cucumber, cut into short sticks
115g/4oz/1⅓ cups beansprouts
2 spring onions (scallions), sliced
1 ripe tomato, quartered
225g/8oz cos, romaine or iceberg lettuce leaves

For the coconut dipping sauce

30ml/2 tbsp coconut cream
30ml/2 tbsp granulated sugar
75ml/5 tbsp boiling water
1.5ml/¼ tsp chilli sauce
15ml/1 tbsp Thai fish sauce (nam pla)
juice of 1 lime

1 First, make the coconut dipping sauce. Spoon the coconut cream, granulated sugar and fresh boiling water into a small screw-top jar. Add the chilli sauce, Thai fish sauce and freshly squeezed lime juice, then screw the lid on tightly. Mix the ingredients together thoroughly by shaking the jar vigorously.

2 Trim both ends of the pineapple with a sharp, serrated knife, then cut away the outer skin and remove any "eyes". Remove the central core with an apple corer. Alternatively, quarter the pineapple lengthways and remove the portion of core from each wedge with a sharp knife. Chop the pineapple into small chunks and set aside with the other fruits.

3 Bring a small pan of lightly salted water to the boil over a medium heat. Add the trimmed and halved green beans and cook for about 3–4 minutes, until just tender but still retaining some "bite". Drain well, refresh under cold running water, then drain again and set aside.

4 To serve, arrange all the fruits and vegetables in small heaps on a platter or in a shallow bowl. Pour the coconut sauce into a small serving bowl and serve separately as a dip.

NUTRITION NOTES	
Per portion:	
Energy	188kcal/785kJ
Protein	4.5g
Fat	3.0g
saturated fat	2.3g
Carbohydrate	39.0g
Fibre	5.1g
Calcium	78mg

beetroot and red onion salad

THIS SALAD LOOKS especially attractive when made with a mixture of red and yellow beetroot. Try it with roast beef or cooked ham as it tastes excellent with these rich meats.

Serves 6

500g/1¼lb small beetroot (beets)
75ml/5 tbsp water
60ml/4 tbsp olive oil
90g/3½oz/scant 1 cup walnut or
   pecan halves
5ml/1 tsp caster (superfine) sugar, plus a
   little extra for the dressing
30ml/2 tbsp walnut oil
15ml/1 tbsp sherry vinegar or
   balsamic vinegar
5ml/1 tsp soy sauce
5ml/1 tsp grated orange rind
2.5ml/½ tsp ground roasted
   coriander seeds
5–10ml/1–2 tsp orange juice
1 red onion, halved and very thinly sliced
15–30ml/1–2 tbsp chopped fresh fennel
75g/3oz watercress or mizuna leaves
handful of baby red chard or beetroot
   leaves (optional)
salt and ground black pepper

1 Preheat the oven to 180°C/350°F/
Gas 4. Place the beetroot in an oven-proof dish just large enough to hold them in a single layer and add the water. Cover tightly and cook in the oven for about 1–1½ hours, or until they are just tender.

2 Cool, then peel the beetroot, then slice them or cut them into strips and toss with 15ml/1 tbsp of the olive oil. Transfer to a bowl and set aside.

3 Meanwhile, heat 15ml/1 tbsp olive oil in a frying pan and cook the walnuts or pecans until they begin to brown. Add the sugar and cook, stirring, until the nuts begin to caramelize. Season with 2.5ml/½ tsp salt and lots of pepper, then turn the nuts out on to a plate and leave to cool.

4 In a jug (pitcher) or bowl, whisk together the remaining olive oil, the walnut oil, vinegar, soy sauce, orange rind and coriander to make the dressing. Season to taste and add a pinch of caster sugar. Whisk in orange juice to taste.

5 Add the sliced red onion to the strips of beetroot, then pour over the dressing and toss thoroughly to mix.

6 When ready to serve, toss the salad with the fennel, watercress or mizuna and red chard or beetroot leaves, if using. Transfer to individual bowls or plates and sprinkle with the caramelized walnuts or pecans. Serve immediately.

NUTRITION NOTES

Per portion:	
Energy	248kcal/1033kJ
Protein	3.3g
Fat	22.8g
saturated fat	2.8g
Carbohydrate	7.9g
Fibre	4.0g
Calcium	67mg

baby leeks in red wine with aromatics

CORIANDER SEEDS and oregano lend a Greek flavour to this dish of braised leeks. Serve it as part of a mixed hors d'oeuvre or as a partner for baked white fish fillets.

Serves 6

12 baby leeks or 6 thick leeks
15ml/1 tbsp coriander seeds,
  lightly crushed
5cm/2in piece cinnamon stick
120ml/4fl oz/½ cup olive oil
3 fresh bay leaves
2 strips pared orange rind
5–6 fresh or dried oregano sprigs
5ml/1 tsp caster (superfine) sugar
150ml/¼ pint/⅔ cup fruity red wine
10ml/2 tsp balsamic or sherry vinegar
30ml/2 tbsp coarsely chopped fresh
  oregano or marjoram
salt and ground black pepper

1 Leave baby leeks whole, but cut thick ones into 5–7.5cm/2–3in lengths.

2 Place the coriander seeds and cinnamon in a wide pan. Cook over a medium heat for about 2–3 minutes, until the spices are fragrant, then stir in the oil, bay leaves, orange rind, oregano, sugar, wine and vinegar. Bring to the boil and simmer for 5 minutes.

3 Add the leeks. Bring back to the boil, reduce the heat and cover the pan. Cook gently for 5 minutes. Uncover and simmer gently for another 5–8 minutes, until the leeks are just tender when tested with the tip of a sharp knife.

4 Use a draining spoon to transfer the leeks to a serving dish and set aside. Boil the juices rapidly until reduced to about 75–90ml/5–6 tbsp. Add salt and pepper to taste and pour the reduced liquid over the leeks. Leave to cool.

5 The leeks can be left to stand for several hours. If you chill them, bring them back to room temperature again before serving. Scatter chopped fresh oregano or marjoram over the leeks just before serving them.

NUTRITION NOTES

Per portion:	
Energy	239kcal/998kJ
Protein	2.3g
Fat	20.5g
saturated fat	2.8g
Carbohydrate	7.6g
Fibre	3.2g
Calcium	83mg

broccoli with garlic

THIS LOW-FAT, LOW-CARBOHYDRATE vegetable is high in vitamins and minerals, notably iron and folates. Amazingly, it is an even better source of vitamin C than oranges.

1 Using a sharp knife, trim off and discard the thick stems from the broccoli, and cut the head into large, even-size florets.

2 Bring a large pan of water to the boil. Add the broccoli florets and cook for about 3 minutes, until just tender but still retaining its bite.

3 Drain the broccoli well and arrange the florets in a warmed serving dish.

4 Heat the sunflower oil in a small pan, add the crushed garlic and cook for about 2 minutes, being careful not to let it burn, then remove the garlic with a slotted spoon and discard.

5 Pour the garlic-flavoured oil over the broccoli. Sprinkle with fried garlic slices, if using, and serve immediately.

NUTRITION NOTES

Per portion:

Energy	61kcal/254kJ
Protein	4.9g
Fat	3.7g
saturated fat	0.5g
Carbohydrate	2.0g
Fibre	2.9g
Calcium	63mg

Serves 4
450g/1lb broccoli
15ml/1 tbsp sunflower oil
2 garlic cloves, crushed
fried garlic slices, to garnish (optional)

VARIATION
Use any other steamed or boiled green vegetable such as pak choi (bok choy) or spinach in place of the broccoli.

asparagus with lemon sauce

THIS SOPHISTICATED DISH is higher in carbohydrate than a simple green salad but it makes a wonderful vegetable accompaniment for a special dinner.

Serves 4

675g/1½lb asparagus, trimmed of any
  tough ends and tied in a bundle
15ml/1 tbsp cornflour (cornstarch)
2 egg yolks
juice of 1½ lemons
salt

1 Cook the asparagus, with the tips uppermost, in a pan of salted boiling water for 8 minutes. Drain well and arrange in a serving dish. Reserve 200ml/7fl oz/ scant 1 cup of the cooking liquid.

2 In a small bowl, blend the cornflour with the cooled, reserved cooking liquid, then pour into a small pan. Bring the mixture to the boil, stirring, and cook over a gentle heat until the sauce thickens slightly. Remove the pan from the heat and set aside to cool for a few minutes.

3 In a bowl, beat the egg yolks with the lemon juice, then gradually stir the mixture into the cooled sauce. Cook over a very low heat, stirring constantly, until the sauce is fairly thick. Do not overheat.

4 As soon as the sauce has thickened, remove the pan from the heat and continue stirring for 1 minute. Taste and add a little salt if necessary. Allow to cool.

5 Once cooled, stir the sauce, then pour a little over the asparagus. Cover the dish with clear film (plastic wrap) and chill for at least 2 hours before serving with the rest of the sauce handed separately.

VARIATIONS
This sauce goes very well with all sorts of young vegetables, such as baby leeks and green beans.

NUTRITION NOTES

Per portion:

Energy	126kcal/526kJ
Protein	6.5g
Fat	3.8g
saturated fat	0.9g
Carbohydrate	7.3g
Fibre	2.9g
Calcium	60mg

florets polonaise

STEAMED VEGETABLES are a delicious and extremely healthy accompaniment for any main meal. If you want to reduce the carbohydrate content further, omit the breadcrumbs.

Serves 6

500g/1¼lb cauliflower and broccoli
finely grated rind of ½ lemon
1 large garlic clove, crushed
25g/1oz/½ cup wholegrain
   breadcrumbs, lightly baked or
   grilled (broiled) until crisp
2 eggs, hard-boiled and shelled
salt and ground black pepper

NUTRITION NOTES

Per portion:	
Energy	73kcal/305kJ
Protein	5.7g
Fat	2.7g
saturated fat	0.7g
Carbohydrate	7.1g
Fibre	1.5g
Calcium	33.4mg

1 Trim the cauliflower and broccoli and break into florets, then place in a steamer over a pan of boiling water and steam for about 12 minutes. If you prefer, boil the vegetables in salted water for 5–7 minutes, until just tender. Drain the vegetables well and transfer to a warmed serving dish.

2 While the vegetables are cooking, make the topping. In a bowl, combine the lemon rind, garlic and breadcrumbs. Finely chop the eggs and mix into the breadcrumb mixture. Season with salt and black pepper to taste, then sprinkle the chopped egg mixture over the cooked vegetables and serve.

VARIATIONS
Sprinkle the egg topping over other steamed vegetables such as courgettes (zucchini) or spring greens (collards).

braised lettuce and peas with spring onions and mint

THIS IS BASED on the traditional French way of braising peas with lettuce and spring onions in butter. It is delicious with simply cooked fish or roast or grilled duck.

Serves 4

50g/2oz/¼ cup butter
4 Little Gem (Bibb) lettuces, halved lengthways
2 bunches spring onions (scallions), trimmed and cut into 5cm/2in lengths
5ml/1 tsp caster (superfine) sugar
400g/14oz shelled peas (about 1kg/ 2¼lb in pods)
4 fresh mint sprigs
120ml/4fl oz/½ cup chicken or vegetable stock or water
15ml/1 tbsp chopped fresh mint
salt and ground black pepper

1 Gently melt half the butter in a large pan. Add the lettuces and spring onions.

2 Turn the vegetables in the butter, then sprinkle in the caster sugar, 2.5ml/ ½ tsp salt and plenty of black pepper. Cover and cook very gently for about 5 minutes, stirring once.

3 Add the peas and mint sprigs. Turn the peas in the buttery juices and pour in the stock or water, then cover and cook over a gentle heat for a further 5 minutes. Uncover and increase the heat to reduce the liquid to a few tablespoons.

4 Stir in the remaining butter and adjust the seasoning. Transfer to a warmed serving dish and sprinkle with the chopped mint. Serve immediately.

VARIATIONS
• Braise about 250g/9oz baby carrots with the lettuce.
• Fry 115g/4oz chopped pancetta with 1 small chopped onion in the butter.

NUTRITION NOTES

Per portion:

Energy	181kcal/757kJ
Protein	6.7g
Fat	11.0g
saturated fat	6.3g
Carbohydrate	15.1g
Fibre	6.8g
Calcium	42mg

fried spring greens

GREEN LEAFY VEGETABLES make an excellent choice for a low-carbohydrate accompaniment. They are rich in essential nutrients and full of valuable fibre.

Serves 4

15ml/1 tbsp olive oil
75g/3oz rindless smoked streaky (fatty) bacon, chopped
1 large onion, thinly sliced
2 garlic cloves, finely chopped
900g/2lb spring greens (collards), shredded
salt and ground black pepper

VARIATION

Use shredded red cabbage in place of the spring greens. Leave to simmer for 10 minutes longer as red cabbage is tougher and requires longer cooking.

1 In a large frying pan, heat the oil and add the bacon. Fry for 2 minutes, then add the onion and garlic and fry for 3 minutes more until the onion begins to soften.

2 Reduce the heat, add the spring greens and season. Cook, covered, over a gentle heat for about 15 minutes until the greens are tender. Serve immediately.

NUTRITION NOTES

Per portion:	
Energy	197kcal/823kJ
Protein	10.4g
Fat	12.3g
saturated fat	2.5g
Carbohydrate	11.7g
Fibre	8.5g
Calcium	488mg

radicchio and chicory gratin

BAKING SALAD VEGETABLES in a creamy sauce creates a dish that is wholesome, warming and sustaining. Serve with grilled meat for a filling meal that does not load on the carbohydrate.

Serves 4

2 heads radicchio, quartered lengthways
2 heads chicory (Belgian endive),
    quartered lengthways
25g/1oz/½ cup drained sun-dried
    tomatoes in oil, coarsely chopped
25g/1oz/2 tbsp butter
15g/½oz/2 tbsp plain (all-purpose) flour
250ml/8fl oz/1 cup milk
pinch of freshly grated nutmeg
50g/2oz/½ cup grated Emmenthal cheese
salt and ground black pepper

1 Preheat the oven to 180°C/350°F/ Gas 4. Grease a 1.2 litre/2 pint/5 cup ovenproof dish and arrange the radicchio and chicory in it. Sprinkle over the sun-dried tomatoes and brush the vegetables with oil from the jar. Season and cover the dish with foil. Bake for 15 minutes, then uncover and bake for a further 10 minutes.

NUTRITION NOTES

Per portion:	
Energy	173kcal/723kJ
Protein	6.6g
Fat	13.4g
saturated fat	6.9g
Carbohydrate	8.1g
Fibre	0.7g
Calcium	217mg

2 To make the sauce, place the butter in a small pan and melt over a medium heat. When the butter is foaming, add the flour and cook for 1 minute, stirring. Remove from the heat and gradually add the milk, whisking all the time. Return to the heat and bring to the boil, then simmer for about 3 minutes to thicken. Season to taste and add the nutmeg.

3 Pour the sauce over the vegetables and sprinkle with the cheese. Bake for about 20 minutes until golden. Serve immediately.

VARIATION
Use fennel in place of the radicchio and chicory. Par-boil the fennel first.

mexican-style green peas

THIS DISH, USING FRESH PEAS, is a delicious accompaniment to any meal. Use vine tomatoes and organic peas if possible.

Serves 4
2 tomatoes
15ml/1 tbsp olive oil
2 garlic cloves, halved
1 medium onion, halved and thinly sliced
400g/14oz/scant 3 cups shelled
   fresh peas
30ml/2 tbsp water
salt and ground black pepper
fresh chives, to garnish

1 Plunge the tomatoes into a bowl of boiling water. Leave them for 3 minutes, until the skins split, then drain, plunge into cold water and peel the skins off. Cut the tomatoes in half and squeeze out the seeds. Chop the flesh into 1cm/½in dice.

2 Heat the oil in a pan and cook the garlic until golden. Scoop it out with a slotted spoon and discard.

3 Add the onion to the pan and fry until transparent. Add the tomatoes and peas.

4 Pour over the water, lower the heat and cover the pan tightly. Cook for about 10 minutes, until the peas are cooked. Season with plenty of salt and pepper, transfer the mixture to a heated dish and serve, garnished with fresh chives.

NUTRITION NOTES

Per portion:

Energy	113kcal/476kJ
Protein	6.4g
Fat	4.2g
saturated fat	0.7g
Carbohydrate	13.3g
Fibre	5.9g
Calcium	27mg

mushrooms with chipotle chillies

CHIPOTLE CHILLIES are jalapeños that have been smoke-dried. They are the perfect foil for the mushrooms in this simple salad.

Serves 6
2 chipotle chillies
450g/1lb/6 cups button (white) mushrooms
60ml/4 tbsp vegetable oil
1 onion, finely chopped
2 garlic cloves, crushed or chopped
fresh coriander (cilantro), to garnish

NUTRITION NOTES

Per portion:

Energy	109kcal/455kJ
Protein	1.8g
Fat	10.5g
saturated fat	1.1g
Carbohydrate	1.6g
Fibre	2.1g
Calcium	11mg

1 Soak the dried chillies in a bowl of hot water for about 10 minutes. Drain, cut off the stalks, then slit the chillies and scrape out the seeds. Chop the flesh finely.

2 Trim the mushrooms, clean them and cut them in half, if large.

3 Heat the oil in a large frying pan. Add the onion, garlic, chillies and mushrooms and stir until evenly coated in the oil. Fry for 6–8 minutes, until the onion is tender. Transfer to a warmed dish. Chop some of the coriander, leaving some whole leaves, and use to garnish. Serve hot.

okra with coriander and tomatoes

THIS AROMATIC DISH is delicious hot or cold and makes a good accompaniment at any time of the year. It is rich in valuable nutrients including vitamins C and E and potassium.

Serves 4

450g/1lb tomatoes or 400g/
   14oz can chopped tomatoes
450g/1lb fresh okra
45ml/3 tbsp olive oil
2 onions, thinly sliced
10ml/2 tsp coriander seeds, crushed
3 garlic cloves, crushed
finely grated rind and juice of 1 lemon
salt and ground black pepper

1 If using fresh tomatoes, cut a cross in the stalk ends, plunge them into boiling water for about 3 minutes or until the skins start to split, then refresh in cold water. Peel off the skins and chop the flesh, discarding the tough core.

2 Trim off any stalks from the okra and discard, leaving the okra whole. Heat the olive oil in a frying pan and cook the onions and coriander seeds for 3–4 minutes, or until just beginning to colour.

3 Add the okra and garlic to the pan and cook for 1 minute. Stir in the tomatoes and simmer gently for 20 minutes until the okra is tender. Stir in the lemon rind and juice and add seasoning. Serve warm or cold.

NUTRITION NOTES

Per portion:	
Energy	73kcal/305kJ
Protein	5.7g
Fat	2.7g
saturated fat	0.7g
Carbohydrate	7.1g
Fibre	1.5g
Calcium	33mg

tomato and aubergine gratin

THIS COLOURFUL, Mediterranean dish makes the perfect partner to grilled or pan-fried meat or poultry. If you prefer, use thinly sliced courgettes instead of the aubergines.

Serves 6

2 aubergines (eggplants)
45ml/3 tbsp olive oil
400g/14oz ripe tomatoes, sliced
40g/1½oz/½ cup freshly grated
　Parmesan cheese
salt and ground black pepper

NUTRITION NOTES

Per portion:	
Energy	174kcal/734kJ
Protein	5.3g
Fat	14.3g
saturated fat	3.4g
Carbohydrate	6.8g
Fibre	4.8g
Calcium	148mg

1 Preheat the grill (broiler). Thinly slice the aubergines and arrange them on a foil-lined grill rack. Brush the aubergine slices with olive oil and grill (broil) for 15–20 minutes, turning once, until golden on both sides. Brush the second side with more olive oil after turning the slices.

2 Preheat the oven to 200°C/400°F/ Gas 6. Toss the aubergine and tomato slices together with a little seasoning, then pile them into a shallow ovenproof dish. Sprinkle with the grated cheese. Bake for 20 minutes, until the cheese is golden and the vegetables are hot. Serve immediately.

desserts

FOR THOSE WITH A SWEET TOOTH, sticking to a low-carbohydrate diet and avoiding all things sweet and indulgent may sound impossible. However, there are plenty of sweet treats that won't ruin the diet if they are eaten occasionally. This chapter brings together a selection of delicious desserts that are relatively low in carbohydrate and will make the perfect end to a special meal. Round off a summer barbecue with peach and cardamom yogurt ice or, for something more filling, try baked ricotta cakes with red sauce.

baked ricotta cakes with red sauce

THESE HONEY- AND VANILLA-FLAVOURED cakes are a tasty treat for a special meal. Try not to add too much extra honey to the sauce because it will add to the total carbohydrate content.

Serves 4

250g/9oz/generous 1 cup ricotta cheese
2 egg whites, beaten
30ml/2 tbsp clear honey, plus extra
　to taste
5ml/1 tsp vanilla essence (extract)
450g/1lb/4 cups mixed fresh or
　frozen fruit, such as strawberries,
　raspberries, blackberries
　and cherries
fresh mint leaves, to decorate (optional)

1 Preheat the oven to 180°C/350°F/ Gas 4. Place the ricotta cheese in a bowl and break it up with a wooden spoon. Add the beaten egg whites, honey and vanilla essence and mix thoroughly until the mixture is smooth and well combined.

2 Lightly grease four ramekins. Spoon the ricotta mixture into the ramekins and level the tops. Bake for 20 minutes, or until the ricotta cakes are risen and golden.

3 Meanwhile, make the fruit sauce. Reserve about a quarter of the fruit for decoration. Place the rest of the fruit in a pan, with a little water if the fruit is fresh, and heat gently until softened. Remove the pan from the heat and leave to cool slightly. Remove any cherry pits, if using cherries.

4 Press the fruit through a sieve (strainer), then taste and sweeten with honey if it is too tart. Serve the sauce, warm or cold, with the ricotta cakes. Decorate with the reserved berries and mint leaves, if using.

COOK'S TIP

If using frozen fruit for the sauce, there is no need to add extra water because there are usually plenty of ice crystals clinging to the berries. Adding extra water may make the sauce too runny.

NUTRITION NOTES

Per portion:	
Energy	366kcal/1525kJ
Protein	25.9g
Fat	24.8g
saturated fat	12.4g
Carbohydrate	11.3g
Fibre	3.7g
Calcium	747mg

fruit-filled soufflé omelette

A LIGHT AND FLUFFY soufflé omelette filled with fresh, juicy strawberries is a decadent and indulgent treat that is naturally low in carbohydrate.

Serves 3

75g/3oz/¾ cup strawberries, hulled
3 eggs, separated
30ml/2 tbsp caster (superfine) sugar
45ml/3 tbsp double (heavy) cream,
  whipped
a few drops of vanilla essence (extract)
25g/1oz/2 tbsp butter

1 Hull the strawberries and cut them in half. Set aside. In a bowl, beat the egg yolks and sugar until pale and fluffy, then fold in the cream and vanilla essence. Whisk the egg whites in a very large, grease-free bowl until stiff, then carefully fold into the yolks.

2 Melt the butter in an omelette pan. When sizzling, pour in the egg mixture and cook until set, shaking occasionally. Spoon on the strawberries and, tilting the pan, slide the omelette so that it folds over.

3 Carefully slide the omelette on to a warm serving plate. Cut the omelette into three pieces, then transfer to three warmed plates and serve immediately.

VARIATION
Use any type of soft, non-starchy fruit in place of the strawberries. Slices of peach, fresh berries or a combination of several fruits will all work well.

NUTRITION NOTES

Per portion:	
Energy	205kcal/854kJ
Protein	7.6g
Fat	14.2g
saturated fat	6.8g
Carbohydrate	12.5g
Fibre	0.3g
Calcium	51mg

figs and pears in honey

A STUNNINGLY SIMPLE DESSERT using fresh figs and pears scented with the warm fragrances of cinnamon and cardamom and drenched in a lemon and honey syrup.

Serves 4

1 lemon
90ml/6 tbsp clear honey
1 cinnamon stick
1 cardamom pod
2 pears
8 fresh figs, halved

NUTRITION NOTES

Per portion:	
Energy	145kcal/618kJ
Protein	1.9g
Fat	0g
saturated fat	0g
Carbohydrate	36.6g
Fibre	4.8g
Calcium	48mg

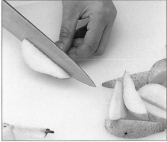

1 Pare the rind from the lemon using a zester. Alternatively, use a vegetable peeler and then cut into very thin strips.

2 Place the lemon rind, honey, cinnamon stick, cardamom pod and 350ml/ 12fl oz/1½ cups water in a heavy pan and boil, uncovered, for about 10 minutes until reduced by about half.

3 Cut the pears into eighths, discarding the cores. Place in the syrup, add the figs and simmer for about 5 minutes, or until the fruit is tender.

4 Transfer the fruit to a serving bowl. Continue cooking the liquid until syrupy, then discard the spices and pour over the figs and pears. Serve.

summer berries in sabayon glaze

THIS LUXURIOUS COMBINATION of summer berries under a light and fluffy liqueur sauce is lightly grilled to form a crisp, caramelized topping. Fresh or frozen berries can be used.

Serves 4

450g/1lb/4 cups mixed summer berries, or other soft fruit
4 egg yolks
50g/2oz/¼ cup vanilla sugar or caster (superfine) sugar
120ml/4fl oz/½ cup liqueur, such as Cointreau or Kirsch, or a white dessert wine

NUTRITION NOTES

Per portion:

Energy	222kcal/932kJ
Protein	4.2g
Fat	6.1g
saturated fat	1.9g
Carbohydrate	29.5g
Fibre	5.7g
Calcium	69mg

1 Arrange the mixed summer berries or other fruit in four individual flameproof dishes. Preheat the grill (broiler).

2 Using a balloon whisk, whisk the egg yolks in a large heatproof bowl with the sugar and liqueur or wine. Place over a pan of hot water and whisk constantly until the mixture is thick, fluffy and pale.

3 Pour equal quantities of the yolk mixture into each dish. Place under the grill for 1–2 minutes, add an extra splash of liqueur and serve immediately.

VARIATIONS
If you want to omit the liqueur, use pure grape, mango or orange juice instead.

fresh fruit salad

A LIGHT AND REFRESHING fruit salad makes a healthy and nutritious end to a low-carbohydrate meal. The natural fruit sugars are kinder to the body than refined sugars.

Serves 6

2 peaches
2 oranges
2 eating apples
16–20 strawberries
30ml/2 tbsp lemon juice
15–30ml/1–2 tbsp orange flower water
a few fresh mint leaves, to decorate

NUTRITION NOTES

Per portion:	
Energy	39kcal/163kJ
Protein	0.8g
Fat	0.1g
saturated fat	0g
Carbohydrate	9.3g
Fibre	1.6g
Calcium	10mg

1 Place the peaches in a bowl and pour over boiling water. Leave to stand for 1 minute, then lift out with a slotted spoon, peel, stone (pit) and cut the flesh into thick slices.

2 Peel the oranges with a sharp knife, removing all the white pith, and segment them, catching any juice in a bowl.

3 Peel and core the apples and cut into thin slices. Using the point of a knife, hull the strawberries and halve or quarter the fruits if they are large. Place all the prepared fruit in a large serving bowl.

4 Blend together the lemon juice, orange flower water and any reserved orange juice. Pour the fruit juice mixture over the salad and toss lightly. Serve decorated with a few fresh mint leaves.

fruit platter with spices

A SIMPLE FRESH fruit platter sprinkled with spices makes a healthy dessert. It is low in fat and offers a range of essential vitamins and minerals that are needed for good health.

Serves 6

1 pineapple
2 papayas
1 small melon
juice of 2 limes
2 pomegranates
ground ginger and ground nutmeg,
   for sprinkling
mint sprigs, to decorate

1 Peel the pineapple. Remove the core and any remaining eyes, then cut the flesh lengthways into thin wedges. Peel the papayas, cut them in half, and then into thin wedges. Halve the melon and remove the seeds. Cut into thin wedges and remove the skin. Arrange the fruit on six individual plates and sprinkle with the lime juice.

2 Cut the pomegranates in half using a sharp knife, then scoop out the seeds, discarding any pith. Sprinkle the seeds over the fruit, then sprinkle the salad with a little ginger and nutmeg to taste. Decorate with sprigs of fresh mint and serve immediately.

VARIATION
The selection of fruit can be varied according to what is available. Guava and mango make an exotic combination but oranges and plums are also good.

NUTRITION NOTES

Per portion:

Energy	55kcal/229kJ
Protein	1.0g
Fat	0.3g
saturated fat	0g
Carbohydrate	12.9g
Fibre	2.3g
Calcium	25mg

frozen melon

FREEZING SORBET in hollowed-out fruit, which is then cut into wedges, is an excellent idea. The refreshing flavour makes this dessert irresistible on a hot summer's day.

Serves 6

50g/2oz/¼ cup caster (superfine) sugar
30ml/2 tbsp clear honey
15ml/1 tbsp lemon juice
60ml/4 tbsp water
1 medium cantaloupe melon or Charentais melon, about 1kg/2¼lb
crushed ice, cucumber slices and borage flowers, to decorate

1 Put the sugar, honey, lemon juice and water in a heavy pan and heat gently until the sugar dissolves. Bring to the boil, and boil for 1 minute, without stirring, to make a syrup. Leave to cool.

2 Cut the melon in half and discard the seeds. Carefully scoop out the flesh using a metal spoon or melon baller and place in a food processor, taking care to keep the halved shells intact.

3 Process the melon flesh until very smooth, then transfer to a large mixing bowl. Stir in the cooled sugar syrup and chill until very cold. Invert the melon shells and leave them to drain on kitchen paper for a few minutes, then transfer them to the freezer while making the sorbet.

4 If making by hand, pour the mixture into a plastic container and freeze for about 3–4 hours, beating twice with a fork or a whisk, or processing in a food processor, to break up the ice crystals and produce a smoother texture. If using an ice cream maker, churn the melon mixture until the sorbet holds its shape.

5 Remove the melon shells from the freezer, pack the frozen sorbet tightly into the melon shells and level the surface with a sharp knife.

6 Use a dessertspoon to scoop out the centre of each filled melon shell to simulate the seed cavity, then freeze the prepared fruit overnight until firm.

7 To serve, use a large knife to cut each melon half into three large wedges. Serve on a bed of crushed ice either on a large platter or individual plates, and decorate with the cucumber slices and borage flowers.

COOK'S TIP

If the melon sorbet is too firm to cut when taken straight from the freezer, let it soften in the refrigerator for 10–20 minutes. Take care when slicing the frozen melon into wedges. A serrated kitchen knife is easier to work with.

NUTRITION NOTES

Per portion:	
Energy	87kcal/364kJ
Protein	1.7g
Fat	0g
saturated fat	0g
Carbohydrate	21.3g
Fibre	1.7g
Calcium	32mg

peach and cardamom yogurt ice

LOW-FAT FROZEN DESSERTS that rely on natural fruit for their sweetness make the perfect low-carbohydrate dessert. This yogurt ice provides a useful source of calcium and vitamin C.

2 Chop the peaches and put them in a pan. Add the crushed cardamom pods, with their black seeds, and the measured water. Cover and simmer gently for about 10 minutes, or until the fruit is tender. Remove the pan from the heat and leave to cool.

3 Pour the peach mixture into a food processor or blender, process until smooth, then press through a sieve (strainer) placed over a bowl.

4 Add the yogurt to the sieved purée and mix together in the bowl. Pour into a plastic freezerproof tub and freeze for about 6 hours until firm, beating once or twice with a fork, electric whisk or in a food processor to break up the ice crystals.

5 To serve, scoop the ice cream on to a large platter or into individual bowls.

Serves 4

8 cardamom pods
6 peaches, total weight about 500g/1¼lb, halved and stoned (pitted)
30ml/2 tbsp water
200ml/7fl oz/scant 1 cup bio natural (plain) yogurt

COOK'S TIP

Use bio natural (plain) yogurt for its extra mild taste. Greek (US strained plain) yogurt or ordinary natural yogurt are both much sharper, and tend to overwhelm the delicate taste of peach.

1 Put the cardamom pods on a board and crush them with the base of a ramekin, or use a mortar and pestle.

NUTRITION NOTES

Per portion:

Energy	126kcal/596kJ
Protein	8.2g
Fat	6.9g
saturated fat	4.3g
Carbohydrate	8.0g
Fibre	1.2g
Calcium	168mg

mango and lime fool

CANNED MANGOES are used here for convenience, but the dish tastes even better if made with fresh ones. Choose a delicious, fragrant variety like the voluptuous Alphonso mango.

Serves 4
400g/14oz can sliced mango
grated rind of 1 lime
juice of ½ lime
150ml/¼ pint/⅔ cup low-fat
  crème fraîche
90ml/6 tbsp low-fat Greek (US strained
  plain) yogurt
fresh mango slices, to decorate (optional)

2 Pour the crème fraîche into a bowl and add the Greek yogurt. Whisk the mixture with a balloon whisk until it is thick and then quickly whisk in the mango purée.

3 Spoon the mango and lime fool into four small cups or glasses and chill for approximately 1–2 hours. Just before serving, decorate each glass with fresh mango slices, if you like.

COOK'S TIP
When mixing the crème fraîche and yogurt mixture with the mango purée, whisk it just enough to combine, but take care not to lose the lightness of the crème fraîche mixture. If you prefer, simply fold the mixtures together lightly, so that the fool is rippled.

1 Drain the canned mango slices and place them in the bowl of a food processor or in a blender. Add the grated lime rind and the freshly squeezed lime juice. Process or blend until the mixture forms a smooth mango purée. Alternatively, mash the mango slices with a fork or a potato masher, then press the mixture through a sieve (strainer) with a wooden spoon until you achieve a smooth purée.

NUTRITION NOTES

Per portion:	
Energy	120kcal/512kJ
Protein	4.4g
Fat	0.4g
saturated fat	0.2g
Carbohydrate	26.5g
Fibre	1.3g
Calcium	53mg

pistachio kulfi ice cream

THIS CLASSIC INDIAN DESSERT, made from milk and nuts, contains more carbohydrate than some other desserts, but it can still be enjoyed as an occasional treat. The milk and nuts provide a good source of protein.

Serves 4

1.5 litres/2½ pints/6¼ cups semi-skimmed (low-fat) milk
3 cardamom pods
25g/1oz/2 tbsp caster (superfine) sugar
50g/2oz/½ cup pistachio nuts, skinned plus a few to decorate
a few pink rose petals, to decorate

1 Pour the milk into a large heavy pan and bring to the boil. Lower the heat and simmer for one hour, stirring occasionally.

2 Crush the cardamom pods in a mortar with a pestle, then add them to the milk. Simmer the mixture for 1½ hours, or until the milk has reduced to 475ml/16fl oz/2 cups.

3 Strain the reduced milk into a bowl or jug (pitcher), and discard the cardamom pods and seeds. Stir the sugar into the milk and set the mixture aside to cool.

4 Meanwhile, place half the nuts in a blender and grind to a smooth powder. Cut the remaining nuts into thin slivers and set them aside for decoration.

5 Stir the ground nuts into the cooled milk mixture. Pour into four kulfi moulds and freeze overnight until firm.

6 To unmould the kulfi, half fill a bowl with very hot water. Stand each mould in the water and count to ten. Immediately lift it out and invert the ice cream on to individual serving plates. Decorate with sliced pistachio nuts and rose petals and serve immediately.

NUTRITION NOTES

Per portion:

Energy	272kcal/1135kJ
Protein	14.6g
Fat	12.9g
saturated fat	4.6g
Carbohydrate	26.3g
Fibre	0.8g
Calcium	464mg

rhubarb and ginger yogurt ice

FROZEN YOGURT flavoured with fruit makes a healthy alternative to ice cream. It is low in fat and high in calcium, which is essential for good bone health.

Serves 6

300g/11oz/scant 1½ cups set natural
(plain) live yogurt
200g/7oz/scant 1 cup mascarpone
350g/12oz/3 cups chopped rhubarb
30ml/2 tbsp clear honey
3 pieces preserved stem ginger, finely
chopped

1 Whisk together the yogurt and mascarpone. Pour the mixture into a shallow freezerproof container and freeze for about 1 hour.

2 Meanwhile, put the chopped rhubarb and honey in a large pan and add 45ml/3 tbsp water. Cook over a very low heat, stirring occasionally, for 15 minutes, or until the rhubarb is soft. Remove the pan from the heat and set aside to cool. When the fruit has cooled, place it in a food processor or blender and process to a purée.

3 Remove the semi-frozen yogurt mixture from the freezer and fold in the rhubarb purée. Beat well until smooth, breaking up the ice crystals, then fold in the chopped ginger.

4 Return the yogurt ice to the freezer and freeze for 2 hours. Remove from the freezer and beat again, then freeze until solid. To serve, scoop the yogurt ice into individual serving bowls.

NUTRITION NOTES

Per portion:	
Energy	84kcal/350kJ
Protein	5.0g
Fat	3.9g
saturated fat	2.5g
Carbohydrate	7.7g
Fibre	0.2g
Calcium	159mg

COOK'S TIPS

• To make serving easier, take the yogurt ice out of the freezer and transfer it to the refrigerator about 15 minutes before serving to allow it to soften sufficiently to scoop easily.
• Make sure that you remove all traces of the leaves from rhubarb as they contain the poison oxalic acid.

checking carbohydrate content

THE FOLLOWING list shows the glycaemic index (GI) and carbohydrate content of many common foods. On a low-carbohydrate diet, try to choose foods with a low GI (55 or less), which indicates that they are absorbed slowly into the bloodstream, as well as a low carbohydrate content.

FOOD	PORTION	GI	CARB
apple	1 fruit	38	18g
apple juice	250ml	40	33g
apricots	3 fruits	57	7g
dried	5 (40g)	31	15g
bacon	2 rashers	0	0g
bagel, white	1	72	35g
baked beans	120g	48	13g
banana			
ripe	1 fruit	55	32g
unripe	1 fruit	30	11g
barley	80g	25	17g
beef	120g	0	0g
beetroot (beet)	60g	64	5g
biscuits (cookies)			
arrowroot	3 biscuits	63	15g
Digestives (graham crackers)	2 biscuits	59	21g
morning coffee	3 biscuits	79	14g
Rich Tea	2 biscuits	55	14g
shortbread	2 biscuits	64	19g
black beans	120g	43	16g
black-eyed beans (peas)	120g	42	24g
bread			
baguette	30g	95	15g
bread roll, soft	45g	69	21g
chapati (Baisen)	1	27	38g
chapati (Bajra)	1	57	42g
fruit loaf	1 slice	47	18g
hamburger bun	50g	61	24g
oat bran and honey loaf with barley (Burgen)	2 slices	31	21g
pitta bread	1 piece	57	38g
pumpernickel	1 slice	41	35g
rye bread	1 slice	65	23g
white	1 slice	70	15g
white (gluten-free)	2 slices	90	37g
wholemeal (whole-wheat)	1 slice	69	14g
breadfruit	120g	68	17g
breakfast cereals			
All-Bran	40g	42	22g
Bran Buds	40g	58	17g
Cheerios	30g	74	20g
Cocopops	30g	77	29g
Cornflakes	30g	84	26g
Golden Grahams	30g	71	30g
muesli (granola)	60g	56	32g
porridge (oatmeal)	245g	42	24g
puffed wheat	30g	80	22g
Rice Krispies	30g	82	27g
Shredded Wheat	2 biscuits	67	30g
Special K	30g	54	24g
Sultana Bran	30g	52	28g
Sustain	30g	68	30g
Weetabix	2 biscuits	74	28g
broad (fava) beans	80g	79	9g
buckwheat	80g	54	57g
bulgur wheat	120g	48	22g
butter (lima) beans	70g	31	13g
cakes			
angel food	60g	47	50g
banana	1 slice	47	46g
carrot	85g	62	45g
sponge	120g	33	22g
carrots	60g	71	3g
cheese	120g	0	0g
cherries	100g	22	12g
chicken	120g	0	0g
chickpeas, canned	4tbsp	31	22g
chocolate, milk	30g	49	19g
Mars bar	medium bar	68	43g
Snickers	medium bar	41	29g
corn	85g	54	16g
corn chips	50g	42	33g
cornmeal	40g	68	30g
couscous	120g	65	28g
crispbreads (rye)	2	69	14g
croissant	1	67	27g
crumpet	1	69	22g
custard	175g	43	24g
dhal	1tbsp	54	8g
dates, dried	3	103	29g
doughnut	40g	76	16g
eggs	120g	0	0g
fish	120g	0	0g
fish fingers (breaded fish sticks)	5 fingers	38	24g
flour tortilla	1 wrap	38	38g
fructose	1tsp (5g)	23	5g

pasta			
fettucini	150g	32	40g
linguine	150g	43	39g
macaroni	140g	45	35g
macaroni and			
cheese (boxed)	250g	64	38g
ravioli	250g	39	45g
spaghetti, white	180g	41	56g
spaghetti wholemeal			
(whole-wheat)	180g	41	56g
tortellini	180g	50	21g
tortellini			
(cheese-filled)	320g	50	49g
pastry	65g	59	25g
peaches	1 fruit	42	7g
canned	120g	30	12g
peanuts	75g	14	11g
chocolate	47g	33	17g
pear	1 fruit	38	21g
peas	80g	48	5g
dried marrowfat	60g	39	12g
pineapple	2 slices	66	10g
juice	150ml	46	20g
pinto beans,			
cooked	60g	39	9g
pizza	2 slices	60	57g
plums	3 fruits	39	7g
popcorn	20g	55	10g
pork	120g	0	0g
potatoes			
baked	120g	85	14g
boiled	120g	56	16g
canned	100g	61	13g
crisps (US chips)	50g	54	24g
French fries	120g	75	49g
mashed	120g	70	16g

glucose	1tsp (5g)	100	5g
gnocchi	145g	68	71g
grapefruit	½ fruit	25	5g
grapefruit juice	250ml	48	16g
grapes	100g	46	15g
haricot (navy)			
beans	90g	38	11g
honey	15ml	58	16g
ice cream	2 scoops	61	10g
low fat	50g	50	12g
jam (strawberry)	2 tsp	51	7g
kidney beans	4 tbsp	27	20g
kiwi fruit	1 fruit	52	8g
lamb	120g	0	0g
lentils	95g	30	16g
lucozade	250ml	95	40g
lychees, canned	7 fruits	79	16g
mango	1 small fruit	55	19g
marmalade	30g	48	20g
melba toast	4 toasts	70	21g
milk,			
full-fat (whole)	250ml	27	12g
skimmed	250ml	32	13g
soya	200ml	31	18g
muesli (granola) bar	1 bar (33g)	61	20g
muffin			
apple	80g	10	44g
blueberry	1 bun	59	31g
noodles	85g	46	55g
nuts (see peanuts)			
oatcakes (Scottish)	1 triangle	57	10g
orange	1 fruit	44	10g
juice	250ml	46	21g
squash (drink)	40ml	66	12g
papaya	½ fruit	58	14g
parsnips	75g	97	8g

pretzels	50g	83	22g
pumpkin	85g	75	6g
raisins	40g	64	28g
rice			
brown	25g	55	20g
risotto	150g	69	53g
white basmati	180g	58	50g
white glutinous	175g	98	37g
wild	50g	54	39g
rice cakes	2	82	21g
romano beans,			
cooked	60g	46	8g
rye	25g	34	16g
sausages	2	28	12g
semolina	25g	55	19g
shellfish	120g	0	0g
soup			
green pea	200ml	66	19g
lentil	200ml	44	24g
split pea	200ml	60	28g
tomato	200ml	38	14g
soya beans	100g	14	12g
split peas	60g	32	13g
swede (rutabaga),			
boiled	60g	72	2g
sweet potato	80g	54	16g
sweets (candies)			
jelly beans	small bag	80	29g
Skittles	small bag	70	27g
taco shells	2	68	16g
taro, raw	80g	54	16g
tuna	120g	0	0g
water biscuits	2 bisc	63	12g
watermelon	150g	72	8g
yam, boiled	80g	51	24g
yogurt, fruit	200g	33	26g

index

NOTES

NOTES

NOTES

NOTES

NOTES

NOTES